Personality and the Teaching of Composition

Writing Research

Multidisciplinary Inquiries into the Nature of Writing

edited by Marcia Farr, University of Illinois at Chicago

Arthur N. Applebee, *Contexts for Learning to Write: Studies of Secondary School Instruction*

Barbara Couture, *Functional Approaches to Writing*

Carole Edelsky, *Writing in a Bilingual Program: Había Una Vez*

Lester Faigley, Roger Cherry, David Jolliffe, and Anna Skinner, *Assessing Writers' Knowledge and Processes of Composing*

Marcia Farr (ed.), *Advances in Writing Research, Volume One: Children's Early Writing Development*

Sarah W. Freedman (ed.), *The Acquisition of Written Language: Response and Revision*

George H. Jensen and John K. DiTiberio, *Personality and the Teaching of Composition*

David A. Jolliffe (ed.), *Advances in Writing Research, Volume Two: Writing in Academic Disciplines*

Judith Langer, *Children Reading and Writing: Structures and Strategies*

Bennett A. Rafoth and Donald L. Rubin (eds.), *The Social Construction of Written Communication*

Leo Ruth and Sandra Murphy, *Designing Writing Tasks for the Assessment of Writing*

Jana Staton, Roger Shuy, Joy Kreeft, and Leslie Reed, *Dialogue Journal Communication: Classroom, Linguistic, Social and Cognitive Views*

William Teale and Elizabeth Sulzby (eds.), *Emergent Literacy: Writing and Reading*

IN PREPARATION

Christine P. Barabas, *Technical Writing in a Corporate Setting: A Study of the Nature of Information*

Robert Gundlach, *Children and Writing in American Education*

Elizabeth Sulzby, *Emergent Writing and Reading in 5–6 Year Olds: A Longitudinal Study*

Personality and the Teaching of Composition

George H. Jensen
Division of Developmental Studies
Georgia State University

John K. DiTiberio
Department of Education
St. Louis University

Ablex Publishing Corporation
Norwood, New Jersey

Printed in the United States of America

LIBRARY OF CONGRESS
Library of Congress Cataloging-in-Publication Data

Jensen, George H.
Personality and the teaching of composition / George H. Jensen, John K. DiTiberio.
p. cm. — (Writing research)
Bibliography: p.
Includes index.
ISBN 0-89391-504-1
1. Authorship—Psychological aspects. 2. Style, Literary. 3. Jung, C. G. (Carl Gustav), 1875–1961—Contributions in typology. 4. Typology (Psychology) 5. Personality. 6. Archetype (Psychology) I. DiTiberio, John K. II. Title. III. Series: Writing research
(Norwood, N.J.)
PN151.J46 1987
808'.02'019—dc19 88-10446
CIP

Ablex Publishing Corporation
355 Chestnut Street
Norwood, New Jersey 07648

Table of Contents

Preface

It was during a lunchtime conversation more than eight years ago that the name of C.G. Jung first came up between us. At the time, George was curious about the content of a workshop which John, a university counseling center psychologist, was preparing. The workshop, designed to help students understand how personality differences influence their preferred learning styles, drew upon Jung's theory of psychological types. Several lunch discussions later, George, the coordinator of Academic Support Services at the university, suggested that the theory might also shed light on how students approach writing. To find out, we generated some hypotheses and then began to test them in a weekly support group for graduate students involved in thesis preparation. We expected to discover an interesting correlation or two, perhaps to fine tune existing programs for dealing with writers' blocks, and then turn our attention to other matters. Almost a decade and several articles on the topic later, we are still at it.

The work that ultimately lead to this book required us each to learn some of the basic language of the other's discipline: personality theory on the one hand, composition theory on the other. Equally important, the work demanded that we develop a means, fortunately facilitated by Jung's theory itself, for monitoring our separate intentions, motivations, and often misinterpreted communications as we continued our collaboration.

Writing the book together has certainly been fun. As must be true for many writers in collaboration, however, different minds, expertise, styles, and personalities present challenges and frustrations in addition to stimulation. We did not include a chapter on personality and collaboration among writers, one of many topics which remain logical extensions of this work. Nevertheless, we have concluded that any composition necessarily involves a psychological collaboration—between writer and co-author, between writer and reader, between writer and fellow members of the discourse community. Furthermore, when we speak of the development of a writer's "voice," we also take into account that person's relationship with different sides of his or her own personality. Many of these complex communications are explicit and deliberate, many subtle and unconscious.

Jung's reminder that people perceive and make judgments differently according to their type does not automatically relieve us from annoyance in the midst of projects with each other. Frustration can usually evolve into appreciative amusement, however, once we gain perspective on the possible intentions of our colleagues and also on reasons we initially reacted as we did. Yet the person and the writer cannot be separated.

As was true for each writer we studied, so too did we as authors wrestle with the tension between poles of psychological opposites. We each tended to prepare our ideas alone before discussing them directly with our partner. While in general this pattern worked well, it contributed to occasional surprises as we responded to each other's drafts. George, in one example, would write a chapter section with a dispassionate analysis of ways to categorize discourse communities; John, typically, concluded that the reader needed warmer and more human examples, and in essence doubled the length of the section. Another time, during final reading before sending the manuscript to the copyeditor, John pencilled in changes in wording to soften or qualify what appeared to him to remain blunt or overly definitive statements; George expressed dismay that what he thought to have been completed long ago was again opened for revision. In the midst of such tension, we wondered how different types of writers ever successfully collaborate. Our work together nevertheless continues. Our differences have helped us each discover strengths in our writing different from those of the other. As a result, we also continue to develop as writers with lessons learned from our partner. The content of this book has facilitated its writing.

For our first acknowledgement, therefore, we point to our years of collaboration with each other, in the beginning as colleagues providing service to students and faculty at the Health Sciences campus of the University of Illinois at Chicago. Neither of us could have written the book alone. Our respective disciplines, one in English literature and composition, the other in counseling psychology, helped to frame our joint efforts.

Others who have supported our work along the way deserve special notice. From our first contact with her at the Conference on College Composition and Communication, Lynn Quitman Troyka of City College of New York gave us encouragement to complete our initial articles on the topic and then to prepare this manuscript. Also helpful in responding to drafts for those first pieces were both Erika Lindemann of the University of North Carolina and George Hayhoe. At the University of Illinois at Chicago, Daniel Lindley and Henrik Eger provided support and data for our early samples. Michael Kleine, Barry Maid, and JoAnne Liebman at the University of Arkansas at Little Rock continue their enthusiastic use of our early recommendations, and also responded to initial drafts of this book.

At Georgia State University, the following colleagues of the first author have helped in many ways: Nancy Chase, Marti Singer, Joan Elifson, Chip Sills, Katharine Stone, Gwen Etter-Lewis, Sheryl Gowen, Frances Grossman-Zeigler, Dawn Latta, Bob Probst, and George Haich. At St. Louis University, the second author has received valuable assistance from Helen Mandeville and Susan Ekberg in applying Jung's concepts within interdisciplinary seminars for Arts and Sciences faculty on students' writing processes.

In the psychological type community, Mary McCaulley of the Center for Applications of Psychological Type has, from the start, been an inspiration to us and given us both comprehensive feedback and encouragement to continue our work. Gordon Lawrence from the University of Florida served as the editor for our first article on the topic, and has graciously agreed for us to include as an Appendix the data which he summarized on learning styles. Allen Hammer from Consulting Psychologists Press has also responded supportively to our research and from his reading of an early draft of the book.

The project has certainly also benefitted from the contributions of colleagues, our students, and participants in workshops over the years who took seriously our notions about personality and writing and helped us to refine them through both experience and reflection. At Ablex, we acknowledge Marcia Farr, the editor for this series, and Carol Davidson, production manager. Lastly, we give heartfelt appreciation to our wives, Donna Jensen and Lisa DiTiberio, for their timeless patience, support, and reactions to the project as we brought it to completion.

1
Jung's Model of Personality Type

> The writing process is as variable and unique as the individual's personality.
>
> Donald Graves, "An Examination of the Writing Processes of Seven Year Old Children," *Research in the Teaching of English*, 1975.

> Various genres can reveal various levels and facets of the individual personality, and individual style can be found in various interrelations with the national language.
>
> M.M. Bakhtin, "The Problem of Speech Genres," 1986 [written circa 1952–1953]

When Donald Graves researched the writing processes of 7-year-old children, he discovered—as Emig (1971) had earlier—that paradigms of *the* writing process had little bearing on how individuals actually composed. Graves found that some children vocalized a great deal while others did not; some had "a need for immediate rehearsal" while others "showed little rehearsal before writing." Graves's response to these varied approaches to writing, which must have initially seemed like random variations, was to divide writers into two categories, *reactive* and *reflective*.

Though Graves's study is often cited in the literature, it has seldom been applied to research or the classroom, probably because a construct of only two types lacks the sensitivity and flexibility needed to account for individual approaches to writing. As T. A. Cowan once quipped, there are two types of people in the world: those who divide people into two types, and those who do not (Mitroff & Kilmann, 1978, pp. 11–12). Although it may be natural to divide people into two categories, the categories are usually too general to describe a wide range of individual differences.

Since Graves's study, researchers have continued to theorize about the influence of personality variables on both the writing process and its end product. For example, Carol Berkenkotter (1984), in a study of students' authority over their texts, wrote: "What I did not anticipate was that the subjects would respond to their readers in significantly different ways depending on the writer's personality, level of maturity, and ability to handle problems." To explain her point, Berkenkotter borrowed concepts from the field of psychology, such as aggression, resistance, and egocentrism. Other researchers have unwittingly discussed personality variables. For example, when explaining why inexperienced writers struggle with term papers, Susan Peck MacDonald (1984) wrote: "Inexperienced writers usually begin college with a tendency to fluctuate wildly between subjective and objective extremes—between immersion in subjective opinion or experience and unintentional plagiarism from encyclopedic works." Even though she seems unaware of it, MacDonald is using personality factors to explain one aspect of how students write. And the same could be said of Perl (1979) when she wrote that an unskilled writer "had 'an event' in mind before writing began," or Hairston (1984), when she wrote that advanced writers "habitually used an abstract and passive style that virtually excludes people from their writing."

It seems difficult to discuss variations found in writing processes or even texts—as Bakhtin has posited—without connecting them to the writer's mind, without intentionally or unintentionally lapsing into a discourse on personality. Yet, despite the time and ink spent on the subject, little progress seems to have been made, perhaps because the research lacks a suitable paradigm (Kuhn, 1962). Graves's construct, though an important contribution to the field, is simply too limited. Bakhtin, although he sensed the importance of personality on the nature of texts, apparently did not have a personality construct in mind to investigate the issue in detail.

In this book, we will present a model of personality that can, we believe, unify and extend the work of Emig (1971), Britton and colleagues (1975), Graves (1975), Perl (1979), Hairston (1984) and others. This model of personality can explain many—certainly not all—of the variables in writing processes and texts, but it is more than a research tool. Its more significant applications to the classroom and writing clinic can allow teachers to understand how individuals differ, to appreciate their varied gifts and potentials, and to make some general predictions about how an individual student will write best and develop into a mature, productive writer.

HISTORY

Perhaps the oddest aspect of the personality model employed in this volume is that it is difficult to name. Though it is usually referred to as Jung's theory of psychological type, it actually emerged from two independent sources. The first source is Carl G. Jung, the Swiss psychoanalyst. The second is Katharine Briggs, who, though well educated, had no formal training in psychology.

Jung initially became interested in how people differed after his break with Freud and Adler. He believed that a more fundamental cause lay behind the split than quibbles over therapeutic issues or the import of symbols; the fundamental cause of the rift, Jung felt, was that he, Freud, and Adler differed in the basic psychological processes that they used to perceive and make decisions. During his "fallow period," from 1913 to about 1918, he began to read extensively in literature, philosophy, and psychology, tracing the evolution of personality constructs from the ancient Greeks to William James. From these studies and his clinical experience, Jung derived a theory of personality type that he presented in *Psychological Types* (1921). In this scholarly, philosophical, and complex work, he explained personality differences in terms of preferences for basic attitudes toward life (extraversion or introversion), processes of perception (sensing or intuition), and processes of judgment (thinking or feeling). To Jung, no single attitude or process was superior to its opposite. No one type was normal and another abnormal. Patterns of mental illness did, as his clinical experience verified, correspond to the types identified in his system, but no one type was more prone to develop a syndrome. Each type could be healthy and well adjusted, as each type could be neurotic.

Across the Atlantic from Jung and independent from professional psychologists, Katharine Briggs began her study of personality near the end of the World War I. Her motive, methodology, and conclusions in many ways mirrored Jung's. Her initial motivation was to understand how friends, neighbors, and family could develop and maintain relationships with spouses who were so obviously different from one another. Using her liberal arts background, reading literature, biography, and history, Briggs hypothesized four types: meditative, executive, sociable, and spontaneous (McCaulley, 1980). When Briggs eventually read *Psychological Types*, she discovered that Jung had independently and more extensively explained the kind of variables in personality that she wished to describe. Briggs (1926, 1928) later expanded her theory to explain differences among types that she called enterprising (Jung's extraversion) and reserved (introversion), observant (sensory perception) and expectant (intuitive perception), and personal (feeling judgment) and analytical (thinking judgment). Her interest in what she called spontaneous types lead to a fourth dichotomy, an extension of Jung's personality theory, which would later develop into a distinction between judging and perceiving types. Ultimately, she wanted, like Jung, to understand how individuals differed without egocentrically valuing one personality type over another.

Over the next 20 years, Briggs and her daughter, Isabel Briggs Myers, used Jung's model to gather observations on individuals and groups, thus extending their understanding of personality types and refining Jung's theory. They also appealed to Jungians to develop an instrument that would help the public understand and work with the apparent random variation of personality variables. Meeting indifference, Briggs and Myers began the task themselves.

Though the task was begun together, Isabel Myers soon became the more active and dedicated researcher, spending long days calculating item analyses by hand. After several stages of development in the 1940s and 1950s, she emerged with the Myers–Briggs Type Indicator (MBTI). In 1962, Educational Testing Service published the instrument but restricted its use to well-controlled studies by research psychologists. The instrument has only become available for broader use by nonresearch psychologists, consultants, and educators since 1975, when Consulting Psychologists Press took over its publication. Since then, the MBTI's use has expanded widely, nurtured in large part by the founding, also in 1975, of the Center for Applications of Psychological Type (CAPT) in Gainesville, Fla., and the forming, in 1979, of the Association for Psychological Type (APT), an interprofessional organization devoted to promoting knowledgeable, constructive, and ethical uses of the MBTI.

In this volume, we will refer to the personality construct that gave birth to the MBTI as "Jung's model." By "Jung's model," we will mean his model as refined and extended by Briggs and Myers.

WHAT IS MEANT BY PERSONALITY TYPE

For many, personality type has unfortunate connotations. Some may feel that personality type is merely a means of classifying psychopathology. In the preceding section, we have already commented on how both Jung and Briggs ran against the grain of much of the psychoanalytic community by formulating a personality construct that appreciated—rather than denigrated—individual differences. Isabel Myers infused even more humanistic values into the system. In *Gifts Differing* (1980), her most comprehensive publication, she used personality type to celebrate, rather than evaluate, the varied ways that individuals may approach even a simple task. The humanistic values behind Jung's model should become even clearer as we begin to discuss individual writers in subsequent chapters.

To others, personality type, even if not focused on psychopathology, is still mere labeling. They argue that a positive label can be as damaging as a negative label, and so it can. A label, however, describes a static trait.

Although the MBTI makes use of key words and letters (as abbreviations for those words) to describe people, these symbols do not signify static traits, but instead indicate a person's preference for a particular cognitive process.

A person's preference for one of a pair of opposite cognitive processes is similar to a preference for either using one's right or left hand. When people sign their name with their preferred hand, they usually do so quickly, effortlessly, almost unconsciously. However, if asked to sign their name with their unpreferred hand, they usually experience more difficulty. The simple task of signing their name takes longer, feels more awkward, and requires more concentration. When asked to use their unpreferred hand, people may feel anxious and inadequate. They may even feel like they are in elementary school, in the process of just learning to write.

As we prefer one hand over the other, Jung's model suggests that we have psychological preferences on a number of bipolar dimensions. For example, we prefer from an early age to direct our energy and attention either outwardly toward people and things (that is, prefer an extraverted attitude toward life), or inwardly toward our thoughts, reflections, and contemplations (an introverted attitude). Because we use the preferred cognitive process more frequently, it matures more rapidly. The unpreferred process, which may be used each day but less habitually, develops more slowly. We may feel, even as adults, childishly awkward when using it.

In this volume, we will be describing an individual writer as an extravert or introvert, a sensing or intuitive type, a thinking or feeling type, and a judging or perceiving type. The language will at times sound like labeling or pigeonholing. It is not so intended. To say that a person is a certain type (e.g., an extravert rather than an introvert) is only to say that he or she prefers the cognitive process of extraversion over that of introversion. In *Psychological Types* (1921), Jung was cautious about how he explained the designation of type, as he is when he describes an extravert in this passage:

> Now, when orientation by the object predominates in such a way that decisions and actions are determined not by subjective views but by objective conditions, we speak of an extraverted attitude. When this is habitual, we speak of an extraverted type. If a man thinks, feels, acts, and actually lives in a way that is *directly* correlated with the objective conditions and their demands, he is extraverted. (p. 333)

For the sake of a simpler style, we may say that a particular writer is an extravert. This should, however, be regarded as a necessary, but potentially misleading, abbreviation. By phrases like "Susan is an extravert," we really mean that "Susan prefers the cognitive process of extraversion" or "Susan's use of the cognitive process of extraversion is habitual."

As we describe student writers, we will attempt to avoid cartooning or caricaturing; readers should be equally cautious about calcifying personality type into mere labels. Reductionistic labels must be avoided because they delimit individuals and slight their potential as human beings. If fully understood, Jung's model can explain fundamental differences among people without reducing them to caricatures. An extravert is simply someone who prefers an extraverted attitude toward life, not someone who uses extraversion exclusively. Jung has stated that it is impossible for an individual to neglect totally any of the cognitive processes described in *Psychological Types*, that it is not even advisable to slight any process. To use introversion to an excessive degree would not produce a superintrovert, but rather a distortion of the innate values of introversion. As Jung (1921) wrote,

> The excessive development of the introverted standpoint does not lead to a better and sounder use of the subjective factor, but rather to an artificial subjectivizing of the consciousness which can hardly escape the reproach "merely subjective." This is then counterbalanced by a desubjectivization which takes the form of an exaggerated extraverted attitude, an attitude aptly described by Weininger as "misautic" [the absence of reflection or subjectivity]. (p. 375)

Myers (Myers, 1980, pp. 181–188; Myers & McCaulley, 1985, pp. 14–15) described "good personality development" as becoming comfortable with relying principally on one's preferences (an introvert feeling comfortable with being an introvert) while developing unpreferred processes to a useful level of adequate competency (an introvert being able to interact comfortably in the outer world). Type development does not mean that one's fundamental personality changes. Theoretically, people's preferences remain unchanged throughout life, but they can develop their unpreferred processes. They will never truly become, as Martin Luther King claimed to be, an ambivert, but they may become so well rounded as individuals that their preference is not readily apparent. Yet, as Jung (1921) explains, the preference still exists:

> it may easily happen that a personality appears to us both introverted and extraverted, so that we cannot decide at first to which attitude the superior function belongs. In such cases only a thorough analysis of the qualities of each function can help us to form a valid judgment. We must observe which function is completely under conscious control, and which functions have a haphazard and spontaneous character. The former [the preferred

> process] is always more highly differentiated than the latter [the unpreferred process], which also possesses infantile and primitive traits. (p. 341)

Even though everyone uses both extraversion and introversion every day, individuals prefer one over the other, and their preference will seem be more fully developed and mature.

One of the most useful aspects of Jung's model is that it affirms everyone, but in different ways. The typology can help us to understand how we and those around us have preferences for certain cognitive processes, but it is not static. When Jung originally described his model, as we will do in subsequent sections, he had to describe, for the sake of simplicity, pure types. For example, he had to describe a pure extravert in contrast to a pure introvert. But he also cautioned that there are no pure types. People are flexible: They can and do use both extraversion and introversion (and all of the other processes as well) everyday. People also change and develop; they learn, as they mature, to use unpreferred processes with greater skill, confidence and ease. We cannot say, therefore, that all extraverts are alike. Some can more skillfully employ extraversion than others. Some extraverts, when one watches their behavior, may never seem to introvert, while others may seem to introvert almost as frequently as they extravert. It is important to remember that Jung was interested in describing an individual's preference for certain cognitive processes; he was not interested in merely categorizing behavior. Personality type relates to behavior, but it does not determine behavior. Extraverts are usually more talkative and outgoing than introverts, but not always.

What follows is a description of the three dichotomies of Jung's model (Extraversion–Introversion, Sensing–Intuition, and Thinking–Feeling) and of a fourth dichotomy added by Briggs and Myers (Judging–Perceiving) with examples of how each impacts on learning styles. The discussion on learning styles is drawn from earlier work on applications of type to education (DiTiberio, 1983; Jensen, 1987; Lawrence, 1979, 1982, 1984).

It should be noted that the four dimensions are conceptually and statistically independent (Myers & McCaulley, 1985, pp. 165–174). However, as the reader moves from the presentation of one dimension to the next, distinctions may at times blur between extraversion and sensory perception, intuitive perception and feeling judgment, or between other pairs of preferences. We may naturally associate some preferences because the two appear in combination in ourselves or family and friends. It is natural that the boundaries of the concepts we are about to discuss may be difficult to establish. As we apply these concepts to the writing processes and texts of individual students, distinctions between preferences within and across dimensions should become clearer.

BASIC ATTITUDES TOWARD LIFE: EXTRAVERSION AND INTROVERSION

> We may observe that, in displaying the praises of any humane, beneficial man, there is one circumstance which never fails to be amply insisted on, namely, the happiness and satisfaction derived to society from his intercourse and good offices. . . . Like the sun, an inferior minister of providence, he cheers, invigorates and sustains the surrounding world.
>
> David Hume, *An Enquiry Concerning the Principles of Morals*

> The philosopher who maintains that the "historical process" passes through his study is laughed at. He gets his revenge by settling the accounts of history's absurdities.
>
> Maurice Merleau–Ponty, *Signs*

Eugene Kelly described David Hume as "a man of the world" who "made friends easily" (Navia & Kelly, 1980, p. 188). This stance toward life, Hume's preference for outer experience, is reflected even in his ethics. Rather than praise the lone individual who takes a moral stand against society, Hume praised what could be called a heroic bureaucrat, the moral person actively interacting with other human beings.

In the philosophy of Merleau–Ponty is found a contrasting value. Richard C. McCleary described him as "a philosopher who made men wonder," as a man who built a "studied wall of solitude" around himself (Merleau–Ponty, 1964, p. ix). Rather than focus his energy on interacting with the external world, Merleau–Ponty preferred to view the world from his study and there settle "the accounts of history's absurdities." Hume's and Merleau–Ponty's opposing stances toward life and philosophy exemplify what Jung attempted to explain when he coined the terms extraversion, literally outward-turning, and introversion, or inward-turning.

Extraverts habitually focus their energy outwardly toward interactions with people and things. They may, as was Hume, be social and gregarious, actively involved in conversations, but not necessarily. Some extraverts are more directed toward the "things" of their environment than the people. They may assert their preference for an active life by being involved in careers, avocations, political causes, sports, or crafts.

Some extraverts may initially question that they are extraverted because they highly value quiet moments of contemplation. What they may overlook is that extraverts are usually more intensely involved with outer experience for longer durations than introverts. Extraverts can long for a few moments of solitude as a brief pause from an otherwise busy day, but introverts are more likely even at work or at school to spend the greater part of each day reflecting rather than acting. Indeed, extraverts often feel that they become more energetic when interacting with people, and so can spend long hours at social events without becoming fatigued.

Introverts are more drawn to inner-experience, to their own reflections, contemplations, and plans for future action. They may talk less than extraverts, but they should not be labeled as shy or withdrawn. Many introverts are comfortable and confident in social settings, albeit in a more quiet and reserved manner. They will usually, however, have less stamina at large parties, feeling more comfortable and talkative when interacting with a few close friends. After a relatively short period of social interaction, they may choose to be alone. If that is impossible, they may "space out," psychologically withdrawing from the crowded, busy environment.

In conversations, extraverts are more likely to initiate the topics being discussed, alter the direction of the discussion, and interrupt other speakers. For them, an interruption is an integral part of conversations. Indeed, they may consider a lack of interruptions from others as an indication of apathy or boredom. Introverts are more likely to listen than talk. When they do talk, they take it seriously. After all, they have usually given much thought and consideration to their words before speaking.

As students, extraverts need activity. Since they use their greatest strengths and talents in the external world, they think best when talking and learn well in groups, but they may have difficulty sticking to their books for a long period of time. They are usually able to concentrate more fully when they take frequent *and active* breaks from the typically solitary tasks of reading and writing. Or, they can try to make these typically solitary tasks more suited to their preference for extraversion. They can, for example, form a study group or talk to friends about upcoming writing projects.

Since they value active experience so highly, extraverts tend to leap into tasks with very little planning. Once actively involved, they use trial and error, which naturally suits them, to complete the task. They prefer trial and error because it allows them to think as they think best: while acting or after acting.

Introverted students usually think best when alone, or at least when their inner solitude is uninterrupted. They are more comfortable than extraverts with long stretches of study, but, unless they anticipate questions before hand or are presented some kind of agenda, they may perform poorly during in-class discussions. Because introverts do not always share what they know, teachers may be slow to appreciate their talents and depth of knowledge. In general, they may be more private and show less of themselves to others. They may, as Merleau–Ponty did, make others wonder what they are thinking.

Introverts do most of their thinking before they act. They tend to plan extensively, anticipate problems, and develop solutions to these problems before ever becoming involved in a task or activity. If asked a question, introverts will usually think about their answer, rehearse it, and only then deliver it to their audience. They are unlike extraverts, who are more likely to begin answering questions immediately, thinking of what they want to say as they speak.

WAYS OF PERCEIVING: SENSING–INTUITION

> All ideas, especially abstract ones, are naturally faint and obscure. The mind has but slender hold on them. They are apt to be confounded with other resembling ideas; and when we have often employed any term, though without any distinct meaning, we are apt to imagine it has a determinate idea annexed to it. On the contrary, all impressions, that is, all sensations either outward or inward, are strong and vivid. The limits between them are more exactly determined, nor is it easy to fall into any error or mistake with regard to them.
>
> David Hume, *An Inquiry Concerning Human Understanding*

> First, as concerns the sources of metaphysical knowledge, its very concept implies that they cannot be empirical. Its principles (including not only its maxims but its basic notions) must never be derived from experience. It must not be physical but metaphysical knowledge, namely, knowledge lying beyond experience.
>
> Immanuel Kant, *Prolegomena to Any Future Metaphysics*

The above quotations are gleanings from one of the most fervent debates in the history of Western philosophy. In *An Inquiry Concerning Human Understanding* (1784), Hume argued that all knowledge ultimately derives from sensations, or sensory data, and that these sensations are the clearest and most vivid kind of knowledge. He expressed a deeply held distrust of abstract ideas, which he felt were "naturally faint and obscure." Kant was in direct opposition. In *Prolegomena* (1783) and other works, he set out to prove that *a priori* knowledge does exist and is valid, that a kind of knowledge does come from sources other than sensations. It was from this and similar philosophical debates that Jung conceptualized two opposing processes of perception: sensing and intuition. Each process clearly has strengths and weaknesses.

Sensory perception represents the direct and conscious use of one's senses, the sensations that Hume felt were the purest form of knowledge. Sensing types prefer and more highly value sensory perception, what they see, hear, touch, smell, and taste. They tend to focus on the details of perception, on what is in the here and now; they want to be sure of actualities, certain that what can be verified is verified. Only then will they inductively move on to understand the gestalt-like relationships among objects of perception.

Sensing types do develop general or abstract ideas, but generally after collecting and massaging large amounts of data. After they have *felt* their data, they are more comfortable about making speculations. But at times they may become so engrossed in the observation of concrete data that they fail to think beyond them.

Intuitive perception, in contrast, is less direct and employs impressionistic and even unconscious hunch-trusting. It is the process used to perceive what Kant called the "knowledge lying beyond experience." Intuitive types, those who prefer intuitive perception, first notice the gestalt. They attend to the details or sensations of perception later, if at all. Intuitive types are usually not as observant as sensing types, and are also less practical and down to earth. They are more likely to be perceived as dreamers who are engrossed in the world of possibilities.

As students, sensing types are, in general, practical and realistic; they like to put into use what they have learned. Learning for its own sake does not appeal much to them; application does. They like teachers who give clear directions that are concise and to the point, and they tend to be detailed and precise in their own communications. Most sensing students approach academic tasks as craftspeople or surgeons. They like to learn a skill or procedure, perfect it, and then practice it without much variation.

As students, intuitive types are less likely to be patient with routine or overly structured mechanical approaches to learning. Because they desire and seek the opportunity to let their gut impressions and hunches work, they tend to prefer open-ended instructions.

College-level English instructors tend to be intuitive types in an intuitive world (see Appendix 2). They value imagination and abstract thought so highly that the strengths of students who are sensing types are often overlooked as are the weaknesses of those who are intuitive types. Sensing types are very observant, accurate with facts and details, careful about following directions, skillful at performing the most complex and intricate of kinesthetic procedures, and scientifically cautious in their development of concepts and acceptance of hypotheses. They are, however, often viewed as being unimaginative and merely concrete. Intuitive types are certainly quick to generate abstractions, but these abstractions may be the kind of flighty, inaccurate, or untested hypotheses that are valued only in academia. Intuitives are also sometimes so creative that they have difficulty accurately following even simple instructions. Writing instructors would better serve their students if they consciously realized that each process of perception—sensing and intuition—has strengths and weaknesses.

WAYS OF JUDGING: THINKING–FEELING

> According to one opinion, the principles of morals are evident *a priori*, requiring nothing to command assent, except that the meaning of the terms be understood. According to the other doctrine, right and wrong, as well as truth and falsehood, are questions of observations and experience. But both hold equally that morality must be deduced from principles; and the intuitive school affirms as strongly as the inductive that there is a science of morals.
>
> John Stuart Mill, *Utilitarianism*

> The moral significance of our conduct can only lie in the effect produced upon others; its relation to the latter is alone that which lends it moral worth, or worthlessness, and constitutes it an act of justice, loving-kindness, etc., or the reverse.
>
> Arthur Schopenhauer, *The Basis of Morality*

In the above quote, John Stuart Mill, attempting to summarize a long history of treatises on ethics, concludes that "morality must be deduced from principles." Some philosophers may develop principles inductively, from observations and experience as a sensing type might. Others may seek principles that they believe are "evident *a priori*," as intuitive types might. But both, Mill contends, seek principles on which they can base ethical decisions. Schopenhauer found principles far less appealing. He felt that there existed no system of principles or moral rules that could be followed unequivocally, for rules and principles do not account for "the complicated nature of human affairs." Rather than rely on principles, Schopenhauer based his ethics on personal values, what he called "a feeling in our own mind," and on how one's actions affected other people. Jung used the terms thinking judgment and feeling judgment to describe these opposing processes of making decisions. Jung felt that both thinking and feeling judgment are rational functions, each bringing a different kind of order to our decision making: the objective base of logic, or the subjective base of valuing.

Thinking types, who prefer thinking judgment and use it more frequently, value the objectivity of decision making. They thus prefer to formulate decisions on what transcends human vacillations, on the objectivity of "things" or ethical principles. Whether decisions are mundane or catastrophically important, they seek to be fair, consistent, and just. For example, when phoning someone, they may establish a criterion to help them to decide when to hang up; they may let the phone ring six times and then hang up. When they do not use criteria, thinking types tend to rely on ethical principles. John Stuart Mill believed that ethical decisions should be based on "the greatest happiness principle," that we should do what promotes the greatest happiness for the greatest number of people. Because thinking types tend to base decisions on criteria or principles, they are—when at their best—consistent, tough minded, truthful, and forthright. At their worst, they may slight the "people issues" of making decisions. They may fail to consider extenuating circumstances (e.g., that Bill has been going through a divorce) or how the decision will affect other individuals (whether someone's feelings will be hurt or someone may feel left out).

Feeling types, who prefer feeling judgment, value the "people issues" of decision making. Whereas thinking types base decisions on criteria and principles, which transcend people and can be applied to all people consistently, feeling types base decisions on personal values, which evolve from people and have meaning only as long as they are attached to people. Rather than establish criteria or principles, feeling types seek to clarify their own values. They strive to understand what Schopenhauer called "a feeling in our own mind." They attempt to determine what they care about most and how they are personally invested. Since feeling types also value affiliation and harmony, the establishing of networks with others, they often base a decision on how it will affect the people around them. They want others to feel valued, and they strive to promote group harmony. At their best, feeling types are supportive, warm, tactful, and sensitive. At their worst, they may be reluctant to offer even constructive criticism and be sentimentally wishy-washy.

As with other dimensions, one's preference toward thinking or feeling judgment significantly influences communication styles. The talk of thinking types usually reflects their thought process, which is rule- or principle-based and syllogistic. They often explain their decisions by counting off "reasons" on their fingers: "the first reason is . . . the second reason is . . . the third reason is . . . ." They also frequently punctuate their talk with the markers of an orderly, syllogistic thought: thus, therefore, in conclusion. Their discourse is what Kinneavy (1971, p. 88) calls "thing-centered." They concentrate on content, what is being said, rather than on process, how the message is connecting with the audience. They may, as a result, come to their point too quickly, or express it too bluntly.

Since the thought of feeling types is based more on forming hierarchies of values, their talk is more likely to be expressive, filled with markers like "I feel," "I believe," or "I like." Their discourse is more "people-centered" (Kinneavy, 1971, p. 88). They more naturally add qualifications to soften criticism or adjust messages to the audience.

As students, thinking types tend to perform to the best of their ability when given a clearly presented set of performance criteria. They also need a logical rationale to learn best; they want to know that their learning will lead toward a greater understanding of the systematic way that the world works and of the principles that underlie systems. In contrast, feeling types need to know that what they are about to learn can be put to work for people they are concerned about or in the service of personally held convictions and values. They are best motivated when their hearts are in their work. While all students certainly are at their best when *both* sets of conditions prevail, thinking types are less likely, as long as they are given a logical reason for doing it, to complain about dry, uninteresting writing assignments, and feeling types, unless given personal encouragement, may find many tasks boring and unrewarding.

ORIENTATIONS TO THE OUTER WORLD: JUDGING–PERCEIVING

> Although [Merleau–Ponty] was more involved politically than his friend Sartre when they founded *Les Temps Modernes*, and never stopped speaking out for political freedom and lucidity, his aesthetic fascination with the visible and his metaphorical multiplication of perspectives subsequently led Sartre to ask whether he had not adopted the politically ineffectual position of contemplating them all without choosing any.
>
> Richard M. McCleary, Translator's Preface to Merleau–Ponty's *Signs*

Though Sartre and Merleau–Ponty were both actively involved in French political life, each was, as McCleary explains, involved in his own way. Sartre seems to have considered fewer political options than Merleau–Ponty and reached his decisions more quickly. Merleau–Ponty seems to have been less concerned about adopting a position and adhering to it. He was more concerned with exploring all options in great depth before reaching any conclusion. Both were involved with outer-experience, but in distinctively different ways. Briggs and Myers added a fourth dimension to Jung's typology to differentiate between judging types (who tend to adopt a position and adhere to it) and perceiving types (who delay closure in order to explore a wide range of options).

The judging type's orientation to the outer world is structured, planful, and decisive. Judging types principally seek to structure the world around them for the purpose of getting things done. The perceiving type's orientation is an adaptive one, flexible, often spontaneous, and inquisitive. Perceiving types principally seek to leave the world around them unstructured for the purpose of examining it, understanding it, or engaging with it in its free, unaffected state. While judging types tend to move toward closure, arriving at conclusions expediently, perceiving types prefer to defer decisions until all of the possible evidence is in. At their best, judging types are productive and task-oriented while perceiving types are thorough. At their worst, judging types rush to decisions, become controlling or even pushy as they rigidly stick to their plans to meet an approaching deadline. At their worst, perceiving types are indecisive procrastinators.

As students, judging types tend to be overachievers. Their natural desire to reach closure leads them to meet deadlines by keeping commitments limited and focusing on one task at a time. Teachers often view them as being more organized and motivated than perceiving types. The natural style of perceiving types, which leads them to overcommit themselves, work on several projects at once, and delay closure until the 11th hour, may make them appear unmotivated. Teachers need to realize that the apparent procrastination of perceiving types is often as productive as a judging type's rush to meet a deadline. Perceiving types may delay beginning or finishing projects so that they can more thoroughly conceptualize or research them.

INTERACTION OF THE DIMENSIONS: DOMINANT AND AUXILIARY PROCESSES

As just described, Jung's model of personality has four bipolar dimensions:

Extraversion (E) .... Introversion (I)
Sensory Perception (S) .... Intuitive Perception (N)
Thinking Judgment (T) ... Feeling Judgment (F)
Judging (J) .... Perceiving (P)

The letters that follow each preference are useful symbols for showing how an individual's preferences on the four dimensions combine and interact, for it is easier to write the abbreviation ESFP than "extraverted–sensing–feeling–perceiving type." Using the letters, Myers diagrammed the 16 possible types thus:

	SENSING (S) TYPES		INTUITIVE (N) TYPES		
INTROVERTS (I)	ISTJ	ISFJ	INFJ	INTJ	JUDGING (J) TYPES
INTROVERTS (I)	ISTP	ISFP	INFP	INTP	PERCEIVING (P) TYPES
EXTRAVERTS (E)	ESTP	ESFP	ENFP	ENTP	PERCEIVING (P) TYPES
EXTRAVERTS (E)	ESTJ	ESFJ	ENFJ	ENTJ	JUDGING TYPES
	THINKING (T) TYPES	FEELING (F) TYPES	FEELING (F) TYPES	THINKING TYPES	

As we cite examples of individual writers in subsequent chapters, we will be commenting on how a student's preference on a single dimension (say, a preference for sensory perception) influences his or her writing process or text. Because it is impossible to isolate purely any single preference, we will also supply the student's preference on all four dimensions of the MBTI within parentheses (ISTJ). An introverted–sensing type will not generate ideas in the same way as an extraverted–sensing type will, nor will a sensing–thinking type develop a topic exactly as will a sensing–feeling type. More importantly, an ISTJ may write more like an ESFP than an INTJ even though the ISTJ and the INTJ may seem, at first glance, to have more in common.

Jung felt that one of the preferences on the Sensing–Intuition or the Thinking–Feeling dimension is more highly developed and thus serves as the foundation of the personality. If one of the preferences were not dominant, then people would tend to be in constant conflict, flip-flopping from one preference to the next. The ISTJ is a dominant sensing type; the INTJ a dominant intuitive type. The two types are so different because the ISTJ's greatest strength is an INTJ's greatest weakness and vice versa.

The dominant can be determined by employing the following system, which was developed by Briggs and Myers:

Extraversion (E) .... Introversion (I)

[This dimension determines whether a person's dominant preference is used in the outer or inner world. Extraverts use their dominant preference in the outer world; introverts use their dominant preference in the inner world.]

Sensory Perception (S) .... Intuitive Perception (N)
Thinking Judgment (T) ... Feeling Judgment (F)
Judging (J) .... Perceiving (P)

[This dimension determines whether one uses a judging or a perceptive process in the outer world. Judging types use either thinking judgment or feeling judgment in the outer world; perceiving types use either sensory or intuitive judgment in the outer world.]

The formula, thus, can tell us which of the middle preferences (the SN and TF dimensions) are used most frequently in the outer world and which of these is the dominant, or the most highly developed.

Let us look at the ISTJ type as an example. This type has a preference for judging on the fourth dimension, which means that the ISTJ uses his or her preference for thinking judgment in the outer world. This person would be structured and task-oriented in dealing with the external world (J), but in a way that is basically objective, logical, systematic, analytical, and perhaps at times cool and impersonal (T). The person would tend to use his or her preference on the other middle dimension (sensory or intuitive perception) when dealing with the internal world of reflections, ideas, considerations, and anticipations. The ISTJ would, then, use his or her preference for sensory perception in the internal world. Since the ISTJ, as an introvert, prefers the internal to the external world, the preference that he or she introverts is called the dominant. It is the most highly developed of all of the middle processes. The ISTJ, then, is called a dominant sensing type.

Let us look at the ENFP. As a perceiving type, the ENFP will tend to use his or her preference for either sensory or intuitive perception in the external world. This type will tend to be flexible and spontaneous in the external world (P), constantly exploring new ideas and possibilities (N). (If the person were a sensing type, he or she might be constantly exploring the concrete nature of the here and now.) The ENFP uses his or her preference for thinking or feeling judgment in the internal world. This type is very sensitive, but his or her sensitivity may sometimes surprise people because it is often internalized. The ENFP's preference for extraversion means that his or her dominant process is the one used in the outer world. The ENFP is a dominant intuitive type.

Once we have established the dominant, we can make some assumptions about the strength of the other cognitive processes.The ENFP's dominant is intuitive perception, which is the most highly developed process. The next most highly developed process, the auxiliary, is the person's other preference, or feeling judgment. The third most highly developed process, the tertiary, is opposite the auxiliary, or thinking judgment. The weakest of the processes is opposite the dominant, which for this type is sensory perception.

Though we will not extensively deal with such complex interactions in this book, it is important to realize that the dimensions are not simply additive. The formula can also help us to understand communication styles better. A person will tend to communicate with whatever preference is extraverted. An ESFP, who extraverts a preference for sensory perception, will tend to talk most about what is concrete, thus communicating the raw data of his or her life. An ENFP, who extraverts a preference for intuitive perception, will tend to talk most about abstract ideas, general impressions, and possibilities. Though the two types seem highly similar, they may, unless they can connect on a shared preference for feeling judgment, have some difficulty communicating with each other.

AN EXAMPLE OF INTERACTIONS AS DISCOURSE COMMUNITIES: ST, SF, NF, NT

In the previous section, we discussed the interaction of dimensions abstractly and rather formulaically. In this section, we will provide a concrete example: the interaction of the Sensing–Intuition and the Thinking–Feeling dimensions as related to discourse and discourse communities. The discussion will be drawn from four sources. First, Hayden White's *Metahistory* (1973) and *Tropics of Discourse* (1978). In these works, White uses the four major tropes (metonymy, synecdoche, metaphor, and irony), which he feels are "useful for understanding the operations by which the contents of experience . . . can be prefiguratively grasped and prepared for conscious apprehension", to analyze different approaches to historiography. White does not overtly tie his work to personality theory, but parallels can be drawn. Second, Mitroff and Kilmann's *Methodological Approaches to Social Science* (1978). They use Jung's personality theory to analyze four scientific methodologies. Although they do not use the term, they are actually describing discourse communities in the social sciences. Third, Stephen North's *The Making of Knowledge in Composition* (1987). North attempts to define different methodological approaches to research in the field of composition, producing categories that are remarkably similar to those that Mitroff and Kilmann find at work in the social sciences in general. Fourth, a classroom exercise. We divided students into four groups (ST, SF, NF, NT) and asked them to describe time to a Martian. With the results of this exercise, we hope to show that personality type influences the thought of these ad hoc discourse communities.

Sensing–Thinking Types (ST)

A metonymy is an expression in which a part of the whole stands for the whole, for example, "fifty sails" stands for "fifty ships." White sees a metonymy as a microcosm–macrocosm relationship, an analytical reduction of the whole into a representative part, which leads to a scientific, materialistic, causal interpretation of phenomena. Of Tocqueville, who employed the metonymical mode, White says:

> He purported to discern long-range trends, of a political, social, and cultural-historical nature, which indicated by his lights the decline of one of the types of society (the aristocratic) and the rise of the other (the democratic). And he suggested that the decline of the aristocratic type is a function of the rise of the democratic type, which means that he viewed the whole democratic process as a closed system, containing a finite amount of usable energy, in which whatever is gained in any process of growth must be paid for by some loss in another part of the system. The system as a whole, viewed as a process, was thus mechanistically conceived, and the relationship between the parts were conceived in mechanical-causal terms. (*Metahistory*, p. 195)

This is an apt description of the thought process of STs. They tend to view experience as a closed system, one that can be broken down into parts (e.g., types of societies) and analyzed.

The STs, according to Mitroff and Kilmann (1978), can be labeled as Analytic Scientists. As supreme empiricists, they believe that knowledge is value-free, impersonal, and unambiguous. Data must be collected via a method that is reliable and precise, and they must be analyzed objectively and logically (see Table 1). Mitroff and Kilmann do not assert that all empiricists are STs, but they do feel that predominantly ST populations were probably behind the rise of positivism and are currently the caretakers of empirical values.

In the field of composition, North (1987) calls these researchers the Experimentalists; they assume that "the world is an orderly place, a place of non-random causes and effects, that order exists quite apart from our experience of it, and that the principles of order are accessible to human inquiry" (p. 146). North points out that, even though the Experimentalists have produced a large volume of work, their findings have had relatively little influence on practice. This is probably due in part to the lack of training that the average composition teacher has in empirical methodology, but it may also be related to the low number of STs in the field. Most practitioners seem to be NFs or NTs (see Appendix 2).

The metonymical mode of thought (the breaking down of the whole into discrete parts) and empirical values even emerge in the writing of our students. A group of ST students wrote the following description of time:

1. Time is a measurement of duration.
2. Time is based on the position of the sun during the day.
3. A unit of time is a second
    (A) 60 sec. make a minute
    (B) 60 minutes make an hour
    (C) 24 hours make a day
        (1) A day is a rotation of our planet earth
    (D) 365 days in a year
        (2) 1 year is 1 revolution of our planet around the sun.

For these ST students, time is not a mushy concept; it is something that can be measured precisely and can be understood by breaking it down into parts.

Sensing–Feeling Types (SF)

A synecdoche is an expression in which a part of the whole stands for some quality of the whole, e.g., "He is all heart." In this expression, "heart" is part of the man, but it also symbolizes his compassion. White feels that a synecdoche represents a movement from the part to the whole and is, thus, integrative rather than reductive. He believes that Ranke, the 19th-century Prussian historian, employed this mode:

> Ranke stated that his purpose had been to relate the histories of the nations "in their unity." But the comprehension of that unity could come, he maintained, only through a consideration of particulars. He admitted that his concentration on "particulars" might give a "harsh, disconnected, colorless, and tiring" aspect to his narrative. But the "sublime ideal" to which his work aspired, "the event in its human intelligibility, its unity, and its diversity," could be attained only by a movement from the particular to the general, never by the reverse. (*Metahistory*, p. 165)

Ranke wanted history to be "solidly rooted"; his thought was generally concrete and rule-governed, but it was also less objective than Tocqueville's. Ranke's ambition was "to grasp the divine intentions of history." He dealt with data *and* values (*Metahistory*, p. 172).

Ranke was very much a part of his historical narratives, and it is this involvement of the scientist with his or her data that Mitroff and Kilmann (1978) find distinctive of SF science, which they label the Particular

Table 1. Characteristics of the Analytic Scientist (ST)

	Evaluative categories	Attributed characteristics
External relations	Status of science as a special field of knowledge in relation to other fields	Occupies a privileged and a preferred position: vaue-free, apolitical, cumulative, progressive, disinterested, clearly separable from other fields, clear lines of demarcation, autonomous, independent, strict hierarchical ordering of scientific fields from precise to less precise fields
Internal properties	A. Nature of scientific knowledge	Impersonal, value-free, disinterested, precise, reliable, accurate, valid, reductionistic, causal, apolitical, cumulative, progressive, clear standards for judgment, realistic, antimystical, unambiguous, exact
	B. Guarantors of scientific knowledge	Consensus, agreement, reliability, external validity, rigor, controlled nature of inquiry, maintenance of distance between scientist and objects studied
	C. Ultimate aims of science	Precise, unambiguous, theoretical and empirical knowledge for their own (disinterested) sake
	D. Preferred logic	Aristotelian, strict classical logic, nondialectical and indeterminate
	E. Preferred sociological norms (ideology)	Classical norms of science
	F. Preferred mode of inquiry	Controlled inquiry as embodied in the classic concept of the experiment
	G. Properties of the scientist	Disinterested, unbiased, impersonal, precise, expert, specialist, skeptical, exact, methodical

Source: Mitroff and Kilmann, *Methodological Approaches to Social Sciences* (1978)

Humanist (see Table 2). They feel that SF science reflects a mythical mode of thought:

> Mythical thought, with its emphasis on personalization and storytelling, is analogous to the relationship between the parts and the wholes of the SF's world. In our everyday world and in ordinary science, the parts of an entity are strictly subordinate to the whole. This is not true of mythical thinking, where the part is more than just a part. By its very presence, the part signifies the whole and becomes, as it were, identical with it. (p. 100)

Table 2. Characteristics of the Particular Humanist (SF)

	Evaluative categories	Attributed characteristics
External relations	Status of science as a special field of knowledge in relation to other fields	Does not occupy a privileged and special position; may be subordinate to poetry, literature, art, music, and mysticism as older, "superior" ways of knowing
Internal properties	A. Nature of scientific knowledge	Personal, value-constituted, interested; partisan activity; poetic, political, action-oriented; acausal, nonrational
	B. Guarantors of scientific knowledge	Intense personal knowledge and experience
	C. Ultimate aims of science	To help this person know himself or herself uniquely and to achieve his own self-determination
	D. Preferred logic	The "logic" of the unique and singular
	E. Preferred sociological norms (ideology)	Antithesis of classical norms of science
	F. Preferred mode of inquiry	The case study; the in-depth, detailed study of a particular individual
	G. Properties of the scientist	Interested, "all-too-human," biased, poetic, committed to the postulates of an action-oriented science

Source: Mitroff and Kilmann, *Methodological Approaches to Social Sciences* (1978)

This epistemology is well suited to case studies and enthnography, but ST researchers often regard it as sloppy and imprecise.

The SFs' methodological ideal, as exemplified by Ranke, is to immerse themselves in the richness and uniqueness of the particular and then move to the general; the ideal, as North (1987) points out, raises their fundamental methodological problem:

> However much [ethnographers] may reduce our puzzlement about the people and places studied, though, these fictions have their limits as knowledge. One such limit lies in the insularity of investigations: the difficulty of somehow extending the findings of an investigation in any one community to any other. Ethnographic findings are made in the context of, and thus tied to, the specific phenomena accounted for. (p. 278)

An SF scientist might retort that whatever is lost in generalizability is compensated for by a rich and complex understanding of the particular.

The merging of the perceiver's values and the particular is apparent in the following description of time, written by a group of SF students for a Martian visitor:

1. sun's movements
2. 5 bleep-bleeps Martian time equals 1 hour our time
3. explain hours and minutes
4. months in a year
5. seasons in a year, colors of trees indicate seasons
6. temperature indicates season
7. rotation
8. revolution
9. time zones
10. belly-aches indicate meal times
11. drooping antennae indicate sleep time
12. alarm clock means to get up
13. shadows indicate changing times
14. movement of ocean indicates changing times

As with the STs, this description is sensory and concrete, but it is far from objective. The SFs do more than simply break time down into measurable units. In a very personable and humorous way, they move from the particular to the general. The phrase "shadows indicate changing times" moves from sensory data (shadows) to a general implication (indicate changing times).

Intuitive–Feeling Types (NF)

A metaphoric expression "asserts that a similarity exists between two objects in the face of manifest differences between them," e.g., "my love is a rose" (*Metahistory*, p. 34). The expression is meant to be taken figuratively, to fuse symbolically a shared quality of "my love" and a "rose." Jules Michelet, according to White, employed the metaphorical mode when writing about the French revolution:

> Michelet strove for a *symbolic fusion* of the different entities occupying the historical field, rather than for a means for characterizing them as individual symbols. Whatever uniqueness there is in history was conceived by Michelet to be the uniqueness of the whole, not of the parts that comprise the whole. The individuality of the parts is only apparent. Their significance derives from their status as symbols of the *unity* that everything—in history as in nature—is *striving to become*. (*Metahistory*, p. 150)

Table 3. Characteristics of the Conceptual Humanist (NF)

	Evaluative categories	Attributed characteristics
External relations	Status of science as a special field of knowledge in relation to other fields	Does not occupy a privileged and preferred position, is not clearly separable from other fields; no clear lines of demarcation; not autonomous and independent; all fields of knowledge depend upon one another. Science is not value-free; it is political.
Internal properties	A. Nature of scientific knowledge	Personal; value-constituted, interested activity; holistic; political; imaginative; multiple-causation; uncertain; problematic; concerned with humanity
	B. Guarantors of scientific knowledge	Human conflict between knowing agent (E) and subject known (S); inquiry fosters human growth and development
	C. Ultimate aims of science	To promote human development on the widest possible scale
	D. Preferred logic	Dialectical behavioral logics
	E. Preferred sociological norms (ideology)	Economic plenty, aesthetic beauty, human welfare
	F. Preferred mode of inquiry	Conceptual inquiry; treatment of innovative concepts; maximal cooperation between E and S so that both may better know themselves and one another
	G. Properties of the scientist	Interested; free to admit and know his biases; highly personal; imaginative, speculative, generalist; holistic

Source: Mitroff and Kilmann, *Methodological Approaches to Social Sciences* (1978)

The metaphorical mode is symbolic, holistic, idealistic, and fluid. History, for Michelet, was a Romance of society becoming "the pure love of unity" (*Metahistory*, p. 151).

Mitroff and Kilmann feel that the science of NFs, whom they call Conceptual Humanists, is as idealistic as the history of Michelet. NFs want to investigate the complexity of human interactions, but their ultimate goal is to improve the human condition (see Table 3). In the field of composition, NFs are probably active in approaches that North calls the Practitioners as well as the Clinicians. Of the Clinicians, North wrote:

> To a far greater extent than in most Experimental studies, the Clinical investigator depends on her relationship with the subjects to get the

> information she wants. Asking people to compose aloud while you and a tape recorder sit with them; stimulated recall, where you go over such tapes or other materials, asking them to remember how they felt and thought at the time; background interviews, where you ask them to tell you their habits, fears, fantasies—all these and other typical Clinical techniques demand not only that subjects trust you as an investigator, but that they be willing to work very hard, as well, and to concentrate in unusual ways. (p. 208)

Although researchers of any personality type might employ this methodology, the NF is particularly adept at developing trust and motivating others.

That NFs value this kind of social interaction is apparent in the following description of time, written by NF students:

1. method of social organization
2. label marking changes so we can communicate
3. circles of cycles
4. sands of sea
5. the eternity of possibilities

Their description is metaphorical ("circle of cycles" and "sands of sea"), clearly more abstract than the description of either the STs or SFs. The NFs' description is value-laden, as was the SFs, but it represents a more holistic value (social organization and communication) that is similar to Michelet's "pure love of unity."

Intuitive–Thinking Types (NT)

Irony is a form of negation. To state ironically that "my love is a rose" is to say that my love is *not* a rose. Irony then, according to White, is "the self conscious awareness of the possible misuse of figurative language" (*Metahistory*, p. 37). White feels that irony "provides a linguistic paradigm of a mode of thought which is radically self-critical with respect not only to a given characterization of the world of experience but also to the very effort to capture adequately the truth of things in language" (*Metahistory*, p. 37). The ironic mode is characterized by a "skepticism in philosophy." It is symbolic, but not idealistic as is the metaphorical mode. It "conceives the world as trapped within a prison made of language, the world as a 'forest of symbols' " (*Metahistory*, pp. 231–233). White found in Jacob Burckhardt a historian of irony:

> Burckhardt called his "philosophy of history" a "theory of history," and presented it as nothing more than an "arbitrary" arrangement of the

> materials for purposes of presentation and analysis. He could not attempt to give the "real nature" of the events, because his pessimism denied him the luxury of assuming that events had any "nature" at all. (*Metahistory*, p. 237)

Not all NTs are as pessimistic as Burckhardt, but they do tend to build symbolic models of reality rather than attempt to deal with reality itself. While they are very concerned about the internal logical consistency of their models, they may be relatively unconcerned about how these models relate to phenomena.

Mitroff and Kilmann (1978) call these researchers Conceptual Theorists. They "deeply value broad-ranging ideas" but "do not demand that these ideas be tied down to 'reality' in the sense of being verified by accepted theories and facts" (p. 55). In the field of composition, North (1987) refers to them as Formalists:

> The object in all of these kinds of Formalist inquiries is model building. An Experimentalist sets out to sort through competing theories by attempting to isolate the features of some portion of the empirical world and working to correlate the relationships among them. A Formalist, by contrast, investigates by what amounts to analogy. The basic idea is to construct, usually in a formal language, a model whose internal logic in some specifiable ways resembles that of the phenomenon under study. (p. 239)

Rather than slowly build "the big picture" step by step, NTs present fully formed models, which may not perfectly correspond to the empirical domain. As the weaknesses of the model become evident, it is—through a process of successive approximation—reworked and refined. What some researchers may not understand is that NTs usually regard their models with a certain degree of skepticism or irony. North explains:

> What makes all this [model building] difficult for outsiders is that it can be hard not to mistake the elements of a Formal model for the "real" things to which they correspond in some way. . . . For instance, Flower and Hayes . . . create a model in which there seem to be three major elements: "the task environment," "the writer's long term memory," and "the writing process." These labels illustrate the problem clearly enough. They sound like they ought to be empirical entities, but in fact they are essentially place holders, nouns which represent some set of formal properties assumed to be traceable also in the "system" by which humans produce written texts. However, an outsider reading them or seeing them depicted in an illustration is very likely to mistake the model for a description, and so think that the model "shows" or "demonstrates" that writers "have" long term memory, a task environment, and a writing process.

Of course, even NT researchers may reify their abstract models, but are they more likely to value models that are intriguing or logically consistent than models that explain the particulars of the "real world" (see Table 4).

Some of the qualities of an NT researcher can be found in the following description of time, written by NT students:

1. Based on earth's rotation around the sun
2. Time is used as a point of reference to synchronize our activities on earth.
3. Time is measured in years, which break down into seasons, months, weeks, days, hours, minutes, seconds (and nano seconds)

Table 4. Characteristics of the Conceptual Theorist (NT)

	Evaluative categories	Attributed characteristics
External relations	Status of science as a special field of knowledge in relation to other fields	Occupies a privileged and preferred position, but is not clearly separable from other fields; no clear lines of demarcation; not autonomous or independent, no strict hierarchical ordering of fields; all depend upon one another; science is, however, value-free and apolitical.
Internal properties	A. Nature of scientific knowledge	Impersonal, value-free, disinterested, holistic, valid, apolitical, imaginative, multiple-causation, purposeful ambiguity, uncertainty, problematic
	B. Guarantors of scientific knowledge	Conflict between antithetical imaginative theories, comprehensive holistic theories, ever-expanding research programs
	C. Ultimate aims of science	To construct the broadest possible conceptual schemes; multiple production of conflicting schemas
	D. Preferred logic	Dialectical logics, indeterminate logics
	E. Preferred sociological norms (ideology)	Norms are a function of one's theoretical perspective and cannot be separated from one's conceptual-theoretical interests
	F. Preferred mode of inquiry	Conceptual inquiry; treatment of innovative concepts from multiple perspectives; invention of new schemas
	G. Properties of the scientist	Disinterested, unbiased, impersonal, imaginative, speculative, generalist, holistic

Source: Mitroff and Kilmann, *Methodological Approaches to Social Sciences* (1978)

4. Time is also measured through our life. When someone is born, how long they live, or when they die, and through life the development of the body from infancy to adulthood.
5. We would send a martian to someone who knows astrological math to explain how to break time down.

The NTs description is as abstract as that of the NFs but more objective, without the idealistic concern for social communication. Some of their comments express a lack of concern for the details of reality; the NTs would rather send the Martian to someone who knew astrological mathematics than explain time themselves. Other comments embody a degree of irony. They say that "time is *used* as a point of reference," not "time *is* a point of reference." Unlike the STs, they seem to have an awareness that time is an artificial and arbitrary construct.

In this section, we have suggested that personality type—especially once combinations are considered—can explain how historians conceive of and present their content, how scientists, including composition theorists, conduct research, and even how students describe a commonplace concept such as "time." No doubt, the distribution of personality type within a discourse community also affects the practice of its members.

THE MYERS–BRIGGS TYPE INDICATOR AS AN INSTRUMENT

The Myers–Briggs Type Indicator (MBTI) can help to identify a writer's personality type. It is a measure of one's expressed preferences on each of the four dimensions discussed earlier in this chapter. It is not, however, a performance test and does not measure how well people use their preferred cognitive processes. Form G of the MBTI (emerging from 30 years of development) is a 126-item pencil-and-paper inventory. The new edition of the manual (Myers & McCaulley, 1985) contains extensive information on the instrument's reliability and validity. The recent review of the instrument in Buros (DeVito, 1985), based on the new manual, is extremely positive.

All pencil-and-paper inventories, however, have shortcomings and can be easily misused. The MBTI is one of the most benign of psychological instruments, since it was designed to identify the strengths and gifts of each type. Nevertheless, results from the MBTI can be misused if those administering and interpreting them attach primarily negative connotations to certain types. It is difficult for some to accept that all types have different but equally valid ways of dealing with the world.

If teachers, researchers, and clinicians are to appreciate the subtleties of the instrument, training in the uses of psychological tests and the MBTI in particular is crucial. The Association for Psychological Type (APT) offers training workshops for administering and interpreting the MBTI.

Though results from the MBTI may eventually provide valuable information for composition teachers, we are not suggesting that teachers should administer the instrument wholesale. If teachers do wish to obtain MBTI results on their students, they should either have a psychologist administer the inventory or seek training from APT. If teachers do not wish to administer the MBTI, a knowledge of type and how it affects writing can nonetheless be valuable. At the very least, the teacher will be more aware of and more accepting of individual approaches to writing. Whether working from actual MBTI results or from hunches, *both teachers and researchers should be cautious about typing students.* MBTI results are sometimes inaccurate, and people are not always as they appear to be.

OTHER MEASURES OF JUNG'S PERSONALITY TYPOLOGY

The MBTI is only one of three inventories of Jung's personality typology. Wheelwright and his associates (1964) developed the Jungian Type Survey. It produces scores for the three dimensions of Jung's original typology (Extraversion–Introversion, Sensing–Intuition, Thinking–Feeling), which correlate highly with respective scales on the MBTI. The dominant is indicated by the highest score on either the Sensing–Intuition or the Thinking–Feeling dimension.

The Singer Loomis Inventory of Personality (SLIP) (Loomis, 1982) is a more recently developed instrument, which is more widely used among Jungian analysts. June Singer and Mary Loomis, the Jungian analysts who developed the SLIP, believe that Myers's method for determining types is too rigid and not in tune with Jung's theory about the possible transcendence of opposites. They feel that a person can be highly developed, for example, in both intuitive and sensory perception, and they wanted to develop an instrument that would more fluidly and flexibly measure such developmental differences.

Their instrument differs from the MBTI in two important ways. They do not include a scale to measure a preference for Judging or Perceiving, which was Myers and Briggs's major extension of Jung's model. They also avoided forced-choice items that lead to a single preference score (toward either S or N, for example). Instead, items that measure only one function at a time lead to independent results for each cognitive process, for example, a separate score for both intuitive perception and sensory perception.

THE MBTI AND OTHER INSTRUMENTS THAT MEASURE COGNITIVE STYLE

In this volume, we will primarily be using the MBTI as an indicator of learning style or cognitive style, but it is certainly not the only such measure available. Since 1960, approximately 30 instruments of learning styles have appeared. Some of the more interesting and more frequently used are the *Hidden Figures Test* (1962), *Matching Figures Test* (1965), *Group Embedded Figures Test* (1971), *Student Learning Styles Questionnaire* (1974), *Cognitive Style Mapping Inventory* (1975), Kolb's *Learning Styles Inventory* (1976), and Dunn, Dunn, and Price's *Learning Styles Inventory* (adults, 1977; students, 1978). These and other instruments collectively measure about 20 aspects of learning styles, but none is comprehensive (for a discussion of learning style theory and a bibliography of learning-style instruments, see Keefe, 1982).

We chose to use the MBTI for several reasons. First, the MBTI was more carefully constructed than most instruments of its kind. It was painstakingly developed over a 30-year period. The second edition of the manual contains data from more than 100 validity studies. Second, the MBTI is more conceptually sophisticated and complex than most learning style assessments. Rather than identify a few "styles," for example, field dependent versus field independent, the MBTI can identify 16 types or 16 approaches to learning. Because of its sophistication, it can, as Lawrence (1984) has documented, account for most of the traits identified by other widely used instruments. It is not, however, comprehensive. Nor is any other published instrument. The most significant shortcoming is the MBTI's inability to identify preferences for visual, auditory, and kinesthetic channels of perception and communication (Grinder & Bandler, 1976). Lowen (1982) has hypothesized connections between Sensing and the kinesthetic channel, Thinking and the visual channel, and Feeling and the auditory channel, but his theory remains untested and has yielded mixed results in the clinic and classroom.

What is most striking about the MBTI, and what so empowers it, is that the instrument was developed as, and primarily remains, an assessment of personality type. Most learning style inventories assess how the student is behaving or how the student believes that he or she performs best. With these instruments, teachers can better understand the patterns in a student's learning behaviors, but learning style inventories rarely provide clues as to whether students' behavior truly represents their learning style or how they were taught to learn. Since the MBTI assesses personality type, one is better able to make predictions about how a given student might perform best, which may or may not be consistent with his or her present behavior. Furthermore, teacher preferences can successfully be studied in interaction with those of students (DeNovellis & Lawrence, 1983). We have found the MBTI particularly useful in understanding conflicts between how the writer prefers to write and how he or she was taught to write (Jensen & DiTiberio, 1983, 1984). The case studies presented in Chapter 5 will illustrate this point. A variety of other applications of type theory and the MBTI to higher education have recently been documented by Provost and Anchors (1987).

SURVEY OF THE BOOK

In subsequent chapters, we will be applying Jung's model of personality to various aspects of the teaching and research of composition. Chapter 2 will cover the effect of personality on the writing process. Chapter 3 presents the hypothesis that different personality types follow a distinct rather than a universal pattern of development. Chapter 4 describes how teachers can use Jung's model to help individual writers follow the developmental pattern that suits their personality type. Chapter 5 discusses the influence of personality type on writing anxiety and writer's blocks. Chapter 6 covers the influence of personality type on how teachers evaluate writing. Chapter 7 shows how Jung's model can be used to understand cohorts of writers, such as basic writers. This chapter is followed by a conclusion.

Since development and context also affect how one writes, we will provide with each illustration the writer's educational or professional level as well as his or her type, for example, (ISTJ/Professional). The following categories will be used:

Basic: Basic writers in the developmental studies program at Georgia State University.

Freshman: Freshmen writers in regular English courses at Georgia State.

Regents: Upperclass students, mostly juniors, in a writing class that prepares students for a minimal competency exam in writing.

Graduate: Graduate students at the University of Illinois at Chicago or Georgia State.

Professional: Writers who are members of some professional community, for example, teachers, lawyers, and so forth.

To remind readers that Jung's model of personality type is fundamentally probabilistic, that the model is not deterministic, we will qualify as many statements as possible, e. g., "extraverts tend to . . ." or "sensing types often . . ." We will also occasionally cite counterexamples to illustrate that personality type alone cannot account for all variables among writing processes and products.

2
Individual Writing Processes

When describing the teaching of writing as a process—a doctrine that has rarely, if ever, been seriously challenged—Donald Murray (1980) wrote:

> Theory . . . must return to practice in our field. A writing theory that can not be practiced by teachers, writers, or students and that does not produce increasingly effective drafts of writing must be reconsidered. We also have an obligation to show how the theory can be put into practice. We must show that our students are able to write more effectively and produce pieces of writing that find their own meaning because they understand what happens during the writing act. (pp. 12–13)

Murray's statement sums up the hopes of many recent theorists and researchers: If we understand the writing process and develop a pedagogy to teach that process, then students will know what to say and how to say it. A healthy process, in other words, will give birth to a healthy text.

Writing has arguably always been taught as a process, but the process, which evolved largely from classical rhetoric, was more prescriptive than descriptive. The quasiprocess of invention, arrangement, memory, and delivery–present or implied in most Greek and Latin rhetorical texts—can be found to some degree in the theoretical treatises of the 1950s. Ken Macrorie's *The Perceptive Writer, Reader, and Speaker* (1959), for example, contains a chapter entitled "Perceiving: The Process," in which he discusses generating and arranging ideas. The influence of classical rhetoric was even more apparent, as was the movement toward teaching writing as a process, in D. Gordon Rohman's influential 1965 article, "Pre-Writing: The Stage of Discovery in the Writing Process." He began the article with a definition of writing: "Writing is usefully described as a process, something which shows continuous change in time like growth in organic nature." The process, Rohman continued, can be described as spanning three stages: prewriting, writing, and rewriting. The model, though simple, linear and sequential, engendered several articles on teaching prewriting heuristics and revising techniques, enormously influencing classroom instruction (see Young, 1976).

In 1971, Janet Emig's seminal monograph, *The Composing Processes of*

Twelfth Graders, began a shift of attention from *the* writing process to writing process*es*. Rohman had advocated a single model for all writers: think of what you want to write, write it, and then revise it. From studying interviews, protocols, and observations, Emig instead discovered that different writers may follow divergent processes and yet arrive at equally suitable texts. She found that some writers like to generate ideas from conversations with friends; others prefer to think alone. Some prefer to outline before writing; others afterwards. Some write best when they begin with a specific incident or fact; some when they begin with a general idea or concept. Some tend to write objectively, others personally.

Data from a massive research project begun in 1966, first published in 1975, added support to many of Emig's findings. In *The Development of Writing Abilities (11–18)*, James Britton and his colleagues asserted that, based on their investigation of the writing processes of students in London's public schools, individuals use different writing processes. For example, the incubation process of some students is brief, and for others it may be very long. Since they were studying students as they wrote in class, Britton's group also realized, as Emig had before them, that how teachers teach the writing process and how writers actually write are often at odds: "We found that there were some irreconcilable differences between the way writers work, and the way many teachers and composition textbooks are constantly advising their pupils to set about their tasks" (p. 20). One of the important messages of the Britton study is that composition teachers should stop delivering the same hackneyed advice to all students.

Other researchers, studying 7-year-old children (Graves, 1975), basic writers (Perl, 1979), advanced writers (Hairston, 1984), and other groups (Selzer, 1983; Stallard, 1974), have come to the same conclusion: writing processes vary. Based on this evidence, composition teachers began to realize that no single task or activity—even outlining—is necessary for the development of writing ability or the production of a suitable text. Robert Gorrell (1983) summarized this trend from teaching a single writing process to teaching writing processes by using the metaphor of Mulligan's stew. Just as Mulligan's stew can be made in a variety of ways, so too can writing be produced from a variety of processes. After exhausting the metaphor, Gorrell wrote:

> I'm aware that this is mainly nonsense, but it leads me to some things I want to say about current enthusiasms in research, particularly about what we are calling the composing process. I think we have been learning something about the composing process—not only about the frequency with which a tenth-grader chews a pencil, but also about the psychological

> events attendant on getting something from the mind on paper. I do not propose to criticize—or expand— current theories about the composing process. Rather I want to look at composing as a simple-minded stewmaker, to try to do some summarizing and ordering, and especially to urge that we should be thinking not of the composing process but of composing processes.

Who is to say, Gorrell asks, which recipe or writing process is correct?

The research seems to have lead us to an impasse. If any single process is conceivably as "correct" as any other, then how can we teach writing as a process? Gorrell answers with shrugged shoulders:

> The search for *the* writing process seems to me to push the investigator toward conclusions too general to be useful or too trivial to be significant. . . . The problem is that the writing process is so complex and varied, as much current useful research is showing, that discussions of *the* process seem often to exhibit the zeal, but also face the futility of the medieval alchemist.

Certainly, general conclusions (such as, "good writers revise") are not particularly useful, as specific conclusions (such as, "Janet revises better after receiving oral feedback") are too trivial, but a more troublesome problem is dealing with complex, often contradictory, conclusions. Hillocks's (1986) meta-analysis of research in the field is an enormous step toward reducing the dissonance found among research studies. We must, as Hillocks advises, discard results from studies that are "ill-conceived and badly designed." As faulty studies are eliminated, consensus in some areas may be reached. We should not, however, strive for consensus at the expense of devaluing valid individual differences.

Jung's model of personality types provides at least a partial solution to these problems. It allows research to be more specific, because we can research the writing process of a particular type of student, and it guards against the trivial, because the model directs our attention to fundamental psychological processes. Even more importantly, once personality type is considered, many apparent contradictions in research findings and theoretical controversies among practitioners can be resolved.

EXTRAVERSION–INTROVERSION AND WRITING PROCESSES

In 1960, Milton A. Kaplan wrote in *College Composition and Communication,* which was becoming the theoretical forum of an emerging discipline, that writers need to spend more time planning before they commit words to paper. His position was far from provocative. He only stated what many of his readers no doubt muttered to themselves whenever they read student essays. Kaplan began:

> Before the experienced writer ventures into formal composition, he surveys his material for the implications and the pattern that will dictate strategy, organization, emphasis, tone and even style. Too often the English instructor takes this step for granted and sends his students off without any preparation to gather material and to write papers in the hope that somehow cohesive patterns will emerge. They rarely do.

Interestingly, Kaplan's approach to teaching composition, despite its glaring conventionality, presaged—as did other articles of that period—the process approach. Five years later, Rohman, after stating that "thinking precedes writing," explained:

> Ciardi describes the [prewriting] process introspectively as without end, "but in time the good writer will acquire not only a sense of *groping for* but a sense of having *groped to*: he begins to know when he has finally reached whatever he was reaching for." The paradox gives us an important clue, we believe, to the principle of Pre-Writing: writers set out in apparent ignorance of what they are groping for; yet they recognize it when they find it. In a sense they knew it all along, but it took some sort of heuristic process to bring it out. When it is "out," they have discovered their subject; all that's left is the writing of it.

As conceived by Rohman, the writing process is particularly suited to introverts (he even describes Ciardi as being introspective), for they naturally plan what they want to say and mentally rehearse how they want to say it before they write.

Extraverted views of the writing process followed soon after. In 1970, Ken Macrorie's *Telling Writing* appeared. In *Writing Without Teachers* (1973), Peter Elbow proselytized for free writing and peer feedback. In 1978, Donald Murray's article "Write Before Writing" was published in *College Composition and Communication*. An important correlate in the theory of all three writers is that outer experience and talk are crucial to generating sound ideas. As Murray words it, "The act of voicing experience and connecting it involves . . . fundamentally an aural facility." And, "In teaching the [writing] process we have to look, not at what students need to know, but what they need to experience." Experience and talk had been quite absent from the prewriting strategies Rohman suggested: a journal, meditation, and the use of analogy. Another correlate is that Murray and Elbow believe that meaning develops as one writes. As Murray states, it is important that writers "write what they did not expect to write" and that "they discover that writing is a process of discovery." Rohman felt that writers discover their meaning *before* they write; Murray and Elbow feel that writers discover their meaning *as* they write. Both views can be correct, but not equally for all types of people.

Certainly, all writers plan to some extent, but, as some studies have shown (Matsuhashi, 1981; Rose, 1984), the amount of time devoted to planning can vary. Extraverts, when not blocked, tend to write without extensively planning what they want to say or how they want to say it. When not hampered by anxiety, they tend to leap into writing, use trial and error to get words on paper, and write drafts quickly. This tendency to leap into writing is most evident with younger writers who are given essay-length assignments. As extraverts develop, they learn how to plan more extensively and even outline. Several extraverted professionals have told us that they seldom outlined until they wrote their dissertation. They then learned to outline from necessity: a dissertation is simply too complex to free write. More research is needed to determine if the kind of differences in planning time that Matsuhashi and Rose found in high school and college students is indeed related to personality type and if these kinds of differences persist even in mature, professional writers.

Because many writers are often taught to plan and outline before writing, those extraverts who are novice writers often feel that their own approach to writing, if it precludes extensive planning, is an aberration. They often describe their writing process as "quick and dirty" or doing it "the easy way." One extravert (ESTJ/Regents), dissatisfied with her writing, sent the following note to her professor:

> When writing an essay I need to slow down and organize my thoughts. . . . However, I'm totally aware that my problem is [occurring] while I write. I never start out with a set of ideas to develop, they come as I write. This paragraph is an example of that, my thoughts of what to say came as I wrote.

Cathy (ESFJ/Basic) expressed a similar uneasiness about how she wrote: "Sometimes I wonder what I am thinking when I write papers. Maybe I just write whats in my head without even thinking how it is going to sound."

These writers often compose with less stress if teachers encourage them to accept, when the context allows, their natural approach to writing. Peter Elbow's work, especially when he is discussing free writing, is a particularly valuable resource for extraverts. He has, as illustrated by the following passage from *Writing with Power* (1981, p. 27), a talent for advising extraverts (particularly extraverted–intuitives) to do what they do best: "Write fast. Don't waste any time or energy on how to organize it, what to start with, paragraphing, wording, spelling, grammar, or any other matters of presentation. Just get things down helter-skelter." For many extraverts, reading Elbow is like receiving absolution for their preferred writing process.

Even though novice extraverts are rarely willing to delay writing long enough to perform protracted heuristics, what they do before writing is nonetheless important. Since extraverts are directed toward the outer world of people and things, that is where they seek their ideas. Most extraverts generate ideas best from talking about the topic, interviewing others, or presenting an extemporaneous speech. Extraverts often say that, before writing, they call a friend and generate ideas over the phone. Their reliance on talk may, especially for developing writers, produce in initial drafts a conversational style with the kind of wordiness and repetition found in face-to-face conversation.

Extraverts can, of course, develop ideas in solitude, which is more typical of introverts, but they do seem to develop their best ideas when talking or writing. Indeed, some extraverts, even experienced, adult writers, have said that they come up with good ideas when alone, but they have trouble remembering and developing the ideas until they talk or write about them.

Besides talking, extraverts may generate ideas by becoming actively involved with the world around them. Some extraverts pace around their desk or exercise before writing. Winston Churchill, whom one biographer described as an extraverted intuitive type, dictated his texts, composing them extemporaneously, as he paced back and forth (Manchester, 1983, p. 32). Outer experience can also be a frequent source of inspiration, because extraverts' ideas most frequently evolve from their interaction with the world around them. For example, Debbie (ESTJ/Basic) watches television before writing. She wrote: "It helps me concentrate and I get a lot of ideas." Novice extraverts rarely say that they prefer to write as introverts do, by sitting alone at a desk in a quiet place. As Debbie said, "My weakness as a writer . . . is writing where there is complete silence." As extraverts mature, they seem to find it easier to write in solitude. Also, as Ching (1986) has pointed out, genre influences process. He found that the adult, extraverted poet in his sample (ENFP/Professional) always wrote poetry in solitude.

Writing as a process of discovery, or writing to discover what one wants to say, also seems more naturally suited to extraverts. For extraverts who are inexperienced writers, this may make getting started particularly difficult. Terri (ENFJ/Basic) found introductions difficult but conclusions easy:

> I feel personally the hardest thing for me to do is writing the first paragraph. I just really find it hard to find the right words to express the

> points I'm going to make. . . . I like writing conclusions, I find them very easy to make. . . . It gives me a way to tell the reader I know what I've written about and here is what I think.

Connie (an ENFP who is a graduate student in English) writes in a process that is more typical of mature extraverts. She outlines, to initiate putting words on paper; once she is writing and begins to discover what she really wants to say, she puts the outline aside and writes more spontaneously. The outline is only her entrée. Once she is writing, the ideas that she develops assume hegemony over what she had planned to say. Another ENFP (Professional) said that she used outlines, but in a particularly extraverted way: "I realize that when I do an (60 min.) outline for a short paper, I discover what to say as I outline—I rarely know how the outline will go before I do it." Even when both extraverts and introverts exhibit the same behavior (such as outlining), the process behind that behavior may be quite distinct. An extravert may use an outline to discover ideas, while an introvert may outline to organize ideas that were developed through solitary reflection.

Extraverts of all ages often say that they begin to write without being very sure of what they want to say, but, in the process of writing, they reach a point at which everything "clicks." At that point, they have discovered their message. Alisa (ESTJ/Basic) wrote in class the following essay on how her public image and private self differed. She struggled through the first two paragraphs, but in the third her ideas seemed to materialize:

> My public image differs from my private self in many ways. First, my manners are at its peak. Secondly, my appearance is more appropriate. Thirdly, my English is well spoken. During my private self image I am more relaxed and non-chalant. In the public I am concerned and aware of all happenings.
>
> My manners are much better in public than in private. For example, when I am at a resturant I always use silverware, chew my food and swallow it before I take a sip of my drink, and I constantly wipe my mouth at the corners. Opposed to eating at home, when I used silverware every once and a while, wash my food down with my drink, and only wash my mouth when I am finished eating. Therefore, my manners in public are always better than in private.
>
> When I'm at home I could care less how I look. I am most likely to have on a pair of jogging pants, a cut up T-shirt, two different color socks, and worn out tennis shoes, if any. In public, I always have on neatly pressed pants, a freshly ironed shirt, stockings, and high heel shoes. I go to the restroom from time to time to check my make-up; I also make sure my hair is neatly combed, with every string in place. At home I don't comb my hair and I never wear make-up. My appearance in the privacy of my own home

> is not the proper attire for my public image. I look like Lisa, the Hobo at home. However, I look like Lisa, the "Business Woman" in public.
>
> I attempt to speak fluent English in public at all time. No one wants to talk to someone who basterizes every word in the English language. Well spoken English is a plus. When I tend to let my English drop speaking illiterately at times. But, when I am doing an Oral Report, or talking to an Interviewer I am on my p's and q's, speaking suitable English during the course of discussion.
>
> Thus, my manners, appearance, and English in my public image is different from my manners, appearance, and English during my private self. The things I say and do in my private self image are not sufficient in my public image. Although everyone is free to do as he or she wishes; I feel that the public image should always dominate the private self. "First impressions are lasting impressions"; therefore, everyone should have a good lasting impression.

Alisa's essay reflects her preference for extraversion in several ways. It is reflected in her content, the valuing of her outer life ("the public image should always dominate the private self") and in some aspects of the structure that evolves from her process. But we do not want to imply that a reader can infer process from product; as Murray has said, "Process can not be inferred from product any more than a pig can be inferred from a sausage" (1980, p. 3). But we have found that sometimes—not always—one can find some residue of process in the texts of inexperienced writers. Alisa's text is typical of younger extraverted sensing types who seem to need to "warm up" before they do their best writing. These writers, thus, may need to devote extra attention to the earlier sections of their text during revision.

Discovering a message while writing can have several ancillary effects on the writing process of extraverts. Younger extraverts may not, for example, fully understand directions for a writing assignment until they are into the physical act of putting words on paper. Marjorie (ENTJ/Basic) wrote to her teacher after he had graded one of her essays: "I didn't exactly know what you was looking for. I think that I partly understood the assignment while I was doing it. So at times I knew what I was doing and at times I didn't." Because they discover so much of their message while putting words on paper, those extraverts who are developing as writers often produce long, rambling sentences. After receiving feedback that her sentences were a bit unwieldly, Reba (ESTJ/Basic) responded:

> As for my sentences being "rambling" sometimes I get more than one idea in my head and become side tracked but thank you for the compliment and the critical opinions which I hope there will be less of in the future

> which was my fault. Also it is very hard to complete a thought in a sentence because it is coming from your mind which is just like you were talking, that is to me.

Extraverted sensing types are more likely to write rambling sentences like this because their thought is focused on the specific clause or phrase that they are writing. Each new thought is simply added—in a process more akin to oral communication—to the end of the sentence. Extraverted intuitive types more naturally have a global/conceptual sense of what they want to say and can thus attend better to the structure of the entire sentence.

Since they tend to think better as they write or after they have written, extraverts can often use what are traditionally considered prewriting strategies (questioning strategies, outlining, etc.) after writing as a means of clarifying—rather than generating—ideas. When writing in class, they often produce better essays if they leap into writing, write a few throwaway paragraphs, and then, after their ideas are better formulated, start a new draft that can be turned in for evaluation.

When revising, extraverts often need to clean up a first draft that was written, in Elbow's words, helter-skelter. They may need to bring consistency to the ideas that they discovered during writing, especially by revising early paragraphs, or they may need to cut the wordiness of a typically conversational style. A professional ENFP told us that she writes her rough drafts in a conversational style because that is easier for her. During revisions, she essentially translates her conversational first draft into a more formal, academic prose.

Since their early drafts often touch on a number of ideas and examples, extraverts, while revising, may need to select the most important material and write about it in greater depth. In a letter to President Reagan about Star Wars, Bill (ESTJ/Basic) wrote the following paragraph:

> I also have my doubts about "star wars." There is really no assurance that "star wars" will work because there is really no way of testing it. Do we have the technology to develop it and test it? I also feel that the cost will be to great and that the money could be spent on other things like space travel, education and medicine. I also feel that if "star wars" was developed that it would probably make the Russians more paranoid than they already are and would probably escalate into a huge arms race. Besides "star wars" would not effect cruise missiles or rockets launched from sub-marines.

One of the strengths of extraverted writers is that they tend to develop more ideas than introverts, but they also tend to reflect less intensely on each idea. In this paragraph, Bill produces a plethora of ideas, enough to develop five or six paragraphs, but only shallowly touches on each one.

Because introverts tend to write as composition has traditionally been taught, they are less likely than extraverts to view their writing process as aberrant. Teachers often require students to plan (e.g., write an outline) before writing, which is more suited to introverts, who naturally want most of their ideas clarified, occasionally even worked into a refined prose, before committing words to paper. Indeed, introverts tend to spend a great amount of time thinking about what they will write. In a course that required writing in class twice a week, John (INTP/Regents) invariably spent about 30 of his 60 minutes planning and the rest of the time writing brilliant essays.

Certainly, the need for planning may, as can any natural preference, be carried to an extreme. After 6 years of research and planning, an INTP in a thesis support group still had difficulty writing his doctoral thesis because he wanted to have practically every word thought out before putting anything down on paper. He claimed to write, revise, and edit papers mentally, almost as if his mind were a word processor, and then sit down, sometimes for 4 or 5 hours at a span, and transcribe his mental text onto paper. The physical act of writing seemed as disassociated from himself as pushing "P" on a computer keyboard and watching the text materialize on a page. Since he was a brilliant student, he had been able to use this process to write, with only moderate difficulty, several graduate research papers. With his longer and more complex dissertation, however, he became locked into his introversion and did little but write mentally. Certainly, extraverts also become blocked and unable to get words onto paper, but they do not seem to become as obsessed with planning as do highly anxious introverts.

At their best, introverts may, after thoroughly preparing to write, move quickly to a well-polished prose. At their worst, however, they may find the physical act of writing a boring process of transcription, or they may find it difficult to move from mental text to the physical act of putting that text forth into the world.

Some introverts need to learn that, though their skill at planning to write is an important strength, they can also develop ideas while putting words on paper. When first introduced to free writing, the more natural process of extraverts, they may find it exciting. Then, after becoming open to writing as a process of discovery, they return to a more introverted, but modified writing process. They plan before writing, but less absolutely. They write according to their plans, but less exactly. They become more open to how their text can evolve.

The writing process of introverts may also be markedly characterized by its isolation from external experience. Robert (ISTJ/Basic) described his prewriting phase of his writing process thus:

> Getting started should be the foremost important thing to anyone. Before I get started I usually take a bath and that helps me to relax. After that I sit in my bedroom with some soft, gentle music in the background to help put my mind at ease and to think about the subject more, and this usually takes 40 minutes to an hour. Then after I have all my thoughts in mind I proceed to put my ideas down on paper, and this is called generating ideas.
>
> Some people may say that generating ideas and getting started are one in the same, but my opinion is that generating ideas is just like classifying. When you generate ideas you are more like putting what you want to say in some fashionable order so that your thoughts aren't all jumbled up that it makes no sense to you and the reader.

Robert claims to divide his prewriting into two stages, 40 to 60 minutes of thinking, followed by a period of organizing ideas on paper. He thinks even before he begins to plan on paper, and, throughout the process, he is thinking alone. He does not get ideas from talking to others on the phone or from watching television.

Just as extraverts' proximity to outer experience and talk before writing sometimes affects their text, isolation from such activities may affect the texts of introverts. After her teacher had asked Karen (ISFJ/Basic) to try to include some personal examples in one of her essays, she replied, "I can't think of any personal examples; I don't have that much experience." The texts of introverted writers are sometimes rather dry, lacking the vitality of experience, as will be explained in more detail in the next chapter.

Introverted students also do not naturally seek out others with whom to discuss their ideas. When they generate ideas in groups, often only at the insistence of a teacher, introverts may find the activity useful. The group can encourage them to think about issues that they may not have raised on their own. They will, however, express more reservations about the group process than extraverts. When asked to comment on using small groups to generate ideas, Veronica (ISTJ/Basic) wrote: "The small groups are good for coming up with ideas that you wouldn't normally think of. [There are] things about it I don't like also." In true introverted fashion, Veronica did not elaborate.

Since younger introverts naturally write in isolation, they need to learn that feedback can, at many stages of their writing process, be valuable. Teachers should certainly structure opportunities for introverts to learn the value of peer feedback, but they should also realize that introverts may be slow to involve themselves actively in the process;

indeed, groups with only introverts in them rarely work. Teachers may also fail to realize that introverts, even when silent, are usually intensely processing what others are saying and that, even though they do not generate as many ideas while talking, feedback can affect how they generate ideas once they are alone. Several introverts have said that they felt confused during group discussions, but that the confusion was constructive. It forced them, once alone, to rethink their topic and refine their ideas. Being placed in groups to generate ideas would only be detrimental to introverts if the teacher expected them to write immediately afterwards, not allowing them time to reflect on the discussion and process it internally.

As writers mature, they naturally learn to write in a more balanced way. Mature introverts are far more likely to invite others into their writing process than young introverts. Ching (1986) found that some professions or writing contexts may either strongly encourage or demand the kind of collaboration that forces introverts to bring talk into their writing process. Yet, even when mature, introverts tend to approach interactions with co-authors and colleagues in ways quite different than extraverts. Two extraverted co-authors may schedule long sessions so that they can generate ideas as they talk to each other. Two introverted co-authors may generate their ideas before meeting, then come together to share what they have thought about when alone.

An introvert's preference for reflection and anticipation often extends into the act of drafting. Introverts seem to pause more frequently. Writers may pause for many reasons: they pause because they are blocked (Rose, 1984), and they pause longer before writing abstract statements (Matsuhashi, 1981). Introverts seem to pause to anticipate the direction of their thoughts. Some introverts feel that writing is like playing chess, especially those who are also intuitive types. They believe that the more moves they can anticipate, the more implications they can make of verbal gambits, the more likely they will be successful. They sometimes forget that writing is also unlike chess. In chess, moves are irrevocable. In writing, moves that lead nowhere can be remade, and poor starts sometimes lead to good ideas. It may be quite natural for introverts to write and discard several perfectly good introductions because they do not like the essay that they anticipate will develop from them. Yet, when they are unable to anticipate the direction of their developing text, or when the act of anticipation leads to writer's blocks, they can be encouraged to keep writing in the kind of exploratory fashion that comes more naturally to an extravert.

The tendency of introverts to pause and anticipate, if exaggerated, can impair the cohesion (the tie from one sentence to the next) of their texts. The following introduction to an essay on abortion, written by Terri (ISFJ/Freshman), reads as a series of disconnected thoughts:

> Ten years ago the U. S. Supreme Court passed a law that made abortion legal for American women. Last year the Senate rejected an amendment that would regulate abortion. There should be a law regulating abortion. Abortion should be legal in two cases: health problems and rape. Abortion should not be legal for women who just want to terminate an unwanted pregnancy.

The text uses devices that one would expect to create a great deal of cohesion; it has chronological markers ("Ten years ago" and "Last year") and repeats the word abortion. Yet, the writer's thought does not seem to develop from one sentence to the next. There seems to be a rather pronounced pause after each sentence, and, indeed, that is how she said it was written. She paused for so long after each sentence, sometimes for several minutes, that her flow of thoughts was never transcribed onto paper. As was stated earlier, we cannot accurately infer process from an isolated product. A variety of causes could potentially explain the kind of lack of cohesion found in Terri's text. Jung's theory, however, can allow a teacher to move from a textual feature to the imaginal space of the writer. Knowing the writer's type, or operating on some hunches about the writer's type, can raise some hypotheses about what kind of process may have produced this kind of text. By observing the writer at work or asking the right kind of questions about how she writes, a better understanding of the writer's elusive process can be reached and more effective—and individualized—advice offered.

As Perl (1979) has said, "Composing always involves some measure of both construction and discovery." All writers need to plan, prefigure, or rehearse, as all writers need to discover some part of their message as they put words on paper, but research employing a variety of methodologies is needed to determine whether all writers rely equally on "construction" and "discovery." Introverts seem to emphasize "construction," but to what extent is their writing actually planned or prefigured before they begin the physical act of writing? Extraverts seem to emphasize "discovery," but to what extent do they plan and to what extent do their plans change or develop as they write? How does context interfere with an introvert's preference to prefigure a message and an extravert's preference to discover a message? To what degree does a writer's reliance on planning or discovery alter as he or she matures?

SENSING–INTUITION AND WRITING PROCESSES

In the October 1966 issue of *English Journal,* Duane C. Nichols stated that teachers need to "explain the concept of *essay* sooner and better than we have been doing." To do this, he suggested that "a simplified breakdown of an essay," a five paragraph structure, could help students to gain insight into the essence of an essay's structure. He concluded:

> The kinds of essays we assign, in both high school and college, are highly artificial things, the assignments often arbitrary. Perhaps they bear no relation to reality. Obviously any writing or speaking occasion the student encounters outside the classroom will require much more than three or four hundred words. We justify our assignments, however, by arguing that the techniques of well-ordered explanation are the same in or out of the classroom. Only length changes. I think this is true. Also subject to expansion is this five-paragraph outline. The length of the body is directly proportionate to the limitations of the topic.

Nichols hoped that his "outline" would give students some idea of what goes into an essay and what the teacher expects. He also did not see it as a rigid formula. Less experienced writers might stay closely within its guidelines, but more able writers could improvise upon it. As Nichols wrote: "Perhaps this is one means of showing good and bad writers . . . what kind of writing will be expected of them in freshman English. Simultaneously they must be allowed and encouraged to transcend the formula."

Nichols must have been surprised and dismayed at what followed. His "outline" became *the* structure that many teachers taught, often as a dictum to be followed rigidly. Even when it was taught as one of many patterns to follow that could be extensively adapted, many students interpreted these guidelines and suggestions as an exact description of what the teacher expected. "Prefab" essays, in which the writer states a thesis and three points in the introduction, explains the three points in the body, and repeats the three points in the conclusion, producing little but tedium in the process, became standard fare.

Recently, several diatribes have been issued against the formulaic, banal application of Nichols's five-paragraph pattern. Most notably, Donald Stewart (1983) and Nancy Sommers (1981) have attacked the teaching of the pattern because they feel it prescribes writing. Students, they believe, become so concerned about fulfilling the demands of the structure that they are unable to express themselves. Despite the attacks, some theorists, such as Mike Rose (1984, pp. 94–95), still contend that, for some writers at a certain stage of development, a pattern like that suggested by Nichols can allay concerns about what is expected and free them to concentrate on their message. Although the issue cannot be resolved here, Jung's model of personality might at least help to clarify it.

Sensing types gather perceptions by looking first at the tangible particulars of their environment. Usually their abstractions emerge later, after nurturing their data or after writing a draft or two, though not always. More mature sensing types may sometimes develop abstractions early in their writing process, but they tend to distrust what seems like vague hunches or unsubstantiated generalities. They must collect, sort, and sequence facts and details to verify—rather than develop—their abstractions.

Sensing types' typical sequential processing of perceptions from the concrete to the abstract often proceeds more smoothly if they are given explicit, detailed and specific directions. If given vague or open-ended directions, they are more likely than intuitives to ask for clarifications, such as, "How long should this essay be?" Composition teachers, who, especially on the college level, are predominantly intuitive types, frequently have difficulty understanding and appreciating the sensing type's need for clarity. They may feel that sensing types, as they habitually follow the five-paragraph pattern or some other widely accepted format, are insecure or unwilling to be creative. They are not. They simply want to follow instructions as would any good technical writer.

The frustrations that sensing types experience in writing classes are evident in Robert's (ISTJ/Basic) written response to a graded essay:

> I believe that you want something different on each paper. I'm not having any problem in grammar its just content. I need to find out what you expect in a paper so that I can write accordingly. Once I find out what you expect, I'm sure that my grades will be better.

This sensing type is confident that, if the directions are clearly delineated, he will be able to write exactly what the teacher wants. He also expresses an annoyance and mistrust toward his teacher. He believes, as many sensing types do, that his teacher is withholding the prescriptive rules of writing that will ensure success. Sensing types often believe that if they can gain access to these seemingly secret rules, then they will be able to write well.

Another sensing type (ISTJ/Graduate) complained to his intuitive instructor in a writing clinic: "When I came in here, I thought that you were going to tell me exactly how to improve my writing." He wanted the instructor to give him a clear, step-by-step procedure—or some set of do-it-yourself tips—for improving his writing. Certainly, this sensing student needs to learn that writing is more than following rules and that good writing cannot be programmed. On the other hand, the intuitive instructor would probably have been more effective with this student if he had, at least initially, given detailed instructions and concrete advice on how to generate and organize ideas. Our experience has shown that clear and specific expectations in the early stages of instruction provide sensing students with a sound base for writing, assuaging rather than heightening their need to be correct and to measure up to a teacher's expectations. They are then more likely, in later contacts, to respond imaginatively to open-ended assignments.

When preparing to write, sensing types tend to focus more on the concrete, perhaps assembling a large amount of facts, statistics, and sensory observations. Sensing types frequently say that they write better when they can write about what is known than when they have to conjecture about what may be true. Though they usually write best when dealing with concrete information, they can become overwhelmed by large amounts of data. A sensing type (ISFJ/Graduate) in a thesis support group found it difficult to know which facts to include in the initial draft of his M.A. thesis; each piece of collected data held an importance of its own simply because it was factual. Exasperated, he settled on the only solution that seemed reasonable: He would include as many details as possible and let his adviser decide what to cut. When overwhelmed with data, sensing types tend to either include almost everything or exclude all but the skeleton of an essay. Their prose may, as a result, either be cluttered with unrelated facts and details or marred with sequential gaps.

The tendency of sensing types, especially those who are developing writers, to stay with the facts and not develop overviews underlies many of their difficulties with writing. They may present data undigested and without interpretation, or they may present general ideas and concrete examples that are not clearly connected. Inga (ESFJ/Basic) wrote a paragraph as part of an essay on how college can change your life. The paragraph, typical of the writing of many developing sensing types, has a concrete, sentence-to-sentence cohesion, but it lacks a clear central idea, as the commentary to the left points out:

[Initial sentence.]	From a college education you may also develop a different concept about life.
[Explanation of first sentence:	Your surroundings make up a

"surroundings" cause "a different concept."]	big part of this.
[Explanation of "surroundings" in previous sentence.]	Because you are learning about so many new things and talking with all types of new people you tend to have a new outlook towards life.
[Explanation of "new outlook towards life."] [The word "terrible" is the first indication that the attitudinal change is moral.]	Things you might have thought were good before, you now think are the most terrible things to ever happen.
[Example of how college can change one's values, but the example does not relate to "talking with all types of people," nor is it a change in morality.]	For example, you begin to think that college is the most important thing in the world and if someone doesn't go to college, they would never get anywhere in life.
[Further explanation of attitude toward one who does not go to college.]	You think that people who don't go to college are bums.
[Concluding sentence: the word "morals" seems an appropriate link to "bums" in the preceding sentence. "Morals," however, is quite different than "concept" as used in the first sentence.]	Morals are altered when a college education is acquired.

Each of the sentences in this paragraph has some kind of cohesive tie to the next; there is also an inductive, step-by-step development of thought that is quite typical of sensing types. (Sensing types often refer to their writing as beginning with the "foundation" of a house or at the "roots" of a tree and developing from there.) The paragraph as a whole, however, lacks conceptual coherence. The first three sentences make no suggestion that the "change" will be moral and, given the phrase "new outlook on life," seem to indicate that the change will be a broadening of one's attitudes. Yet, the example illustrates a rather trivial change in attitude that is not truly moral. Though Inga's development of thought is locally cohesive (each sentence seems connected to the next, if only semantically), all of her ideas are not clearly related ("concept" in the first sentence is quite different in meaning than "moral" in the last) and her example does not clearly support any of her general ideas.

The step-by-step development of thought, so characteristic of sensing types, may affect their writing in another way. Several sensing types have mentioned that they can become blocked when a single piece of data is missing. For example, the progression of data developed and presented in an essay could be seen as a string of numbers:

1 2 3 4 5 6 7 8 9

If, as in the following, some of these data are missing, a sensing type will often become blocked:

1 2 4 5 7 9

Intuitive types, who rely less on a linear development of thought, are more likely to infer the missing information or make intuitive leaps over the gaps and continue writing.

Because they tend to deal with isolated facts rather than abstract classes, sensing types may also, especially when developing as writers, have difficulty categorizing information. The instructor of a basic writing class asked his students to interview people in Atlanta on the Russians' downing of a Korean airliner, to categorize the attitudes, and to write an essay that would explain what Atlantans thought of the political controversy. After the instructor discussed the role of categorizing and the class collectively worked through exercises on the topic, the students were split into groups of four or five to organize the attitudes that they had collected. Only one group out of six was comprised exclusively of sensing types, and that group alone needed help from the instructor to get started. The sensing types' essays also reflected their difficulty with the task. Many did not categorize the data at all; others made quasicategories with only one interviewee in each. Jackie (ESFP/Basic) wrote:

> The Russian Killers
>
> The shooting down of the Korean airliner, 007; was it wrong of the Soviet Union to do? When Americans first heard the news of this disaster, we, the nation, were in shock. Many of the questions asked were; why?, what happened?, and what is the president going to do about this incident? A number of concerned Atlantan's spoke out with their ideas and feelings on this subject. The turn out of responses varied. While some Atlantan's expressed their feelings in one word and with not much to say, others seemed to be more involved with either answers or questionable comments. Combined as a whole, many were upset and very mad. The people of Atlanta share their reactions.
>
> Many Atlantan's reacted to the shooting down of the Korean jet liner by the Russians in a one word comment or a bit lightly. All of these people

> seemed to feel the same about this situation. The people were mainly "shocked" by the news. They felt the Russians knew the airliner was a civilian plane, yet the Soviets took drastic measures and shot it down killing harmless people. These Atlantan's also said they did not feel the United States should go to war, but the Soviet Union should definetly apologize. Some of the solutions the Atlantan's came up with are to continue the matters the President of the United States had taken, along with denying Soviet planes in or near other countries. As one could see, these Atlantan's reacted to this situation on the calm side.
>
> Consequently, some other Atlantan's felt more strongly toward the filling of two hundred and fiftynine civilians. They were more questionable to as why this happened. Many of these Atlantan's felt the president should have acted more severely; for example, stopped all exports to the Soviet Union, cut off all travel to and from the Soviet Union and to discontinue relations with them. Although one person worriedly said that if the United States took too drastic measures, this could of ended up in either a cold war, or possibly World War III. These concerned Atlantan's also wondered about unanswered questions, such as; why was the Korean plan shot down if the Soviet's knew it was a civilian plane?, and what happened to the black box? These people feel the Soviets found the black box to hide the answer.
>
> The writer came up with the conclusion that most of the Atlantan's asked were upset, shocked and concerned. The United States will probably never forgive or understand the reason to why the Soviet Union shot down the Korean airliner 007.

Jackie's essay lacks sound categories. For example, it is not clear whether her first category is "people who responded in one word" or "people who reacted calmly," neither of which is particularly meaningful. However, one of the sensing types who developed fairly effective categories did so concretely, by using statistics. Cathy (ESFJ/Basic) wrote the following paragraph:

> Many Atlantans favor the actions taking place. Thirty-seven percent of the interviews taken say they approve of his (the President's) actions, but think it would be good if we greatly reduced the flow of tourism between the United States and the Soviet Union. Out of those in favor, sixteen percent are male. The majority, women, seem to be less violent.

As a general rule, any concrete, tangible method of categorizing will help sensing types to organize their material and write more coherent essays.

Sensing and intuitive types certainly approach organization differently. Sensing types usually find writing easier when they are given a specific framework to follow, such as the five-paragraph pattern. They find the five-paragraph essay particularly appealing because it embodies clearly specified expectations. If a teacher says that he or she wants—or is willing to accept—a five paragraph essay, then the sensing types in the class feel assured that they understand the teacher's expectations, which Nichols stated as an advantage of teaching the pattern. Teachers should not feel, however, that they have to resort to teaching the five-paragraph pattern—or some variation of it—to reassure sensing types. Their need for clear expectations can also be satisfied by providing a variety of models for them to imitate or by allowing them to read the first drafts of other students' essays. Teachers can also skim early drafts and let students know whether or not their approach is acceptable. As an ESFJ (Basic) wrote after a session of peer feedback: "I didn't really understand how I was to write the paper, but after I read some others I realized how it was to be written."

Because sensing types like to learn a skill, perfect it, and repeat it if it works, they may learn one way to organize an essay and then rarely vary it. If they were taught to write in a five-paragraph pattern and received some success with it, they will tend to use the pattern habitually. They may even become blocked if they can think of only two "points" or "reasons" (instead of the required three) to develop into body paragraphs. Such reliance on what worked in the past or on perceived expectations can hinder one's development. Too often, sensing types write the same basic essay 10 times during a composition course and, as a result, fail to develop a broad repertoire of organizational strategies. They may sacrifice long-term development for short-term success.

The sensing type's tendency to follow models or patterns closely can either hinder or aid instruction, as a couple of examples will illustrate. One instructor of a basic writing class asked his students to free write, select one idea from the free writing, and then develop three questions about that idea. The students were then asked to use the questions to explore the topic further and write an essay on it. The instructor intended the questions to be a prewriting exercise, but several sensing types wrote their essays directly from the questions. They wrote five-paragraph themes in which each of the body paragraphs answered one of the three questions. They felt that as long as they had answered the questions, they had fulfilled the requirements of the assignment.

With a different basic writing class, the same instructor had students write a rough draft of an essay. He then revised, using a different style for each, three paragraphs from a few rough drafts and asked the students to use the style of one of these paragraphs as a model for revising their essay. The essays of the sensing types improved enormously, and several of them began to develop their own personal style by incorporating different aspects from one or more models. Most of the intuitive types in the class did not imitate any of the models; one INFP was openly hostile about the idea of having to imitate someone else's writing.

Sensing types seem to benefit enormously from exposure to models, but one caution should be raised. Teachers should introduce only a few options at a time. Otherwise, sensing types may become overwhelmed or confused by too many options. A few at one time will help clarify expectations; too many models at one time will offer too many options, making it more difficult than ever for sensing types to ascertain what the teacher wants.

Once they begin to write, sensing types attend closely to mechanics (grammar, punctuation, and spelling). Even when using a rather poetic metaphor to describe writing, Inga (ESFJ/Basic) does not diminish the importance that she gives to grammar:

> Writing is like a flower. Its beautiful words shinning bright on paper. As we write it grows and develops its subject with its sweet smells of grammar.

Sensing types, as Shaughnessy (1977, p. 8) has said of basic writers, may pay such close attention to mechanics that they fail to generate sound ideas. They may also view revising as principally "correcting" or proofreading, which Perl (1979) observed in basic writers. Sensing types' concern about writing grammatically correct essays may often need to be allayed, but instructors should also realize that sensing types take great pride in grammatical competence. Sensing types want to fulfill expectations, and mastering mechanics is one of the few areas of writing that present relatively clear guidelines and expectations.

Clear directions and prescribed expectations, which influence so much of the sensing type's writing process, are relatively unimportant to intuitive types. They prefer to write from general, open-ended instructions. Indeed, developing a unique approach to the topic seems to be an important part of their initial approach to a writing assignment. When given explicit directions, they often—to the dismay of some teachers—ignore them and write a strikingly original but inappropriate essay.

Though intuitive types' desire for unique approaches may sometimes cause difficulties, instructors (especially those who are intuitive) more frequently reward them for their originality. Leo (INTJ/Basic), when asked to describe his own writing process, wrote:

> There's this guy in my class and my teacher wants me to describe how he goes about writing a paper. So I watched him for a few days and this is what I found out.
>
> When the topic for a paper is given, Leo gets a far-away look in his eyes and you can just see the wheels turning in his head. Occasionally, he will

jerk as if he just received a mild electric shock and you just know he's about to make some profound point. For example, "Can we write the paper from another persons point of view and not make the essay our own narrative." Groans and snorts of disgust usually follow one of his statements, because the class thinks his ideas just make the paper harder to write. Mostly they're right.

After class Leo rides Marta home and sometimes you can see the far-away look in his eyes and you know he's thinking about and getting ideas for his paper. (One thing I have noticed is that Leo always writes in his bedroom after dark or in class. I don't think he can write anywhere else.)

He almost always writes his rough draft in one sitting with only a pause now and then as if he's choosing just the right word. I have never seen him use an outline or any kind of organizational aid before writing. Interesting.

The next day he takes his rough draft to class where he gets his class-mates opinion on how he can write the paper better. Sometimes he uses the comments and advice, but usually all he does is change a few words here and fix some grammar there. He then turns the paper in to be graded. I wish I could do that.

Leo's essay describes and exemplifies his need to find a unique approach to the topic (as an NT, he objectively describes an ideal writing process, rather than how he actually writes). The rest of the class, predominantly sensing types, could hardly appreciate his approach or his need to be original. Kelly, another intuitive type (ENTJ/Basic), used the metaphor of dressing to describe how she approaches writing:

> Writing is like getting dressed in the way that you have a subject that needs to be dressed. You sometimes try different accessories.

Leo, an introvert, develops his unique approach before writing, by thinking with that faraway look in his eyes. Kelly, an extravert, develops her unique approach through experimentation as she writes, by trying different combinations until she finds the right "look."

Once they start to write, intuitive types tend to develop ideas quickly, almost unconsciously. They develop conceptual interpretations of the data more readily than sensing types, and, as a result, have fewer problems with categorization. The following paragraph, written by an ENFJ (Basic), is typical of many of the essays that intuitives wrote when categorizing views of the Russians' downing of the Korean airliner, an assignment mentioned earlier:

> When speaking with the women from the Atlanta area, the response was one of violence towards Russia. The women were not really concerned over governmental matters, but seemed appauled that the U.S.A. is not

> fighting back. Women felt striking back would be our best option, since this is not the first time the Soviet Union has reacted like this. Three fourths of the women polled, agreed that if the United States does not strike back; and not with just weak sanctions, the Soviet Union won't hessitate to do something like this again.

Intuitive types rarely have difficulty, even when they are developing writers, with categorizing or interpreting their data, but they may fail to support their categories and inferences with concrete examples. On the same topic, Jeff (ENTP/Basic) wrote:

> Men and women of the 18 to 25 age group want some sort of stronger action taken provided it is not of a military nature. For the most part people of this age do not support a grain embargo towards the Russians, believing it would hurt us more than the Russians because they would just go somewhere else to buy their grain such as Canada.

Jeff has no difficulty categorizing data from his interviews and making general statements. He did not, however, see the need to quote anyone whom he interviewed as support. His abstractions often leave his assertions unconvincing and his conclusions vague. When his teacher commented on the vagueness of one of his essays, Jeff replied:

> From your comment it sounds like you want to talk to me which is good. I've not been told I was vague before. Maybe it's because I've had easy teachers or I just didn't explain myself well enough. There are lots of possibilities as to my vagueness. I'll have to find out why.

Unfortunately, teachers (especially intuitive teachers) often perceive that intuitive types are better writers than they actually are, in part because they can write abstractly. As Jeff apparently was in high school, intuitives may be seen as being more highly developed writers than sensing types who, even though at a comparable stage of development, may include fewer abstractions. While sensing types need to learn how to abstract from the evidence that they tend to describe undigested, intuitive types need to learn the value of including specific illustrations. Otherwise, intuitive types may confuse their readers, or even themselves. Intuitive types in our Thesis Support Group often mentioned that they can become confused by the escalating complexity of their own ideas. As they develop implications from their implications, moving farther and farther from direct experience, their ideas become obtuse. One of the major tasks that intuitive types need to accomplish when revising is to clarify and refine their ideas by grounding them with sensory data.

Myers feels that there is a bias in education, especially at the higher levels, toward intuition, which causes sensing types some difficulty as they progress through high school and into college (1980, pp. 147–156). Her general observation also seems true of the field of composition. Once students reach college, about 90% of their composition teachers may be intuitives. We have spent more time discussing the writing process of sensing types because we feel that it is important for instructors to understand how sensing types tend to compose and to appreciate their need for focusing on concrete data, carefully following instructions, and distrusting general ideas or hunches. Instructors should also understand that the sensing type's need to follow directions accurately, to write the kind of essay that they feel the teacher expects, may lead to difficulties. They may appear less creative, become more locked into rigid rules (Rose, 1980), or apply "rules" inappropriately. They may, for example, write five-paragraph essays on topics that clearly elicit narratives.

We do not want, however, to imply that sensing types are less competent writers. Ted (ISTJ/Basic) wrote the following letter about "Star Wars" to President Reagan:

> Dear Mr. President:
>
> I am an 18 year old freshman at Georgia State University in Atlanta and my class is currently studying the possible causes and effects of nuclear war. This letter is written in regard to the proposed development of a "Star Wars" type defense system.
>
> I would like to start by saying that I think your position on the development of "Star Wars" technology was a tremendous help in bringing the Soviets back to the bargaining table after their walkout in Geneva. It was a good move on your part, sticking with the idea as you did. This achieved the reaction of a definite threat to Soviet power and is a great bargaining chip.
>
> On the other hand I have mixed emotions about how far "Star Wars" can go. The nation is already in debt by two trillion dollars and this system will cost three trillion to build. This project is just too expensive. Even though our technology is already far superior to that of the Soviets, it will still take several scientific breakthroughs before we will be prepared to make it work.
>
> My feelings are that "Star Wars" should be a limited project. We should continue to perfect the laser technology and the computer technology before we start to build the defense weapons. The Soviets are continuing research for a land based system and they already spend more on civil defense than the United States. For this reason alone, the idea of a "Star Wars" defense should not be abandoned.
>
> This is a controversial and confusing issue with many arguments over whether it will or will not work. A popular writer on nuclear arms says it could work if the satellites could be inactive until they are needed, making the system undetectible until activated. Another writer argues that it

> could never work because of capacity limitations. If 30 warheads were intercepted and destroyed the Russians would just send 60 making the system ineffective.
>
> Right now we have enough nuclear weapons to destroy the world more than three times over so I think the "Star Wars" defense is certainly a better idea than the continued arms proliferation of the past. Peace is maintained through strength not weakness, therefore, we must maintain a strong retaliation capability of some sort in order to maintain the peace.
>
> I would sincerely appreciate your sending me any unclassified information that would better help me to understand the aspects of a "Star Wars" defense system. Thank you for your continuing efforts on our behalf and for allowing me to express some of my thoughts and concerns.

The essay—though not without some faults—is quite an exceptional effort for a basic writer. As is often characteristic of good writing (a point that we will discuss further in Chapter 3), the letter reflects his type but also transcends it.

Typical of sensing types, Ted begins with a fact: "I am an 18 year old at Georgia State University in Atlanta. . . ." He also grounds his writing in data. However, Ted's letter has a broadly conceived theme (usually more typical of Ns), shows an appreciation for the complexity of the issue (a strength often found in the essays of NPs), makes contact with the audience without being abrasive (more typical of the discourse of Fs), and is well developed (which is quite atypical of the essays of developing ISTJs). Type is not destiny. All writers can learn to write well, as Ted illustrates.

THINKING–FEELING AND WRITING PROCESSES

Frank J. D'Angelo, in *A Conceptual Theory of Rhetoric* (1975), states that rhetorical patterns, which he believes are reflections of basic cognitive processes, cannot only be identified but can also be effectively used as a heuristic. He writes:

> If thought processes and conceptual patterns of discourse display a close fit, and if, as some rhetoricians believe, the topics are symbolic manifestations of thought processes, then it follows that there is a similiarity of form between the topics [of invention] and conceptual patterns of discourse. Therefore, conceptual patterns of discourse are topical and may accordingly serve a heuristic function. To illustrate this argument, let us consider three basic processes of mind: analyzing (or dividing into parts), classifying, and comparing. We consider these to be fundamental mental processes. Analogous to these mental processes are their symbolic manifesta-

> tions in discourse which take the form of conceptual patterns of discourse. In other words, there are paragraph patterns and extended patterns of discourse which we label "division into parts," "classification," and "comparision." But these mental processes can also be thought of as topics and can accordingly be used to probe a particular subject in order to find out more about it. Therefore, analysis, classification, and comparison can be considered from different points of view as being mental processes, or topics, or patterns of organization. Conceptual patterns of discourse are in fact inseparable from their topical counterparts and thus may serve a heuristic function.

For D'Angelo, form precedes content; indeed, form generates content.

When commenting on two case studies, which compared an unskilled and skilled writer, Nancy Sommers (1981) took a position that appears diametrically opposed to D'Angelo's:

> We tell our students: Be correct! Be concise! But above all: Discover! Yet we rob our students of this important part of the discovery process—this discovery of structure—by forcing them to write formulaic five paragraph essays. We impose rigid structures upon students at the risk of turning out terribly mechanical writing . . . for a fixed structure often inhibits the discovery of ideas, and, therefore, the process of significant revision. If we can teach our students the logic of a paragraph, then we can have the confidence to allow them to discover their own structure to match the meaning of what they have to say.

Sommers feels that structure is more likely to "inhibit the discovery of ideas" than generate them. Donald Murray (1980) has similarly advised against teaching too much before students write because "a student might get the dangerous misconception that writers know the form before they know the content."

The structure that Sommers feels produces mechanical writing is the five-paragraph theme, which is a more simplistic approach to teaching structure than what D'Angelo advocates. Nonetheless, D'Angelo feels that structure either consciously or unconsciously precedes content; Sommers and Murray feel that structure is discovered either after or as the writer writes. Though diametrically opposed, the two approaches are both valid. Thinking types tend to use structure to develop ideas, while feeling types tend to develop their structure organically from their content.

Even before they have an organizational structure, thinking types need a rationale. For example, a teacher can say: "It is important for you to learn how to define terms because definition is a fundamental part of academic writing." Once thinking types have accepted the stated or implied rationale of the assignment, they will usually not complain about a topic being banal or routine. However, they may (especially if also introverted) express discomfort about writing personal narratives, for they usually prefer to write objectively and analytically. When younger thinking types are given a personal or expressive topic, they may not perform as well or they may simply objectify it. For example, when asked to write on personal topics such as, "What do you like about the South?", they may depersonalize the topic. Rather than use the personal pronoun "I," as the topic almost demands, they may use the pronoun "one" and write about the objective advantages to living there.

Yet, from the moment they begin to incubate ideas, thinking types rely on what Elbow (1985) calls spatial structure. They prefer the structure of symmetry, an architectonic structure of how ideas and data are logically related. An ENTP (Basic), who as an extravert, found his inspiration in the outer world, wrote of getting ready to write:

> When I get home in the afternoon I like to relax before I start anything new and music from groups like Pink Floyd, The Beatles, & Queen help me to do this. It helps me because it isn't harsh or unpatterned. The beat is slower & more organized. Music from these groups helps me think clearer when I'm working on a project.

This thinking type likes structured, patterned music, for the structure of the music seems to allow him to think more clearly.

Once they begin to write, thinking types rely on structure, an outline or a mental blueprint, both to help them make organizational decisions and to generate ideas. To make organizational decisions, they will include material that is specified in the outline or pattern and exclude the material that is not specified there. Without some kind of structure, they lack the objective criteria so important to their decision making process. For example, an ISTJ (Basic) wrote the following in response to a comment that her essay was unorganized: "I found it hard to think of any pattern that I [could] do. I believe I could have developed my paper more. I realize I put certain sentences out of order." As a sensing type, she prefers to follow a widely accepted organizational structure (such as the five-paragraph theme) or a pattern that she has used successfully for previous assignments. Since she is also a thinking type, she needs a criterion to guide her decision making. And since this writer was unwilling or unable to originate a pattern to guide her thought, she not only wrote a disorganized essay, she also wrote one that was underdeveloped.

Thinking types may, especially when developing, write essays that are too structured. Robert (ISTJ/Basic), who once said that he revises his essays until they achieve "grammatical structure," was asked to observe a person in a public place and then describe him or her. He wrote an essay that has the flavor of a grocery list:

> While wandering around the neighborhood on a bright, sunny day I came upon a male speciman. While observing him for about 20 minutes I came up with this:
>
> He has short black hair, medium length sideburns and a mustache. He has average height. To be a little more specific he is 5 feet 9 inches tall and weighs about 150 lbs.
>
> His personality is strange and is kind of hard to describe. He is the type of person that acts like a 10 year old. While sitting there he started to play with children that were a lot younger than he was. And I came up with the assumption that he is fond of kids.
>
> He has different types of personality traits. He is a phlegmatic and a sanguine in the positive sence and he is also an extravert.
>
> The tonality of his voice is medium, but the volume is deep. During altercations his voice becomes loud, but it doesn't have any power to produce any result or meaning.
>
> His sentence is poor because he speaks in fragments and chops his words into pieces. I believe his main difficulty is, that he studers and has trouble getting the words out.
>
> His facial expressions isn't overwhelming. He hardly ever smiles but, sometimes he walks around with a frown on his face thinking that something is wrong. The very next minute he will be smiling.
>
> His body behaviors were somewhat interesting. He likes to imitate people on the way they walk, which I think isn't too amazing. But one thing I noticed was that he likes to flex his body to keep in shape. This concludes my observation.

The structure of Robert's essay is a rather simple enumeration; the simple structure almost seems to hide his truly interesting observations. In contrast, the structure of Tim's (INTP/Regents) essay, which defines a gentleman, is more complex:

> Is chivalry dead in America? I think so, but it did not die of natural causes, it was beaten to death. Until about 20 years ago one of the highest compliments a man could receive was to be considered a gentleman. In the last 20 years though the term gentleman has in many cases become synonymous with male chavinist. There is a place in society for the gentleman, but he will have to have up-to-date views.
>
> The Victorian definition of a gentleman is somewhat different from a 1980's gentleman. During the Victorian era a man obeyed a fairly strict set of rules if he wished to be considered a gentleman. A gentleman had a good well rounded education, giving him the ability to speak on most any subject. He was strong and agile, being proficient in such manly activities as horseback riding, hunting, and fencing. And most of all, he was ever

> vigilant toward the needs of ladies, considering it an honor to open a door for a lady or to entertain her with his charming wit. But, to the Victorian gentleman a woman was closer to a pretty plaything than an equal.
>
> The gentleman of today must walk to the beat of a different drum. He has no strict set of rules to abide by. He is the man who works hard to provide for his family. He must be proficient in different areas than the Victorian man. He too must have a good general education, but he must also have an area of expertise. The 1980's man is more likely to be considered a gentleman if he can run five miles than if he can hunt down a bear. Most of all the new gentleman must have a proper view of women. He should think of women as equals: more as comrades than as pretty playthings.
>
> The gentleman of the 1980's is not the male chavinist of the the 1970's, but a considerate, well adjusted person. He is a person who is successful but not at the expense of others. He is a friend to all and holds no prejudices, and his obvious enjoyment of life radiates to others around him.

What is interesting about Tim's essay is that structural elements seem to help him generate ideas. He seems to use the statements made about Victorian gentlemen in the second paragraph to generate statements about 1980s gentlemen in the third. Even the structure of the last sentence in the second paragraph is echoed in the last sentence of the third paragraph.

Within the overall structure of a thinking type's essays, one may find yet more structure. They are more likely to use a logical development of their topic than discuss personal examples. Jeff (ENTP/Basic) wrote the following paragraph to explain how security could be increased at shopping malls:

> At most malls around Atlanta they could increase the security of workers by providing a well lit & guarded employee parking lot somewhere close to one of the mall's exits. However, most malls still ask their employees to park out away from the stores where it is poorly lit and difficult to guard due to the fact that there is so much space to watch and so few people to watch it. If malls had an employee lot it would be easier to guard because it would be all in one well maintained spot. The employee lot would also be safer due to the fact that all the employees of all the shops would have to move in groups to get to their cars and thus you have the security of moving in numbers or pack safety. In conclusion, one employee lot makes it easier for mall security forces to guard people and makes people travel in groups which automatically makes them safer.

Jeff's writing is densely packed with markers that signal logical development: "however," "due to," " if," " thus," and "in conclusion."

When writing, indeed whenever communicating, thinking types are most concerned about presenting the content clearly in a well-organized format. They are less concerned about the process of communication, about how they are relating to their audience. As a result, their essays may be clear and structured but also dull, similar to the archetypical dry, academic treatise.

For feeling types, the initial stage of the writing process—selecting a topic—is often crucial. If they do not select a topic that they can bind to their personal values, writing may become a meaningless burden. As Ron (ESFJ/Basic) wrote: "The conditions I write best under are when I know alot about the subject and I can express my total feelings on the subject." We have noticed that the grades of feeling types may fluctuate wildly throughout a composition course. If they find a topic boring, they write poorly. It the topic is interesting, they write well. Those feeling types who are more skilled as writers can often adapt a boring, objective topic to their own aims. For example, when asked to write about one's favorite sport, an experienced feeling type might write about walking her dog, adroitly describing every aspect of the activity in sporting terms.

When initially exploring a topic, feeling types may prefer to delay the kind of objective analysis behind many prewriting heuristics. They first, as Robert Baden (1975) has advised, need to explore their subjective responses to the topic. He wrote:

> that, before valid thought can take place and certainly before meaningful writing can occur, the *feelings* of the writer must be stimulated to the extent that he is willing and able to make an emotional, sensuous commitment to the task. . . . Once an emotional response occurs, thought has its place to explain, temper, and clarify that response and to facilitate the organization and techniques that can best communicate the feeling to an audience, although one might argue that good writing can come as a direct response to feeling without passing through a *conscious* thinking period. Whether the means employed is expository, narrative, argumentative, descriptive, or lyric, the presence of feeling is what is going to make the expression genuine and effective.

Jung (1921, p. 357) stated that feeling types can only think clearly after they have felt. Certainly, we need to teach, as Baden suggests, prewriting strategies that explore feelings and attitudes as well as those that generate ideas or clarify thought.

From early in the writing process, feeling types are concerned as much about the process of communication, that is, how they are connecting with their audience, as about the content. Ron (ESFJ/Basic) wrote: "My strengths as a writer are, I like to write, I like to put a part of myself into the things I write and I think the reader realizes that and [it] makes them enjoy more what they are reading. And I also think I can entertain the reader by the big words I use." Feeling types, especially the extraverted-sensing types like Ron, may be so concerned about entertaining the readers, finding just the right word or phrase to capture their attention, that they fail to develop or adequately explain their ideas.

At their best, the desire of feeling types to put their heart into their writing and connect with the audience creates very lively, endearing prose. Rather than develop their topics objectively and logically, feeling types are more likely to write expressively or employ personal examples. When asked to write an argumentative essay on whether or not the space program should be continued after the explosion of the space shuttle in January 1986, a topic that would usually elicit logical appeals, Olivia (ENFP/Freshman) wrote the following essay:

> I remember sitting somberly in my living room listening to television reports of the tragic challenger explosion and tears were streaming down my face as the President recited these sad lines from a sonnet by John Gillespie Magee, Jr., " . . . with silent, lifting mind I've told the High, untrespassed sanctity of space, Put out my hand, and touched the face of God."
>
> I was reminded of the eerie feeling of imbalance when Pres. Reagan was shot—this dark feeling of uneasiness hovered over me. I sat there trying to see beyond my tears, looking, groping desperately for something positive that could be said. Somehow it was not enough to know that those seven fragile humans, Ellison Onizuka, Christa McAuliffe, Gregory B. Jarvis, Judith A. Resnick, Michael J. Smith, Francis R. Scobee, and Ronald E. McNair, would go down in history as heros. These seven fragile humans had been effaced from the face of the earth but surely not from the minds and the hearts of those who had remained behind.
>
> There are still many questions in my mind about what went wrong with the Challenger shuttle but I've come to realize the importance of space exploration. There is always some sort of danger involved in embarking upon unknown, unexplored frontiers. It is perhaps that sense of danger that makes exploration so thrilling. How are our children to dream and vision new horizons if we place a roof upon our skies?
>
> Space exploration is very vital to our study of science and technology. Yes, we could send shuttles up that are controlled by machines but it's difficult to comprehend the splendor of space simply through pictures. We need the reactions, emotional feedback that only humans can give. Yes, there are risks but the astronauts are quite aware of the dangers they face, and yet, they still long for the opportunity to travel through space and time. Perhaps, NASA, in reviewing this tragedy, will decide to send up shuttles without astronauts until they have perfected the program. But NASA should not completely discontinue manned flights of space shuttles. Look at the following milestones in the U.S.'s space program:
>
> May 5, 1961 First American, Alan Shepard, is launched into space.
> Feb. 20, 1962 John Glenn orbits the Earth

> Dec. 21–27, 1968 Apollo 8 mission sends astronauts to circle the moon
> July 20, 1969 Apollo 11 astronauts Neil Armstrong and Edwin Aldrin land on the moon, as Michael Collins remains in orbit
> May 25, 1973 Skylab station is launched.
> July 17, 1975 Americans join Soviets in Apollo–Soyuz flight
> April 12, 1981 First Shuttle Columbia is launched
> April 12, 1985 Shuttle takes Sen. Jake Garn up as a "guest" astronaut
>
> Can you honestly look at these accomplishments and not feel slightly curious and envious at the same time? If given the opportunity to fly through space, to visit Saturn or Jupiter, wouldn't you take your chances and sign up with NASA? I would.

The essay does not rely on logical appeals, more typical of the argumentative essays of thinking types; rather, it relies on the expression of values and emotions to persuade.

Feeling types may develop outlines or search for organizational patterns, but they are less likely to follow them. Connie (ENFP/Graduate), as mentioned earlier, said that she makes outlines but only uses them for a few paragraphs. Then, once she begins to discover what she really wants to say, she ignores the outline and follows "the flow" of her own personal thought process, organically developing structure from her own reactions to the subject matter. By following the "flow," feeling types usually mean following how one statement leads to and triggers another. Their structure is what Elbow (1985) calls temporal. It is the structure of how the essay unfolds to the audience in time. As June (ESFP/Basic) wrote: "Writing is like a summer breeze in that it cools your senses by releasing your thoughts and feelings. It allows a person to 'let themselves go' and let the pen and paper take total control of mind and hand. Writing is freedom and freedom is beautiful."

Outlines or organizational patterns can be too constraining for writers who follow the "flow." When her teacher asked her if the five-paragraph theme was compatible with her style of writing, Jackie (ESFP/Basic) wrote:

> I'm not sure if a five paragraph theme is good for me. Its really the only one I learned, but everything seems to get jumbled up when I write. I also seem to get C's on my papers. I must be doing something wrong and a lot of it probably deals with the body of my papers. I'd like to try another approach to writing a paper, I'm not sure how they are constructed though.

Jackie exemplifies the difficulty that many SFs experience with writing. As sensing types, they want to write "correctly," as they feel the teacher expects them to write. This leads them to adopt and habitually rely on spatial patterns, such as the five-paragraph theme. Yet, these patterns do not allow the flexibility they need to write their best. The fixed structure does not allow them to follow the "flow," thus inhibiting the development of their ideas. They need to be encouraged, as Sommers (1981) said, to discover their own structure.

Certainly, the nature of a given topic almost demands that the student employ a particular cognitive process, even if the process is an unpreferred one. When asked to write on the value of a college education, the kind of topic that elicits five-paragraph themes, Cathy (ESFJ/Basic) wrote what she felt was expected:

> A college education can change your life in many different aspects. After and beyond graduation this person should acquire social aspects, financial know-how and responsibility.
>
> At college, you learn everything you need to know in later life such as responsibility, maturity and independence. Since you've taken the pains to go to the right college, you should feel secure enough to indulge in the most of that college's activities. At every school, from one campus to another, there will be a broad variety of fraternitys and sororities. When becoming involved in a social group, the membership in a club forms strong ties.
>
> After deciding upon a profession, that you can talk about at future social gatherings, you now face the task of actually going to school for two or more years to obtain this degree. Once the college degree is received, this document can now be used to open many doors in your trade or profession depending on how much schooling each individual has had.
>
> A responsible person is one who can account for his or her actions and a college education can help an individual further his responsibilities. A college graduate should be one who can be reliable and responsible in everything they do.
>
> In conclusion, the collegiate years are a final opportunity to sow wild oats, a chance to live the carefree life to the fullest. When the four years are over, you will be expected to assume the duties of adulthood.

The five-paragraph structure came to her preordained. She mechanically, as an artist painting by the numbers, filled in the prescribed structure with routine ideas, an immature expression of her sensory attention to detail and to what she believes is expected of her. When asked to write a short narrative, a structure more naturally suited to feeling types, her more mature dominant feeling preference comes to the fore. She begins to relate an experience but then follows the flow of her thoughts:

> Early Monday morning I arrived at the Avondale station. I was looking at the many sleepy eyed and tired faces, occasionally checking their watches, while waiting for the train. I noticed how many women are part of the

work force, many who are single parents, or working along with their husbands just to help make ends meet.

As I watch, I wonder about their children. Where do they spend most of their time? In school learning or at day care centers waiting? These children probably have their physical needs taken care of but what about their emotional needs? Does each child have one person that comforts them when they are hurt? Who are the people that share their joys and frustrations of growing up?

As I remember when I was younger how my brother and sisters all played together and how well behaved we were. Because if we did not behave in a proper enough manner we were spanked or punished.

These children are not getting enough discipline and are more or less being ignored. Who would be the best possible babysitter or day care center for my child in the future? It is a very frightening feeling to me because I would like to have the option to work after I have started a family.

What is the future for the children of the working mothers?

The latter essay has structure, but it is a more subtle structure that was developed organically as she wrote. Not only is the temporal structure of the second essay more appealing, but, interestingly, her ideas also seem more original and mature.

Certainly, the temporal structure that feeling types develop almost unconsciously as they write may at times be more chaotic than subtle. During revisions, they may need to clarify content and refine organization. Whereas thinking types will usually revise by concentrating on perfecting their spatial structure, feeling types usually accomplish similar ends by shifting from the "flow" to a concern for how the reader will react to their writing. Thinking types may add a definition because it will serve as a premise for the development of their arguments. A feeling type may add a definition because he or she feels that the audience may be confused (or, even more importantly, frustrated) without it. Of course, such changes may improve the organization or worsen it. Since the basic organization of a feeling type's essay may simply be the objectification of the "flow," his or her train of thought, making additions or deletions can create breaks or gaps in the "flow." Frequently, a lack of cohesion in the essays of feeling types can be traced back to isolated revisions, those made locally without an awareness of the initial train of thought behind the essay.

The Thinking–Feeling dimension may prove to have important interactions with how writers—especially those who are less experienced—adapt to or ignore the demands of a given topic. Thinking types seem to objectify personal topics, gravitate toward logical appeals, and may even write what has traditionally been called an expository essay (especially if also introverted) on a narrative topic. Feeling types (especially if also extraverted) seem to prefer expressive, narrative topics. When writing on argumentative topics, they seem to rely more heavily on personal examples, metaphors, and values. More research is needed on how topics affect thinking and feeling types, how each type adapts to different kinds of topics, and what modes they use to develop them.

JUDGING–PERCEIVING AND WRITING PROCESSES

In *Writer's Guide and Index to English*, a fairly typical composition textbook, Ebbitt and Ebbitt give the following advice to students who are about to write their first research paper:

> In a research paper, with its considerable length and numerous details, an exact formulation of the thesis or purpose is especially important. Often writing the paper calls for a good deal of juggling and testing of ideas. The point is to force yourself, as soon as your research permits, to define the purpose of your paper to *yourself*. (1978, p. 324)

The authors feel that—by achieving an early, if only tentative, closure—the student will be able to avoid "duplications and irrelevancies." In *A Writing Teacher Teaches Writing*, Donald Murray offers advice with a different focus:

> The amateur thinks that the writer has an idea, perhaps a vague thought, and a few facts. He doesn't. He has shelves of reports, miles of tape-recorded interviews, notebooks of quotations and facts and ideas and possible connections. It takes thirty gallons of sap to make a gallon of maple syrup; it takes hundreds of pages of notes to make one *Reader's Digest* article.
>
> The good writer is wasteful. He saws and shapes and cuts away, discarding wood ends, shavings, sawdust, bent nails—whatever doesn't fit and doesn't work. The writer cannot build a good, strong, sturdy piece of writing unless he has gathered an abundance of fine raw material. (1968, p. 6)

In contrast to Ebbitt and Ebbitt, Murray seems to advise students, and other writers, to delay closure, to continue to collect as much information as long as possible. Variations among writers pertaining to when and how they begin to seek closure are related, at least in part, to personality type.

Judging types, who prefer to complete tasks expediently, tend to limit their topics quickly and set goals that are manageable. Before writing, they usually devote time to what Flower and Hayes (1981) call process goals (how to get things done), which ideally include plans to stop at key intervals to analyze and revise objectives.

Judging types at their best are very good at planning to complete a task, following that plan and finishing the task early or on time. Yet, sometimes they may follow those plans too rigidly. An INTJ recounted how he developed a plan to complete a graduate research paper. He then followed his plan without evaluating or revising it, realizing only a few days before the assignment was due that the "plan" was simply unworkable. To avoid being locked into unproductive plans, judging types need to allow time to rethink and revise them. They should, in other words, plan to be spontaneous.

Much of the writing processes of judging types reflects their need to complete the first draft expediently. They may begin to write before they have researched the topic adequately, make stylistic and organizational decisions quickly (sometimes arbitrarily), and their quickly written first drafts are often shorter than later ones. Because judging types tend to make decisions that are based on relatively little input, they may fail to understand the importance of supporting evidence when writing and naturally exclude it from the their essays. Cathy (ESFJ/Basic) developed the following material before beginning to write an essay on why Americans overeat:

Dieting   The big workout.
Common goal
Staying fit   All ages, sex is not the major factor.

Health clubs: American Fitness, Richard Simmons, Australian Body Workout

Aerobic classes   Jazzercise   Never Say Diet

I. Social Aspects   —Why do people join clubs
Meeting people   —Talk about $$
—involvement
Confidence   —setting goals
—better outlook on yourself
Aggressiveness
Enthusiasm
Enjoyment

II. Health as 2nd Major Role
A. Adrenalin   —beautiful face

B. Heart Rate —jazzercise, weight lifting, aerobic class

C. Energy Level

Releases tension, stress that arises throughout the day
feel better mentally, socially, physically = improvement
slim and trim

The rich accumulation of ideas and details was not exploited when Cathy wrote her essay. She produced a short and relatively underdeveloped piece:

> In today's society, dieting and staying fit is a common goal for people of all ages. Many hours of hard earned money are spent in local health clubs, spas and aerobic classes. But the results, in the end, are satisfied by each individual. Americans exercise for enjoyment as well as health purposes.
>
> Many people join an exercise group for contentment and confidence in one's abilities. Once one enters a perspective club, he becomes involved in the social aspects which create fulfillment as well. Thus, to share the same outlook and enthusiasm to reach a set goal promotes further enjoyment.
>
> Health also plays a major role in the body beautiful fad. One's adrenalin, heart rate, and energy level increases with every leap and bound. Jazzercise, aerobics and free weight lifting help release tension and stress that arises through out the day. People tend to believe that in feeling better mentally and socially, exercise on the whole provides an improved outlook.
>
> In conclusion, Americans exercise to help promote social enjoyment as well as a slimmer, trimmer, healthier lifestyle.

Illustrative material, such as the different kinds of health clubs, or ideas, such as "talk about $$," which could be easily used to develop the threadbare essay, are excluded or only briefly mentioned.

When revising, judging types need to compensate for their initial expedience. They may need to re-evaluate decisions that have been made hastily or arbitrarily, to consider more thoroughly the implications of their data or ideas, and (especially if they also have a preference for thinking) to expand their writing to clarify or qualify bluntly worded statements.

Perceiving types, who prefer to delay closure in order to take in more information, and whose concern for thoroughness outweighs their concern for meeting deadlines, tend to select broad topics and dive into reading without narrowing their focus. They discover a multitude of interesting, possibly related studies and sources in a literature search, often without knowing clearly what they will do with the information they gather. Terri (an ISFP nursing student) said that whenever she wrote a term paper her dorm room was cluttered with library books. Other perceiving types have said that they feel like there is always one more article or book to read, and they often express insecurity about their knowledge of the topic, even after they have extensively researched it. As a perceiving type in a thesis support group said: "Data collection is easy; writing is hard." Their topics may be limited only as the deadline approaches. How effectively they limit their topic will determine whether they finish the assignment at the last minute, late, or at all.

Perceiving types often say that they do their best writing under pressure. Whether or not they are right deserves further research. When they do produce fairly respectable prose at the 11th hour, writing under pressure may increase their writing anxiety and may limit their revisions. They may simply leave themselves little or no time for rethinking and reformulating their text. As one ENFP (Professional) commented: "Usually I haven't left myself enough time, so the second draft ends up being the final copy."

When writing, they may pause more frequently than judging types, not to reflect or anticipate as an introvert does, but to entertain the possibility of numerous alternatives. Their first drafts tend to be long and thorough but also too inclusive, which may at times disrupt the cohesion of the text. Kris (ESTP/Basic) wrote the following analysis of a print advertisement after his teacher had lectured on persuasive writing:

> Advertising agents have found that the surest way to influence an audience to buy is to appeal to their emotions. Writing advertisements relate heavily to the study of psychological effects. The advertiser should relate to his reader through ethical, emotional, and logical appeals. Printed advertisements usually have a headline and a main illustration called "stoppers." In this particular advertisement the words tough and beautiful are in bold letters signifying the appearance of a floor after the product is used. The bottle of "future" is beautifully lighted and its picture is uniquely enhanced by the flawless rose in the background. The rose in this, for instance, symbolizes two important topics: being as beautiful as its fiery red bloom and tough as its nail like thorns. This particular writer uses the logical side of the reader's thoughts.

Even though the essay is short, quite atypical of perceiving types, it is far too inclusive. Kris seems to have felt the need to include every idea that his teacher mentioned in the lecture on persuasion, whether it belongs or not. On the topic of categorizing attitudes toward the Russian downing of the Korean airliner, Kris wrote a six-page introduction that, typical of a sensing type, recounted all of the facts of the incident from beginning to end. After he wrote the introduction, he spent one paragraph categorizing the attitudes of those he had interviewed. He said that he would have spent still more time categorizing these attitudes, but he felt that the essay was getting too long. When revising, perceiving types such as Kris usually need to cut unrelated or vaguely related data and ideas. They can then focus on the essential points and adequately develop them.

At their best, perceiving types write essays that are comprehensive and well thought out. They may not, however, believe that their work is adequately inclusive. Writers who are INFPs seem especially blessed and cursed in this regard. They consider their ideas at length before they make them public (I), have a vivid imagination for ways to approach a topic (N), weigh the meaning of each word or phrase for its potential to either stimulate or turn off their readers (F), and research their topic at length (P).

The pitfall of a psychological preference for perceiving may be characterized by the following comments from an INFP graduate student: "I find it hard to narrow in on a topic. I feel like I need to read everything that has been written about that topic (and in fact I do read about it—a lot). When I start writing . . . every sentence I write seems to need so much more background, implications, qualificatons, etc. that I get bogged down." The strength of perceiving types, not often appreciated by deadline-conscious instructors, lies in their capacity to view writing as a process of investigation and exploration. Indeed, perceiving types so enjoy exploring a topic that, even when asked to write a persuasive essay, they may write at length about both sides of the issue.

Research (O'Donnell, Griffin, & Norris, 1967) has shown that, as writers develop, they produce longer essays, but gross indicators—such as number of words per essay— may be slighting equally important qualitative changes in these texts. Judging types certainly seem to develop as they learn the value of providing support for their propositions, but perceiving types seem to struggle more with learning to exclude extraneous ideas and data, by learning to say "enough is enough." Although the essays of perceiving types may become generally longer as these writers develop, qualitative research may reveal that their writing improves as it becomes more focused and concise.

INTERACTIONS OF THE DIMENSIONS

In this chapter, we have discussed, mostly in isolation, how the four dimensions of Jung's model affect an individual's writing process. Yet, as we mentioned in Chapter 1, the dimensions interact dynamically rather than simply addititively. The entire model is greater than the sum of its parts.

The process of how different thinking types organize an essay can serve as an example. Sensing–thinking types tend to adopt widely accepted organizational formats, such as the five-paragraph essay, or formats that have proven successful with previous assignments. Intuitive–thinking types are more likely to develop a unique structure for each essay. If intuitive–thinking types are also introverted, they will tend to develop their unique structures before writing; those who are extraverted are more likely to develop unique structures while writing a first draft. Such additive effects are relatively easy to predict.

Some dynamic interactions, however, are less obvious. Sensing–feeling types are often drawn to the five-paragraph format (or some other established pattern) because, as for most sensing types, they want to use a format that they feel will be accepted by their teacher. Yet, since they, as feeling types, write best when following the "flow," their own personal train of thought, such patterns may be restricting. To develop as writers, sensing–feeling types need to resolve this conflict between two of their preferences. Further research may reveal that resolving such conflicts are important developmental issues for other type combinations as well.

Another interesting interaction is related to preferred styles of developing a topic. Extraverts (E) tend to write longer essays than introverts because they tend to develop a broader range of ideas and their essays often have the kind of wordiness found in a more conversational style. On another dimension, intuitive types (N), who may expand their ideas by making inferences from inferences, tend to produce longer essays than sensing types, who value being factual and concise. Feeling types (F), who add words to soften their message, often write longer essays than thinking types, who are more blunt and value getting directly to the point. Perceiving types (P) are much more inclusive than judging types and, thus, tend to write longer, sometimes rambling, essays. Individuals with each of these four preferences (ENFP) do indeed tend to write rather long essays compared to those of other types, especially when writing in a basically narrative format. (Preliminary data indicate that INTs may write longer expository essays.) If the interaction of preferences on each dimension were simply additive, one would also expect that ENTPs would write relatively long essays, but they do not. Adequately developing a topic is usually most difficult for ENTPs; at times, they are even belligerently resistant to expanding upon ideas or providing supporting data or examples.

Why are the essays of ENTPs so much shorter than those of ENFPs? It relates to how intuitive–thinking types develop topics. As thinking types, they prefer a logical development. As intuitive types, their logical development is founded on general ideas, not data and concrete examples. Rather than write long paragraphs replete with personal examples, detailed description, or facts, they are more likely to write short paragraphs that may contain a single threadbare syllogism or a series of enthymemes.

There is a danger that Jung's model can be applied in fragmented ways that do not appreciate the complexity of a writer's composing process. Even if we acknowledge that there is more to personality than this system can explain, we still must recognize that *within* the system, the subtleties of interaction of one's four preferences (not to mention the even more complicated interaction of those with the four unpreferred modes) are profound.

WRITING SITUATIONS AND PERSONALITY

Jack Selzer (1984) has argued that researchers too often ignore the writing situation. He believes they should acknowledge whether their subjects were writing an essay in class, a memorandum on the job, or a letter to a friend, and the influence that each situation exerts on the individual's writing process. A business executive will not use the same writing process to compose a memorandum and a poem, nor will a student use the same process to draft a term paper at home as he or she will to write an in-class essay exam.

Ching (1986), in a study of the writing processes of seventeen university faculty, found that indeed extraverts relied on talking about ideas more than introverts. Six of the 10 introverts disliked talking about ideas at all, but the other four found that the nature of their profession or the nature of their department almost demanded that they spend a fair amount of time talking about various projects. Ching concluded, quite rightly, that the "role of the writer and the nature of the genre of writing should be taken into consideration together with the kind of persons with whom a writer works when considering whether extraverting or introverting situations are beneficial to a certain writer."

At times, individuals may be able to adapt their own preferred writing process to the demands of a certain situation. Introverts prefer to plan extensively, for days if not for weeks, before writing. When writing in class, they cannot plan as extensively as they might wish, but may still spend the first half of a 60-minute period thinking about what they want to write. Extraverts prefer to write sloppy first drafts in a free-writing process and then polish their prose later. We have seen extraverts quickly write a skeletal draft and then rewrite it within 60 minutes.

At other times, writers must temporarily abandon their preferred writing process and embrace a less comfortable one. As stated earlier in this chapter, intuitive types generally want to develop a unique approach to each writing project. When faced with technical reports, they may have to be satisfied with writing in the kind of process that comes more naturally to sensing–thinking types. They may have to follow directions carefully and shape their ideas within the format of a standard technical report. When possible, they nonetheless rely on their more preferred attention to the big picture. As one INFP (Professional) put it: "My writing related to business, proposals, case reports, etc. usually has to do with relating facts of one sort or another. I sort of scan the data and list pertinent items to include in the writing. My personal communication is usually more spontaneous than this."

Radical alterations to one's writing process can be disconcerting and stressful. As writers mature, however, they develop a broader range of strategies and skills and can more adroitly shift from their preferred writing process to one that meets the demands of a particular situation. Mature writers may be more open to adapting their writing processes, but they will still have a preferred writing process.

CONCLUSION

We hope that this chapter can reinforce the pleas of Emig, Britton, Graves, and other researchers, that we should better appreciate the varied approaches that individuals take to writing. As teachers, we should also be more tolerant of writing processes that are quite different than our own. Unfortunately, it is all too easy to make our particular way of writing the standard from which to judge our students. Even in the work of Emig and Britton, who have done more than anyone else to help us appreciate individual approaches to writing, prejudices are evident. For example, Emig wrote:

> For the less able student some species of mode present almost insuperable difficulties—for example, the impersonal argument in which the writer is to present "dispassionately" more than one side, or aspect, of a case. Consequently, if a teacher gives an assignment requiring writing in this submode, certain students may be unable to complete adequately, or even begin, such an assignment. Along with being intellectually unable to perform the assignment, the student may also be unmotivated or psychologically unable to perform the assignment. Such "blocks" may emanate from strikingly different sources: the student may find the task too boring, or he may find the task too threatening. (1971, pp. 38–39)

Certainly, immature writers of a particular type (usually feeling types) may have difficulty writing dispassionately, and may find some topics boring, but they may excel at writing expressively or about topics that deeply interest them. Should these students be viewed as any more deficient than thinking types, who find it easy to write dispassionately but may produce dry, pedantic prose?

Britton and his colleagues demonstrate a bias against a different kind of writer: "It needs to be said that children can often become involved at the extrinsic level of satisfaction at getting it right, seeing a folder mount up, without being intrinsically in the writing and what it is achieving" (1975, p. 8). Britton and his colleagues seem to see no value in writing to get the writing done, as a judging type would. They also apparently ignore the opposite problem, more typical of the perceiving type, of becoming so intrinsically involved in the process of writing that no writing is ever finished.

Perhaps one of the most fruitful applications of the MBTI to the field of composition may be to teacher education: Jung's model of personality and the MBTI can powerfully deliver the message that writing processes differ, that a writer's strengths and weaknesses are related, and that not all writers follow the same developmental path. If brilliant scholars like Emig and Britton can sometimes—if only on rare occasions—fail to see the strengths of a particular approach to writing, so too can the average teacher.

3

Differences in the Process of Writing Development

In a 1983 interview, Andrea Lunsford was asked about research needs in the field of basic writing. She replied: "We simply do not yet understand what constitutes 'development' in writing at the college level and in adults, nor do we know how such development is related to cognitive development, cognitive style, or a host of affective variables" (Stuckey, 1983). Implicit in Lunsford's statement is a schema of gaps, a model of broad topics that need to be researched and synthesized. To understand how students develop into mature writers, researchers need to investigate cognitive development, the development of writing abilities, how cognitive style may alter developmental patterns, and how affective variables may inhibit or promote development.

A few theorists have explored the effect of the writer's cognitive development on his or her writing ability. From the works of Piaget, Vygotsky and Buber, James Moffett (1965, 1968) formulated his I–You and I–It continua, the most comprehensive model of how cognitive development and writing intersect. The I–You continuum, or the rhetorical dimension, reflects an increasing distance between speaker/writer and audience, or an ability to adapt to audiences that are less and less familiar. It reflects a development akin to what Piaget terms decentering, from thinking (reflection) to conversation to correspondence to publishing. The I–It continuum, or the referential dimension, reflects an increasing distance between speaker/writer and subject, a development from immediate experience to memory, generalization and then speculation. Even though Moffett's model is the most widely known, others have been presented. Bradford (1983) has suggested a more purely Piagetian model, and Hays (1983) has applied Perry's model of cognitive development to student writing. Also worthy of notice are Wilkinson's model of writing maturity, which touches upon stylistic, affective, cognitive, and moral variables (Sternglass, 1982), Kohlberg's model (Miller, 1980), and Fowler's model (Elifson & Stone, 1985).

Rather than apply models of cognitive development to writing, other researchers have investigated diachronic changes in texts that might objectively plot the development of writing ability. For example, Hunt uses T-units, or terminal units, to measure syntactical maturity. He believes that mature writing has more words per T-unit, more clauses per T-unit, and more words per clause (Hunt, 1977; O'Donnell, 1976). The validity of this and similar measures has been questioned (Faigley, 1980), and, even if valid, such measures do not adequately describe mature writing or suggest how writers learn to produce mature texts (Shuy, 1981). A writer may produce a "mature" text, as assessed only on surface features, that embodies simplistic, naïve thought.

These and other investigations into the development of writing maturity tend to map development as a basically linear or sequential process, which begins roughly at the same point and moves through a preordained series of steps or stages. For example, Moffett (1968, p. 29) believes that "growth is toward internal complexity and external relationships." At least with complete units of discourse, Moffett feels that writers mature as they are able to develop more abstract forms of discourse for more distant audiences. Although individuals may differ as to when they move on to a "higher" stage and may integrate stages at different rates, they all move through the same stages in the same sequence (Moffett & Wagner, 1976, p. 29). Moffett's model may allow for some flexibility, but, as is typical of most developmental models, it fails to account for cognitive style. For virtually all developmental theorists, every individual is presumed to follow the same sequence of developmental steps or stages.

An overlay of cognitive style with developmental theory may allow for a more complex paradigm, as did Vygotsky's separation of external and internal speech. Once separated, Vygotsky could posit that the two develop in opposite directions: external speech from the particular to the whole and inner speech from the whole to the particular (1962, p. 126). In a similar way, writers of different personality types may develop in opposite directions, adding complexity to some models of development and raising questions about others.

In this chapter, we will concentrate on how the four dimensions of Jung's model can suggest individual patterns of development. In Chapter 4, we will comment on how instructors can use this model to encourage growth in student writers. In Chapter 5 we will discuss how affective variables may interfere with that growth.

JUNG'S MODEL AND DEVELOPMENT

Jung believed that we mature within the context of our personality type, that we develop our preferred cognitive processes early in life and our unpreferred processes later. To develop a fully integrated personality was, as Jung saw it, a lifelong goal. Similarly, Myers believed that "good type development" involves two necessary conditions: "First, adequate but by no means equal development of a judging process (thinking or feeling) and a perceiving process (sensing or intuition), one of which predominates; and second, adequate but by no means equal facility in using both the extraverted and introverted attitudes, with one predominating." Balanced development, she believed, "does not refer to equality of two processes or of two attitudes; instead it means superior skill in one, supplemented by a helpful but not competitive skill in the other" (Myers, 1980, p. 182). Early in life as well as in times of transition or stress, individuals develop most smoothly by employing and refining first (and sometimes exclusively) those aspects of their personality that are most psychologically inherent and natural. Full and integrated development, what Myers calls "balanced development," of all processes (preferred and unpreferred alike) is rarely, if ever, fully achieved. When it is approached, it is best done by employing the unpreferred cognitive processes in the service of a preferred process. Myers, a dominant feeling type (INFP), once described how she, while developing the MBTI, strove for this kind of balance:

> If you operate solely on just feeling and intuition, you don't criticize the course that you are usually joyfully setting out on. There may be something awfully wrong about the particular hypothesis you're using. You may not have enough of a sample to support this "enchanting improvement." And so it behooves you to ask your thinking if there are any flaws in the idea before you go out telling it to people. And you ought to ask your sensing, "Why don't we get a whole lot more data before we consider that we've got a big enough sample?" The only way I can bring myself to call on thinking and sensing—and to shut off my two favorite processes so I can really listen to them—is on the explicit assurance that they are helping me in the service of my favorite [or dominant] process. That way, you see, feeling is not abdicated. Feeling is simply waiting in line to listen to its servicers with what they can contribute and give you in pursuit of your own goals. So I have done unending days and weeks of "coolie-work" with my sensing—scoring and item analysis and the like—because it is in the service of my main goal. (Myers, 1977, p. 4)

Most teachers would like their students to work in the well-balanced way that Myers describes, but "balance" does not come easily or quickly.

Recent research suggests that beginning, or immature, writers are less able to carry out as many cognitive actitivites in a given period of time than more advanced writers (Schumacher, Klare, Cronin, & Moses, 1984). The immature writers, because they are less familiar with the task of writing, must concentrate on each cognitive activity, such as generating content, organizing ideas, and attending to mechanics. They are, therefore, less capable of dealing with the complexity of writing. If they concentrate on content, their mechanics may suffer. If they concentrate on mechanics, their organization may fall apart. More experienced writers, for whom many of the tasks of writing are automatic or habitual, are better able to juggle several cognitive activities. They can attend to content without ignoring organization and mechanics.

Since developing writers are not able to attend to all of the cognitive activities required to produce mature prose, what they usually attend to first are the cognitive activities associated with their preferred processes. As Myers (1980) indicates below, this naturally leads to a temporary neglect of the opposite cognitive process:

> When people prefer sensing, they are so interested in the actuality around them that they have little attention to spare for ideas coming faintly out of nowhere. Those people who prefer intuition are so engrossed in pursuing the possibilities it presents that they seldom look very intently at the actualities. (p. 2)

As writers mature, the application of their preferred process to writing becomes more habitual and they are more capable of turning their attention to unpreferred processes. Once both preferred and unpreferred can be employed, they are better able to produce a more balanced and mature product.

FROM INNER MONOLOGUE TO OUTER DIALOGUE: THE WRITING DEVELOPMENT OF INTROVERTS

Jung believed that extraverts live closer than introverts to the outer world; they collapse the distance between external experience (what Jung called "the object") and internal reflection (what Jung called "the subject"). They develop a broader, but less intense, fund of experience. He wrote that "the particular nature of the extravert constantly urges him to expend and propagate himself in every way " (1921, p. 332). We might then expect the work of immature extraverted writers to include undigested reports of the events of their lives and to deal with a wide range of ideas and information. Moffett categorizes this brand of writing as *what is happening* on his I–It continuum. He describes it through the example of sitting in a public cafeteria eating lunch:

> I am bombarded with smells of food, the sounds or chatter and clatter, the sights of the counter, the tables, the clothing, the faces, the gesticulations

> and bending elbows. But I am not just an observer; I am eating and perhaps socializing as well. . . . My perceptual apparatus is recording these moments of raw experience, not in words but in some code of its own that leads to words. . . . It is difficult to separate this sensory recording from the constant stream of thoughts that is going on simultaneously and parallel to the sensory record but may often depart from it. (1968, p. 36)

In his 1965 article, Moffett said of this stage: "My symbolic representation in this case would entail the least processing of matter by mind." The following journal entry, written by Jackie (ESFP/Basic), illustrates the closeness between writer and phenomenal reality that Moffett mentions:

> Today I was supposed to of worked 9–2 but I felt terrible, I had a bad cold and shivers so I left at 12:30 & went to sleep until 6:00. Benny went to play tennis with John. Last night I told him that they are hiring part-time at Guest Quarters. He wasn't too thrilled with the idea, but it would be $4.50 per hour, 24 hrs per week, only 3 days a week. (Two would be weekend) 10–6 Saturday & 7–3 Sunday, also one day during the week. Which is a lot better than (4) 5–11 days at Richway.

Jung believes that extraverts, when immature, may be so involved in outer experience that they skim across the surface of life, as Jackie seems to present a prose veneer of her daily life. She is writing, seemingly without reflection, about what happened a few hours before or about what she is thinking at the moment. The writer almost seems indistinguishable from her experience. As Jung states, "This is the extravert's danger: he gets sucked into objects and completely loses himself in them" (p. 336). The result of an exaggeration of the extravert's outer orientation is what Moffett (1965) calls "raw phenomena." Jung said that when extraversion "is subordinated to objective data, it engrosses itself entirely in the individual experience and accumulates a mass of undigested material" (1921, p. 340).

In her journal entry, Jackie skips from topic to topic, leaving no mental time to develop any of them in depth. In about 100 words, she writes about three or four different topics. The striking strength of such writing is its vitality and the clear connection between the writer's experience and thought. Such strengths are often overlooked by English teachers, who in general tend to value inner reflection over experience.

When Jackie's instructor reviewed her journal, he wrote: "In your journal, you write about a lot of things but cover everything quickly. How do you think it would be to write about a single event but explore it more deeply?" In her next journal entry, she wrote: "Well, we got our journals back today. So I'll continue to write. I'll try not to write a whole bunch of things." She followed with this entry:

> Benny and I have been going out 6 months today (more or less) I say that because we went out in Jan (82) for 7 mo. and he broke up in Sept (82) for reasons like, he needed time, time to study, friends . . . It's pretty hard to explain, but I guess he was just confused. He was very sincere about the whole thing, he had tears in his eyes, & said he could never leave for good. Well, it was 7 months that we ended up being broken up for, but in those 7 months I learned *a lot*!! I don't think I would trade those 7 months for anything. Even though I *always, always* thought about Benny I did have fun. I got to know practically the whole school (people) & I really enjoyed my senior year. I am glad I didn't miss out on any of the things like high school parties, dates, football games, basketball games, dinners, going to Florida with everyone during Spring break. I got to know myself and everyone, my friends so much better, & I think I grew up a bit more. I guess that goes to show you how things work out. I'm glad about this one!

Here, Jackie's inner monologue is no longer swallowed up by the events of her experience; she seems to reflect before composing. The passage is less immediate; she is not writing only about what happened in the last 24 hours, but about what has happened in the past year and a half. She is also exploring the subject in greater depth. The previous 100-word entry dealt with three or four topics; this 200-word passage deals with only one.

We do not mean to suggest that Jackie matured in a matter of hours just by trying to focus on one topic or by writing about events that occurred over a span of time instead of immediate experience. We do believe, however, that her previous journal entry lacked depth, which she can begin to develop by being encouraged to focus on fewer ideas and by distancing herself more from her experience.

As extraverts' writing is experientially close to the outer experience, so too is it experientially close to the audience. Their prose often reads like a dialogue with a close friend, what Moffett calls "conversation." In his 1965 article, Moffett describes conversation or outer vocalization in this way:

> The fact that my account is unrehearsed, face-to-face vocalization, uttered to *this* person for *this* reason at *this* time and place and in *these* circumstances determines to an enormous degree not only the overall way in which I abstracted certain features of the ongoing panorama of the cafeteria scene but also much of the way I choose words, construct sentences, and organize parts.

The following narrative by June (ESFP/Basic) has the qualities that Moffett attributes to outer vocalization. It seems unrehearsed, conversational, and experiential:

> Friendship and drugs don't mix. As I found out the hard way, there is no place for drugs in a good-long standing friendship. It (drugs) entered one of my closest [friendships] once. It was between my friend Dana and I. Dana had started acting strange this one particular week, I mean she was cranky and yelling at everyone and just in an all-around bad mood. I went up to her house (she's my next-door neighbor) and she was yelling at her mother and boyfriend Mario. They said she started the yelling because Mario had made a wise-crack about her blouse and she blew her top. So I left because I didn't want to be next on her list. So the next day—which was on a Friday, I think—it happened a very strong climax in our friendship.

June continues, in the same style, to relate how her friend, under the influence of drugs, accidentally stabbed her.

Another essay, written by Margo (ESTJ/Basic), reflects a similar proximity to an outer-dialogue and expressive approach, even though the topic (students were asked to explain nihilism) would seem to elicit a more formal, expository essay:

> Driving along 285 on my way home, trying to figure out what to write about I first thought about Hitler and Nihilism. (It would take too much research and time is of the essence). Then I thought about the power behind the man Hitler. Questions begin to form. What is power? What makes a powerful man? What makes men, women and children seek power? I then envisualized the universe with all of the people reaching out and upward for something. That something was the *almighty dollar*, in other words M O N E Y.
>
> They call it the "ROOT OF ALL EVIL" ....IS IT? Well, I thought, if money is the root of evil then let me be up to my eyeballs in it. Let me be surrounded by mounds of it.
>
> As I sat there driving the following thoughts occurred (It's 1986 and I live in a technological world) to me:—
>
> a. *CHRISTIANITY*
>
> Have you ever wondered where christianity would be today if there were no preachers or a pope? The maintenance of the church (upkeep) the outgoing mail, the wine that is passed out, the robes that are sent to the cleaners, the bibles and hymn books that are furnished? IT takes MONEY.
>
> b. *POLITICS*
>
> The political arena that functions behind billions of dollars. The private jet, limousines, champaign managers and champaigns. Flyers that are printed, the media coverage. It takes MONEY.

Margo's essay continues in this manner, listing topics that require money.

What is striking about both texts are the print features that the writers use to express the intonation or oral qualities of their discourse. They use parentheses to add little asides (the written equivalent of saying "what I really mean is . . ."), exclamation points, capital letters, underscoring and other textual features to give hints of their spoken emphasis. They employ typically conversational delimiters ("well," "so," "then"), an oral form of punctuation, and their sentences sometimes ramble on, which is more typical of spoken discourse (see Brown & Yule, 1983, pp. 15–16; Chafe, 1986). Margo's essay also employs a typically oral refrain: "It takes MONEY."

We have observed that the writing of extraverts seems to be more naturally dialogic (Bakhtin, 1981, pp. 259–422), developing an energy and vitality from the interplay of different voices. Their essays usually have a clear sense of voice, and their narratives often include more dialogue. June's and Margo's ability to write more conversationally, from outer speech, may at this point of their development be more refined than their ability to write from an inner monologue. We have frequently observed that extraverted basic writers, who may have struggled for weeks to produce an artificial and vague formal prose, begin to write more clearly and fluently when asked to write the text of a speech.

Further research might suggest that extraverts first learn to write from outer dialogue, as if they were talking with or to someone, while introverts first learn to write from inner monologue, a reflective speech to oneself. We should also not assume that writing from inner monologue is necessarily superior. For example, we have noticed that extraverted basic writers are more likely to demonstrate a clear sense of voice, which introverted basic writers can begin to develop by writing the text of a speech rather than an essay. It may be that a sense of voice emanates more easily from an outer dialogue.

FROM INNER MONOLOGUE TO OUTER DIALOGUE: THE WRITING DEVELOPMENT OF INTROVERTS

Introverts tend to spend less time dealing with outer experience, naturally assuming a more distant stance from their topics. Their writing is less likely to be close to "phenomenal reality" because the introvert is as likely to be concerned with his or her inner map of the world as with experiencing the world directly. As Jung (1921) explains,

> The introvert is distinguished from the extravert by the fact that he does not, like the latter, orient himself by the object and by the objective data, but by subjective factors. [Also,] the introvert interposes a subjective view between the perception of the object and his own action, which prevents the action from assuming a character that fits the objective situation. (p. 373)

Moffett, in describing his I–It continuum, has pointed out that a similar effect, an intervention of a subjective factor, is achieved when the writer shifts from writing about *what is happening* to *what happened* or *what happens*. In describing *what happened* in his 1965 article, Moffett comments on how the writer, the "I," or what Jung calls the subjective factor, intervenes between "phenomenal reality" and the text:

> If next I treat the events at the cafeteria as *what happened*, the subject will necessarily partake a little more of my mind and a little less of the original matter. Although the order of events will still be chronological, it is now my memory and not my perceptual apparatus that is determining the selecting. Some things will stick in my mind and some will not, and some things I will choose to retain or reject, depending on which features of the scene and action I wish to bring out. Of the details selected, some I will dwell upon and some I will subordinate considerably. Ideas are mixed with the material from the very beginning, but the recollection of a drama—a narrative, that is—inevitably entails more introduction of ideas because that is inherent in the very process of selecting, summarizing, and emphasizing, even if the speaker refrains from commenting directly on events.

Outer experience is even less present when the writer deals with *what happens*, in which the interlude at the cafeteria is treated as something that recurs. The text is further from "phenomenal reality" because no "primary moments of experience recur."

According to Moffett, as the writer treats topics further back in time, memory and the writer's values (what he or she feels is important) filter out data and specific events. Whether writers are extraverted or introverted, their memory will naturally filter data from the event to the text, but introverts, far more than extraverts, will allow a subjective factor to come into play. As Jung states: "The introvert's attitude is an abstracting one; at bottom, he is always intent on withdrawing libido from the object, as though he had to prevent the object from gaining power over him" (1921, p. 330). The simple fact that introverts tend to think and plan more extensively before they write allows more time for memory and their subjective values to select and digest objective data. But this natural filtering out of data is not necessarily a higher form of development.

The following journal entry, written by Veronica (ISTJ/Basic) about a coworker, illustrates:

> Tommie wants to be a ladies man. He is to some ladies, especially Cheryl. He want Samatha bad for his ego that's all. He wants to use her the way he did Cheryl because she seems niave. He came from Sandersville, Ga. He can give girls the smoothest sweetest lies that sound so true but Samatha knew where he was coming from. He's also trying to get customers phone numbers.

The passage, which reads like the condensation of a soap opera, reflects months, if not years, of intense observation. Veronica does not show the weakness of lack of depth and scattered focus, as Jackie (ESFP/Basic) did. She does not skim across immediate experiences, writing about what happened today or what she is thinking at the moment. She does, however, lack the vitality and clear connection between experience and thought that came so naturally to the extravert. Indeed, the passage is almost devoid of experience. Learning to write about a more immediate experience, *what is happening*, which Moffett calls the "lowest level of verbal abstraction of reality," is a skill that Veronica had not yet developed.

Veronica's instructor continually encouraged her to spend more time explaining her conclusions, practicing free writing, and trying to write about more immediate experiences. Because introverted writers are sometimes reluctant to share their thoughts, he also said to her, "I believe that you have a lot of good ideas in your head, but you don't seem to get them down on paper. I know that it can be a little hard to share your thoughts with someone else, but I would like for you to try." Over the course of the term, the following journal passage, which explored current feelings, rather than conclusions made from extended observations, shows growth in this direction:

> Since I've been in college this quarter, I'm really getting a tough time. My father is jealous of me; he wants me to fail. When he know I'm studying, he turns the TV up as loud as possible. He's always feeding me bull about "if that's what a education does for you . . ." Its always some bull about "you think you're smart . . ." He always try to say I think I'm too good because I'm in college. This is only my first quarter and I'm getting this bull.
>
> I know its wrong to have disrespect, but once I wished the man would drop dead. Him and all 6′3 and 220 pounds of his foolish bull. I know what type of person he wants me to be and he can keep wishing. I'm going to do my best to do what I want. If he's jealous of me and wants a "education" he should have gotten one. I'm not telling where his educational

> history ends but I will say this. He surely wasn't bright or mediocre & you know what's left.

Here, the writer is closer to her experience; she no longer reflects upon experience to a point that she loses touch with its vitality.

Introverts will also tend to assume a more relatively distant stance toward their audience, at least compared with extraverts with other MBTI preferences in common. The highest level of Moffett's I–You continuum is "Publication," an impersonal communication to a large anonymous group. Karen (ISTJ/Basic) wrote the following essay about her mother, in which, despite the intimate topic, she formally addressed her audience:

> Sometimes my mother really gets on my nerves. I don't think she realizes it but she does. I take her to work every morning. She usually waits until we have only fifteen minutes before it's time for us to leave; then, she rushes puts on her clothes for work. This usually takes about thirty minutes. There are days when she fusses all day. She fusses about cleaning the house, moving fast, getting a job, and a number of other things.
>
> I asked her why she argued all day and continued to get ready late. Her response was that she was my mother. I never asked again.
>
> I'm glad she is not always so nerve wrecking. Sometimes she is also very understanding at times. When I am going to have a major exam, she usually doesn't say anything to me about cleaning up. She just tells my sister to do it. Those are the days my nerves are relaxed and I love her the most.

June's (ESFP/Basic) earlier essay in which she described her friend stabbing her, was about a particular event in the past unlike Karen's essay above. Because it was written about a past event, June's writing has some general ideas ("Friendship and drugs don't mix"), but it is still much closer to experential data than Karen's essay. June wrote about *what happened*, a particular event; Karen wrote about *what happens*, about her relationship with her mother as it recurs, spanning years of experience. The introvert (who in this case is also a thinking type, whose writing is more objective) naturally filters out more experiential data than the extravert, but she also writes more formally. Absent are the chatty phrases ("So I left") and conversational asides ("she's my next door neighbor") found in June's more extraverted style of writing (note that June is also a feeling type). In certain situations, Karen's naturally formal style will undoubtedly be more appropriate; in other situations, June's more conversational style will be more effective. As they mature as writers, Karen will need to learn what comes naturally to extraverts; June will need to learn what comes naturally to introverts.

FROM THE TANGIBLE TO THE INFERRED: THE WRITING DEVELOPMENT OF SENSING TYPES

Because of the use of terms such as "external realities" and "internal abstractions," it is often wrongly assumed that extraversion and sensing are automatically correlated, or introversion and intuition. They are not.

Extraversion is a primary turning toward the outer world. That outer world may, for ES types especially, draw the extravert into interacting with tangible actualities; EN types, in contrast, are more interested in how the world around them can be changed and remade.

Introversion is primarily a turning toward the inner world. IN types step back from the world and put their imagination to work to create inner models of how the world as a whole might be conceived. IS types carefully gather precise information about the world around them, not for the purpose of interacting with that world as an ES might, but to have the data ready for understanding how it works.

Sensing types who are still developing as writers, whether extraverts or introverts, may concentrate so intently on their preferred process of sensory perception that their essays never proceed beyond the tangible. They may never seem to rise beyond the *what happened* stage of Moffett's I–It scale, or they may even, since their thought and writing remains concrete, seem to be in Piaget's Concrete Operational stage of development.

Tara (ESTJ/Basic), in the following passage, exhibits those qualities that might be confused with the Concrete Operational stage. When asked to relate briefly a story in one paragraph and then connect it to a proposition or moral, she chose to narrate the events of her senior cruise:

> The day had finally arrived, the day we were leaving for our Senior cruise. There were only five of us but we were determined to have fun. We had all met at 10:00 at Cherokee Plaza (we were taking a bus to Miami). When we got there, there were about 20 elderly couples, not really old but older than us. We each said good bye to our families and boarded the bus. Cindy and Danielle had come well prepared with big pitchers of magaritas, and a bottle of Rum, with Coke. We had planned on drinking all of it but the only thing that had gotten drunk was the coke, because we had all fell asleep. . . .

The "paragraph" continues in this genre for another six pages. Even though Tara participated in class exercises that illustrated what was expected, she never made a proposition or reached any kind of general conclusion. When the last event of the trip was related, her piece of writing ended. Apparently, she was so focused on an accurate recounting of the events of the trip, on "phenomenal reality," that she was unable to make a general, abstract statement about what the trip meant to her. As both an extravert and a sensing type, Tara is especially inclined to focus on the external world to the neglect of reflection and inferences. As Jung said of sensing types, which is perhaps far more accurate of developing than of mature sensing types, "Once an object has given him a sensation nothing more remains to be said about it. It cannot be anything except concrete and real; conjectures that go beyond the concrete are admitted only on condition that they enhance sensation" (1921, p. 364).

When sensing types fail to develop inferences about their data, their essays may lack coherence. The first half of a sentence may even fail to relate to the latter half. When still immature, the abstract statements that they do make may be awkwardly juxtaposed—rather than synthesized—and their tangible data may not clearly support topic sentences and thesis statements. Tara, when writing on the disadvantages of owning a car, produced the following paragraph:

> When you have your own car, you are responsible for the maintenance of the car. This includes all repairs, gas, and being able to budget your money so that, if something does go wrong, you are able to fix it! You are also responsible for the people's lives who ride in your car. With other people in your car, you must be extra careful, which shows responsibility.

That one must maintain a car *and* drive carefully are both responsibilites, but they are only loosely related concepts. Tara apparently connected the two ideas at a fairly concrete level, through the literal, denotative meaning of the word responsibility.

Sensing types are often more able to generalize from their data when asked to revise a single paragraph of an essay, when they are not overloaded with other cognitive activities. In the following revised paragraph, Tara is able to make a general statement about her short narrative, which she failed to do in the first draft, and go on to relate it to her thesis, that the drinking age should be lowered:

> Yesterday, Glen turned 18 and he went to register for the draft. At age 18, you're considered an adult, you're old enough to vote, go to war, legally be responsible for yourself, and if you want you can leave home. Now that Glen is 18, he has a lot of major decisions to make. He is considered legal in

> every aspect except he is, unfortunately, not considered an adult if he goes to buy beer or liquor.

When revising only a paragraph, she is not overwhelmed by the very concrete data that she so values. She is more able to direct her attention to a less preferred intuitive process and can begin to develop the skill of generalizing and inferring from her data, which comes less naturally to her.

FROM THE INFERRED TO THE TANGIBLE: THE WRITING DEVELOPMENT OF INTUITIVES

Intuitive types, especially those who are basic writers, are more likely to concentrate foremost on implications and abstractions because they naturally attend to imaginative possibilities. They may begin with a small amount of concrete data, make inferences from them, and then cavalierly discard the tangible data that no longer seem relevant. For them, data may be nothing more than a means to an end. As Jung noted, as soon as objective data have "served their purpose as stepping-stones or bridges then they lose their value altogether and are discarded as burdensome appendages" (1921, p. 367).

At other times, intuitive types may generate ideas from ideas, as in what Moffett considers to be the highest stage of development on the I–It continuum, *what will, may or could happen*. Moffett explains:

> Finally, in its most distilled form, I might speak or write about the cafeteria experience without referring directly to it at all, even as a brief example, for I might be developing an anthropological theory in which the generalization about how Americans socialize in public places would be combined with other generalizations similarly derived from other material. (1968, p. 39)

This brand of thinking seems more like Piaget's Formal Operations stage, in which the thinker can generate or follow arguments without the need to attend to specific content or data. In Jung's model, Moffett's description is clearly intuitive, perhaps with the suggestion of introversion and thinking as well (INT).

Pat (ENFJ/Basic) exhibits many of these characteristics in her writing, which, though more abstract than Tara's, is equally immature. On the Russians' downing of a Korean airliner, Pat wrote the following as the second paragraph of her essay:

> There are two different sides to the issue: the political and the moral outlook. But there is only one correct and proper conclusion to be drawn from this issue. First, the moral view is that there is no justification for the shooting down of a defenseless plane. Mainly because the disregard of human life can't be tolerated behind the excuse trespassing into Soviet territory. There were several options which the Soviets could have taken but instead ignored. It is strongly felt and believed that the Soviets were aware of this plane being occupied by passengers and not spies. This makes their act even more barbaric and cruel because it eliminates the possibility of being an accident.

The tangible data (or the local opinions of the people she interviewed) behind these ideas were lost somewhere in the composing process. At no point does she quote or paraphrase anyone. She remains with her inferences, but even these are not clear. Her concepts are confusing largely because it is not clear from what they have been inferred. Her prose might be more lucid if she had included some of her tangible data, but attending to direct findings, facts, and evidence, which comes so naturally to sensing types, is quite difficult for developing intuitives. For them, as Jung says, sensation "is a hindrance to clear, unbiased, naïve perception; its intrusive sensory stimuli direct attention to the physical surface, to the very things round and beyond which intuition tries to peer" (pp. 366–367).

Once Pat began to attend to and include concrete examples, her writing ceased being needlessly abstract. Later in the course, the following paragraph was written in support of capital punishment:

> Our society does not learn from its mistakes. It's hard to believe that many murders are committed by an individual who was set free from jail. For example, a young lady which was murdered in a shopping mall was executed by a man which served eleven years for killing another individual. If proper action would have been taken, this incident may never have occurred.

Even though she includes more support for her propositions here than she had before, it is still clear that her sensory perception is not very well developed. Her example remains too abstract, lacking the details that lend emotional force. Her prose also remains awkward. But her ideas, now grounded with concrete examples, are much clearer in this passage.

Even though Pat's earlier writing seems to fit into a higher stage of development, at least according to some models, it is still in many ways as immature as Tara's. Unwittingly, Pat concentrates on her more preferred intuitive perception, producing a very abstract prose. Yet, her perception and her writing are often very flighty, needlessly abstract, and obtuse. She has not mastered what Tara more naturally demonstrates, thinking and writing concretely, which is generally regarded as a skill mastered in prerequisite stages of development.

ANALYZING AND PERSONALIZING: THE WRITING DEVELOPMENT OF THINKING AND FEELING TYPES

Since thinking types base decisions on logical, objective, and impersonal criteria, and feeling types base theirs on personal, subjective values, the writing of each often reflects respectively an analytical or a personal approach to both content and audience. To use Kinneavy's terms, the writing of thinking types is "thing-centered" and the writing of feeling types is "people-centered" (1971, p. 88). The difference further explains yet more qualities of Moffett's I–It and I–You continua.

The distinction can be clearly seen in a set of essays by Glenda and Paulette. During the fall quarter of 1983, the two students formed a close friendship, offering each other support through their first quarter of remedial coursework. In the winter quarter, they were placed in separate basic writing classes. Before they were able to re-establish contact, they both in their own way touched on the friendship when composing their first essay. Glenda's (ESFJ/Basic) essay reflected her personal values, her close friendship with Paulette:

> I have been trying to get in touch with my friend Paulette. We met last quarter and became very special friends. But after the quarter ended we lost touch of each other.
>
> Paulette and I formed a very unique friendship. We were able to laugh and cry with each other. Paulette became a sister to me. We had the type of friendship whereas, we could talk about anything and not feel embarrassed about it. Whenever one of us had a problem we always found a way to solve it together.
>
> The past few days everybody has been telling me that Paulette has been looking for me. I haven't been able to run into her yet. It seems as though something or someone doesn't want us to see each other. I miss seeing Paulette everyday, because we has alot of fun together. I just want the chance to spend some time with my very special friend.

Even though Paulette (ISTP/Basic) greatly valued her friendship with Glenda, her essay reads more objectively. It lacks the personal warmth found in Glenda's essay. It is more thing-centered than people-centered:

> I feel that this quarter I will do well because of my determination in becoming a successful student. In the Remedial Reading course that I took

last quarter, I remembered feeling insecure. Because it was an insult to my intelligence that I had to take a remedial course in college, while the other students were studying degree courses. I felt that I have not accomplished anything at all throughout my high school years.

When I found out that I had to take a remedial course I cried and felt negative about attending college. But I had a few people to talk to me, which made me take a chance to see what the remedial course was like. It turned out that I really needed it and what made it better for me was finding a friend with the same problem. My friend had a reading comprehension problem like myself, but she had something that I admired her for, which was a positive attitude of strengthening her weakness that I envied very much. I knew right off that I needed to stay around her for support and to gain enough respect for myself to make me establish a positive attitude of myself. We shared the same problems and we understood where we both were coming from. We felt comfortable around each other because we knew our problem and was able to talk it out freely and openly without a put on. We supported each other by convincing each other when we felt discouraged about our potentials. We overcame that fear by seeking help which was taking a Remedial course. And we seached for extra help, by going to the Reading Center to dig deeper for finding the problem that we both shared in comprehension.

Now it seems like that positive drive of overcoming the fear that we thought we had erased from our minds seemed to have reversed back into gear from where and how I started off.

I know that I can do well in my Remedial courses. If I maintain good notes and keep up with my assignments.

The important thing for me to do is to associate with people who have a positive attitude about themselves and a positive attitude about life.

Glenda mentions Paulette's name in the first sentence, but Paulette never mentions Glenda's name. Rather than saying that she needs to locate Glenda, Paulette further analyzes and objectifies the relationship by saying that she needs "to associate with people who have a positive attitude."

Glenda's essay dealt with a specific friendship; it was, to use Moffett's terms, *what happened* to her last quarter and how it relates to *what is happening*, how she feels at the moment. Paulette objectifies the friendship and, in the process, abstracts it. Her essay is closer to Moffett's *what happens* stage (as described in his 1965 article), in which the writer makes an "analogy between something in the cafeteria experience and something . . . singled out in a number of other experiences." In this sense, Paulette's essay may be more abstract, but it lacks the personal warmth and sentiment of Glenda's essay. Paulette's more objective approach to writing may, in some situations, be preferable, but certainly not always. With some topics, Paulette will need to write more personally; with other topics, Glenda will need to write more analytically. As these writers mature, they will become more capable of adapting their style to the demands of a particular rhetorical situation.

As thinking types assume a more analytical stance to their content, they assume a more emotionally distant stance to their audience. In general, thinking types concentrate more on the content than the process of communication. They often, especially when immature, present their content clearly but dryly, excluding personal examples and the emotional facet of the topic. Heidi (ISTJ/Basic) wrote the following short narrative of an incident that happened to her while working in a drugstore:

> One night as I was working at Eckerd's, a man and lady walked in. The man walked toward the magazine rack and looked at magazines. The lady stayed at my counter and asked me a lot of questions. I saw him in the distance looking at magazines and also the cigarette cartons. She told me to turn around to get some batteries for her camera and I turned around several times. All of a sudden while I was turned around, I heard something drag across the floor. She said she would come back and buy the things she had put on the counter. She then left and I ran to look at the carton of cigarettes and about 10 cartons of Kool's had been stolen.

Bakhtin feels that the "finer nuances of style are determined by the nature and degree of *personal* proximity of the addressee to the speaker." He feels that "objectively neutral styles . . . select language vehicles not only from the standpoint of their adequacy to the subject matter" (by focusing on content) but also by objectifying the audience. The result is an "almost complete forfeiture of expression" (1986, pp. 96–98). This has seemed to occur with Heidi's narrative. What is missing from the text are possible personal reactions (fear, anger, suspicion) and stylistic features (descriptive verbs, adjectives, and adverbs) that could connect writer and audience. Not only do we wonder if Heidi was personally present in the story, but the factual and emotionally neutral story invites the audience to remain detached as well.

Toward the end of the term, after a great deal of peer feedback from feeling types, Heidi was able to write more personally and with a more interesting style. To explain why college students are often broke, she wrote:

> I drive to school every day. This can take a big chunk of green out of a paycheck. My car drinks gasoline so fast I sometimes think it is leaking. I fill my car up at the beginning of the week. This costs twenty dollars. By the end of the week my car is back on empty. I guess the reason for this is because it takes a lot of gas for a Camaro. I was warned about this by my parents and friends but did I listen?

In this essay, though the improvement may be subtle, she has begun to develop a greater sense of style ("a big chunk of green" and "My car drinks gasoline") and to include human emotions (as in the last sentence), making her writing far more vivid and interesting. She has begun to attend to the process of communication as well as the content; she has perceived the need to connect with her audience.

Though feeling types are far less likely to write dry, academic treatises, they may so closely attend to the process of communication, by attempting to engage the reader, that they neglect content. Ron (ESFJ/Basic) wrote the following paragraph to explain one of the disadvantages of owning a car:

> Maintenance on a car is one disadvantage as discussed previously, but I have the ultimate that can turn anyone against a new car. When you're washing your new car every other day and making it look pretty and shiny and then go to a party and salad dressing is put on your car, let me tell you that will send you into cardiac arrest. I'm still not over the trauma of the salad dressing escapade. It eventually came out but trying to get it out is when I started to panic, should a human being be subjected to such pressure from a car. No.

The stylistic features and emotional effects ("send you into cardiac arrest") that thinking types like Heidi had to learn come more easily to feeling types like Ron. But, as is evident even in a single paragraph, the feeling type has more difficulty developing and organizing content. He discussed maintenance in an earlier paragraph of the essay and begins to discuss it here as well. However, once he begins to discuss maintenance, he is diverted by a personal example that does not adequately explain the difficulties of maintaining a car.

After instruction on organization and peer feedback from thinking types, Ron eventually began to write more logically organized, coherent essays. The following paragraph supports the proposition that videotaped music, as seen on MTV, is superior to mere recordings:

> When one pulls out a set of records at a gathering of friends, the records are being heard but are they actually listened to? Video's I feel change this. By viewing a video, the people of the group can all observe together, therefore the same data perceived is going in at once and a lasting conversation discussing the respective video among the people in the group can be started.

This paragraph (beginning with "one" rather than "I") takes a more objective stance toward the subject, which, though not necessarily preferable, allows the feeling type to gain more control over content. We are not advising feeling types (or anyone else) to avoid the first person, but certainly experimenting with more dispassionate points of view may help them to develop skills that come more easily to thinking types. As they attempt to learn these new skills, the feeling type's natural strengths may temporarily disappear. The paragraph above is far less interesting than his earlier paragraph. Yet, after he has mastered, or begun to master, organization and analysis, he can then be encouraged to return to his strength, his personal approach and his striking style, to which he can then add his new found skill. Composition teachers are too seldom aware that, when a student's writing appears to deteriorate, he or she may be laying the foundation for an important period of growth.

Although an extraverted–feeling type's need to connect emotionally with an audience may sometimes produce qualities associated with Moffett's "conversation" (often leading them toward expressive, narrative genres) and an introverted–thinking type's more objective stance toward an audience may be more suited to most kinds of formal, expository writing, no direct developmental correlation should be forced. Some kinds of formal writing, such as technical reports or scientific studies, in which content is more important than how a writer connects with the audience, are suited to the thinking type's naturally analytical approach. Other kinds of formal writing, such as persuasion, require that the writer readily connect with the audience, which comes more naturally to feeling types. As Myers (1980) stated, "in teaching, in acting and the other arts, in oratory and in that humbler branch of persuasion called salesmanship, in the relations of the clergy to their congregations, in family life, in social contacts, and in any sort of counseling, *it is feeling which serves as the bridge between one human being and another*" (p. 66). Thinking types who are still developing as writers may generate valid arguments for a persuasive essay but fail to connect with the audience or assume an unnecessary and counterproductive antagonistic stance. To be well rounded, writers need to be able to write analytically *and* personally, as they need to present content clearly *and* connect with their audience.

EXCLUSIVE AND INCLUSIVE WRITERS: THE DEVELOPMENT OF JUDGING AND PERCEIVING TYPES

We have already discussed (in Chapter 2) how judging types are more likely to write without first thoroughly investigating the topic and even then they may exclude much of the information that they have developed. In contrast, perceiving types are more likely to delay writing in order to investigate more thoroughly a topic and often feel compelled to include virtually all of the information that they develop. One might assume that judging, the more selective cognitive process, would produce a more abstract prose; Moffett, for instance, considers selectivity to be a form of lower-order abstraction (1968, p. 22).

But whether or not exclusion, or selectivity, leads to a higher degree of abstraction depends on what is being excluded. Judging types who exclude sensory data tend to write more abstractly than perceiving types who include sensory data. Perceiving types who include inferences tend to write more abstractly than judging types who exclude inferences.

In other words, SJs tend to write more abstractly than SPs because SJs exclude some of the raw phenomena or tangible data that, as sensing types, is the focus of their perceptive process. In a similar fashion, NPs tend to write more abstractly than NJs because they explore their intuition, their inferences, more thoroughly and include more of those inferences in their texts.

The writing of Jackie and Veronica, quoted in the E–I section of this chapter, is illustrative. That Veronica's (ISTJ/Basic) early journal entry is more abstract than Jackie's (ESFP/Basic) is partly due to a difference between the two on the Extraversion–Introversion dimension. It is also partly due to Veronica's tendency (as an SJ) to exclude more tangible data than Jackie (an SP).

As stated in previous sections of this chapter, a higher level of abstraction is not necessarily indicative of a higher order of cognitive development. Although SJs are comparatively more abstract writers than SPs (if all other variables were held constant), they are not necessarily more highly developed. Similarily, NPs are not necessarily more highly developed than NJs. All writers, judging and perceiving types alike, can develop, but in their own way.

In general, judging types develop as writers by first stating clearly and forthrightly the conclusions that come to them so naturally, especially in initial drafts. They then enrich their prose, as they develop as writers, by seeking out new possible ways to look at their topics, by qualifying overly definitive statements which may read more like pronouncements and finalities (especially for TJs) and by adapting their rather orderly plans for their writing to unexpected pieces of new information.

Perceiving types develop in the reverse fashion. Naturally inclusive, inquisitive, and curious, they leave most options wide open, which leads to first drafts that may be long and rambling but that can develop toward a healthy, comprehensive view of the topic. As they develop, they learn to enrich their writing by narrowing their focus when appropriate, by sharpening ambiguous concepts (especially if NPs) and by making more solid declarations of their conclusions.

Judging types, who naturally make decisions quickly on very little

Table 1. Writers' Strengths and Weaknesses

Extraversion (E)	Introversion (I)
Physical proximity to topic and audience. STRENGTHS: Es excel at writing from experience. Their prose is likely to be vital and reflect a clear connection between experience and thought. They tend to excel at writing dialogues from outer speech and usually have a clear sense of voice. At their best, they will write a vital, informal prose that reflects an immediacy of experience. WEAKNESSES: Es may write more fragmentally, touching superficially on a broad range of topics (especially if also P). They may not adequately reflect on their topic or fail to differentiate their values from those of their audience (especially if also T). At their worst, they present undigested information in an inappropriate and conversational style.	Physical distance from topic and audience. STRENGTHS: Is will tend to write more intensely about a more limited range of ideas or topics (especially if also J). They will usually reflect on their topic enough to make abstractions from it and clearly perceive the audience as someone with values different than their own. At their best, they will condense ideas into a naturally formal style. WEAKNESSES: Is' writing may be so distant from experience that it lacks vitality or fails to reflect clearly the connection between experience and thought. They may be reluctant to express ideas and feelings, even on paper. At their worst, they will produce a lifeless and needlessly formal prose (especially if also T).
Sensory Perception (S)	**Intuitive Perception (N)**
Focus on concrete, sensory data. STRENGTHS: Ss excel at following directions closely, at attending to concrete observations and accurately presenting data. At their best, they will write accurate descriptions and sound technical reports; they may also be better at dealing with complex data sets than Ns. WEAKNESSES: Ss may fail to present the ideas and concepts behind their concrete data. They may fail to see the unique demands of the rhetorical situation and fail to adjust their writing to meet those demands. At their worst, they will present mere facts in a hackneyed formula.	Focus on generalities, implications, inferences, and possibilities. STRENGTHS: Ns excel at developing unique approaches to a topic. At their best, they will write imaginatively and originally about sound concepts and theories. WEAKNESSES: Ns may leap into the middle of the piece or narrative and fail to provide background information. They may fail to include support (examples, facts, etc.) for their ideas, and they may find it difficult to follow directions. At their worst, their writing is incomprehensibly abstract and complex, based on flighty, inaccurate hunches.
Thinking Judgment (T)	**Feeling Judgment (F)**
Emotional distance from topic and audience. STRENGTHS: Ts excel at the logical development of essays. They tend to write objectively and analytically. At their best, they will present content clearly and	Emotional proximity to topic and audience. STRENGTHS: Fs excel at using personal examples to develop their essays and at writing expressively. They also excel at making contact with the audience and at

Table 1. (*Continued*)

Thinking Judgment (T)	Feeling Judgment (F)
develop sound and consistent organizational patterns.	conveying the deep personal conviction behind their beliefs. At their best, they produce stylish, interesting, and personal prose.
WEAKNESSES: Ts may regard their beliefs as universally held (especially if also E) and thus write abrasively or dogmatically. They may objectify ideas and examples until they lose personal appeal. Their organizational patterns may be too structured. For example, they may make a narrative read like a technical report. At their worst, they may, by writing abrasively or dryly, fail to connect with their audience.	WEAKNESSES: Fs' writing may be gushy or overly sentimental. They often dislike analyses or making critical remarks and may, out of concern for others' feelings, soften criticism until it is unclear or lacks force. Their organization may be so free flowing that their thoughts seem contradictory (especially if also E). At their worst, they write sentimentally and unclearly.
Judging (J)	**Perceiving (P)**
Exclusion of data and ideas to enhance decisiveness.	Inclusion of data and ideas to enhance thoroughness.
STRENGTHS: Js tend to be decisive and can usually reach conclusions quickly and thus forcefully assert a proposition. They tend to write quickly, meet deadlines, and may complete more projects than Ps. At their best, they write expediently and emphatically.	STRENGTHS: Ps tend to investigate their topic thoroughly and present carefully considered ideas. Their writing will tend to be fully developed, and their ideas well supported. At their best, they are thorough and present well-qualified conclusions.
WEAKNESSES: Js, in their haste to meet deadlines, are in danger of reaching premature closure. Their conclusions may be ill-considered or arbitrary. At their worst, their writing is opinionated, unambitious, and underdeveloped; their statements unqualified.	WEAKNESSES: Ps may write on topics that are too broad and, in general, be overinclusive. Their writing may be so thorough that it is tediously long, or it may be rife with digressions. They may be reluctant to assume a position in persuasive essays, open-endedly discussing both sides of the issue. At their worst, their writing may seem to ramble endlessly without clear focus.

data, also need to learn to delay writing in order that they might more thoroughly research or think about a topic. Even when they do thoroughly research a topic, they may exclude many of their findings from the final product. Because they feel comfortable with basing conclusions on very little data, they may naturally assume that their audience will accept their poorly supported conclusions. In general, they need to develop into more careful decision makers who justify and qualify their ideas, theories, and conclusions.

Perceiving types, who prefer to explore a topic openly, are prone to indecisiveness. They may vacillate between what they feel are equally valid solutions, or overqualify the conclusions that they tentatively embrace. Since they value well-researched decisions, their writing is often overinclusive. As a result, the point that they wanted to support with copious research may become lost in a rambling catalog of data, examples, or ideas. In general, perceiving types need to develop into more concise, decisive and emphatic writers who are not overly inclusive of data and ideas.

TYPE AND OTHER MODELS OF DEVELOPMENT

Jung's model of personality may also bear more relevance to developmental issues once the interaction of dimensions is considered. For example, Perry's (1968) model of cognitive development for college students seems to place STJs at the lowest stage of development and NFPs at the highest. The lowest stage in his model is "Basic Duality," in which students see knowledge as being either right or wrong, true or false. Mitroff and Kilmann (1978, pp. 32–53) have commented on how ST scientists have a low tolerance for ambiguity. Students at the stage of "Basic Duality" also feel that knowledge resides in authorities, as SJs frequently do, and that knowledge is gained through hard work and obedience, a belief also typical of SJs. Hays (1983) suggests that writers in the "Basic Duality" stage are especially prone to making broad, unqualified statements, which we have commonly found in the writing of TJs.

The highest stage of Perry's model is "Developing Commitment." At this stage, students accept that knowledge is "contextual and relativistic," typical of NFPs. Also, these students affiliate themselves with and express a commitment to a community. Mitroff and Kilmann (1978, pp. 92–93) characterize NF scientists, whom they call Conceptual Humanists, as forming a commitment to the improvement of mankind. Hays (1983) feels that writers who are at this stage express their relativistic view of knowledge by recognizing the varied facets of an issue, which we have found to be typical of NPs. She suggests that these writers express kinship with a community through a refined sense of audience, which we have found characteristic of feeling types.

We do not intend to say that Perry's model is invalid, but that it and others should be critically re-evaluated from the perspective of Jung's model of personality or some other model of cognitive style. Perry's interpretation of his data may have been influenced by the biases of his own personality type, his sample could have been in some respect skewed, or he could be describing an accurate developmental pattern for college students.

TYPE AND CONTEXTUALIZED APPROACHES TO DEVELOPMENT

In previous sections of this chapter, we have discussed how type might relate to general models of cognitive development and to models of the development of writing ability. These theories almost universally ignore the importance of context.

Writers undoubtedly develop in some general ways that transcend context, but they must also develop by learning how to write in specific modes or genres and by learning to adapt to specific discourse communities. Peter Elbow, when describing his own difficulty with writing expository prose, hints at a developmental issue related to context:

> The answer [to why expository writing is difficult] is that it's not good enough to breathe real, experienced thinking into your expository writing, that thinking must also be disciplined. Thoughts are supposed to be coherent, that is, to begin at the beginning and follow along a single track and end up at the end or conclusion. And there aren't supposed to be any mistakes in logic. But that's not a picture of how the mind usually experiences thoughts. Our habitual thinking is seldom strictly logical but rather associational, analogical, metaphorical. We think and we experience our thoughts, but those thoughts are often rambling or even jumpy—and mixed up with feelings and stories and descriptions. To think three or eleven thoughts in a row, follow logic, and come out with the right answer at the end is something our minds can be trained to do, but we seldom do it out of school or work. Seeing and hearing we do all the time.
>
> No wonder it seems harder to give readers an experience with reports and essays than with creative writing. You must translate more. There is a longer path you must travel from experienced thinking to acceptable expository writing than you need to travel from experienced sensation to acceptable creative writing. (1981, p. 343)

As we have stated before, it is rash to assume that we can accurately "type" a person through inferences drawn from his or her writing alone. Regardless of his own type preferences, however, Elbow here describes, with acute sensitivity, the kind of difficulties that NFs (particularly ENFPs) have adapting to expository or academic writing. Their thinking—which is grounded in experience and tends to be "associational, analogical, metaphorical"—must be translated into a controlled, logical, coherent mode of discourse. For ENFPs, learning to translate their natural thought patterns into an objective form that an academic audience will accept as expository is an important—and difficult—developmental task. And this is a developmental task that other types (say, INTJs, whose natural thought patterns are more logical and syllogistic) may master readily, seemingly without much effort. For INTJs, writing expository prose requires little translation, but producing creative writing might. We need to understand better the kind of discourse that comes naturally to each of the 16 types in Jung's model and how they may need to develop in order to adapt to different genres and discourse communities.

CONCLUSION

The effect of personality type on the development of writing ability is, we are sure, far more complex than we have yet been able to determine. Writers of each type probably grow in two ways. First, they probably develop as their preferred processes mature and they apply these ever-increasingly, more mature preferences to writing. Sensing types learn early how to write concretely, but, as they mature, they learn to process and organize larger and more complex sets of data. Intuitive types learn early how to write abstractly, but, as they mature, they learn to make inferences from their inferences without becoming obtuse, and can develop accurate hunches that penetrate even farther beyond palpable reality. Second, writers mature more fully as they develop their unpreferred cognitive processes and use these to produce a more rounded text. We hope that this chapter has also raised some questions about more generic developmental models. Most of these models depict students moving, in sequential steps or stages, from being concrete to abstract thinkers. One weakness of such models is that they often have rather abstract notions of what it means to think abstractly, perhaps reflective of the personality type of the theorists. Jung's model can account for several kinds of abstraction. Introverts naturally abstract data by maintaining a physical distance, or a subjective buffer, between the self (or subject) and experience (or the object). Intuitive perception, which devalues sensory data, is also an abstracting process. Thinking judgment, which seeks principles that transcend specific people and things, also objectifies and abstracts experience. The exclusion of tangible data for SJs and the unbridled exploration of inferences for NPs may further contribute degrees of abstraction. We need to understand more fully these and other kinds of abstracting processes.

A more important concern is the apparent bias in developmental models. Moffett's model seems to place ESFs at the lowest stage of development and INTs at the highest. Perry's model and Hays' application of it to writing seem to place STJs at the lowest stage and NFPs at the highest. Though some differences in the models exist, the common thread in these and virtually all developmental models is that abstract thought (or intuitive perception in Jung's model) is uncritically viewed as not only being superior but also indicative of a higher stage of development. Jung's model, we believe, raises some doubts that the more abstract processes of introversion, intuitive perception, and thinking judgment are automatically better than those processes diametrically opposed to them, or that these are processes acquired only at a mature developmental stage.

If we hope to understand how individual writers develop, we must better understand the effects of personality type or cognitive style on writing processes and texts. Some developmental models so consistently confuse natural individual differences with developmental traits that it is difficult to determine whether or not a developmental pattern is being described at all. For example, Bradford (1983) feels that many basic writers are fixated in Piaget's Concrete Operations stage. Her description of these students' writing processes and texts may relate more to immature ESFs than to any of Piaget's developmental stages. To illustrate this point, we have added some parenthetical comments to Bradford's description:

> Immature remedial writers still exhibit qualities of Piaget's Concrete Operations stage in their writing. For example, when dealing with imaginative literature, these students' essays will be very concrete; instead of tracing a theme or character, the remedial student will resort to plot summary [Ss tend to focus on the concrete]. Hypothetical, theoretical questions based on reading yield confused and concrete responses [S], usually based not on the reading, but on the readers' own lives or experiences [Es rely heavily on their experience]. This reaction to creative literature suggests another of Piaget's characteristics of the Concrete Operations child: the inability to express in writing any but a context-bound reaction to the work [Jung said of the E, "As he has no ideals connected with ideas, he has no reason to act in any way contrary to the reality of things as they are," 1921, p. 364]. A topic, for example, which compares themes or ideas in two poems will elicit independent and unrelated summaries of each work [Ss find synthesis particularly difficult]. A final characteristic of the early adolescent still very much in evidence in remedial writers is an embarassing egocentrism [Jung feels that Es may at times appear egocentric, 1921, p. 338]. Assignments meant to be logical explorations of a topic based on an experience with an essay of a piece of literature often elicit confessional writing from remedial

> writers [EFs are particularly prone, if immature, to gush; see Jung, 1921, p. 358]. They produce embarrassingly personal pieces impossible to grade without the students construing an attack on their approach to the topic as an attack on their personal feelings [Fs tend to take criticism more personally].

Bradford may be describing either the writing of students in Piaget's Concrete Operations stage, or that of immature ESFs. Certainly some characteristics can be explained by developmental models of writing ability (such as Moffett's) or by generic theories of cognitive development (such as Piaget's or Perry's). Others could be more validly explained by personality type or cognitive style. Research designs must begin in some way to control for naturally acquired individual differences while also examining stages of development.

We need to understand the developmental stages and patterns through which all writers, of all personality types, must pass, but we also need to better understand—and appreciate—the developmental journeys that may be unique to ESFPs, INTPs, ESTJs, and the other types in Myers' extension of Jung's model. Developmental models that ignore the influence of cognitive style, gender, and social class are dangerously simplistic. As Carol Gilligan has already pointed out, once factors such as gender are considered, the neat linearity of most developmental models crumbles:

> The contrasting images of hierarchy [of males] and network [of females] in children's thinking about moral conflict and choice illuminate two views of morality which are complementary rather than sequential or opposed. But this construction of differences goes against the bias of developmental theory toward ordering differences in a hierachical mode. The correspondence between the order of developmental theory and the structure of the boys' thought contrasts with the disparity between existing theory and the structure manifest in the thought of the girls. Yet in neither comparison does one child's judgment appear as a precursor of the other's position. (1982, p. 33)

Gilligan rather convincingly argues that male-generated developmental models fail to recognize the unique developmental paths of females. Almost universally, the male theorists place female traits at the lowest stages of development and male traits at the highest. As Lee Knefelkamp (1984) once said in support of Gilligan's work: "Theory is autobiography." Who we are will bias how we formulate developmental models. Gender and personality type are two themes of our "autobiographies" that we must in some way consider in order to formulate more valid developmental theories.

4
Helping Writers to Develop

In *The Composing Processes of Twelfth Graders* (1971), Janet Emig made a radical statement about how teachers then gave feedback on student essays:

> Much of the teaching of composition in American high schools is essentially a neurotic activity. There is little evidence, for example, that the persistent pointing out of specific errors in student themes leads to the elimination of these errors, yet teachers expend much of their energy in this futile and unrewarding exercise. (p. 99)

The theory, if not the practice, of the teaching of composition is less neurotic now than in 1971. We at least advise teachers to deal with the essence of the text in addition to the accidentals, grammar, punctuation, and spelling. Yet, 11 years after Emig's study, Nancy Sommers discovered that the theory has not yet trickled down to many teachers, who still neglect the writer's purpose and meaning. Echoing Emig, she advised:

> We need to show our students how to seek, in the possibility of revision, the dissonances of discovery—to show them through our comments why new choices would positively change their text, and thus to show them the potential for development implicit in their own writing.

She says, in essence, that we should comment on an essay as if it were a work in progress, not as a static text but as a document of developing ideas.

Emig's and Sommers' work can be extended yet another step, for when we are commenting on the essence of a developing essay, we are to some extent also commenting on the essence of a developing writer. Without some understanding of how individuals develop as writers, we may help a student to perfect a particular text to the neglect of his or her long-range development. A student's first attempt to develop a new skill will likely be awkward, perhaps even incongruent with the developing text. If teachers view these awkward passages only in light of the text, they may criticize when they need to encourage. If the writer is criticized, he or she may be reluctant to try anything like it again, retreating into safe but routine writing. Phelps (Gleason & Mano, 1986) recently suggested that instructors look at a portfolio of each student's writing to abstract a sense of developmental trends. Jung's model can, we believe, provide another means of getting the long view of a writer's development.

In the preceding chapter, we discussed how Jung's model of personality can be used to understand some of the individual differences found in the development of writing ability. In this chapter, we will show how this model can be applied to the classroom such that teachers may better understand how writers are developing and encourage that development with support and, when appropriate, a challenge.

SUPPORT: HELPING WRITERS DEVELOP PREFERRED APPROACHES

As mentioned earlier, inexperienced writers tend to rely primarily—often almost exclusively—on their preferred cognitive processes. Extraverts may write very close to experience, and introverts far removed from it. As writers mature, they learn to implement unpreferred processes in order to produce well-rounded prose and to meet better the demands of different rhetorical situations. Maturation may occur naturally for some writers; others may only mature when supported by instructors.

As a general rule, instructors should first encourage students to develop their strengths, to apply their preferred processes to writing before attempting to produce well-rounded prose. Those students who were never encouraged to write in a way that suited their cognitive style may need support and encouragement even to develop their natural strengths. Judy (ISFJ/Basic), for her first essay of the term, wrote:

> College is an important step to take during a person's life. The person feels a need to continue the improvement of life. Many students go to college so they can be more financially stable than their parents.
>
> Many students go to college to fulfill the dreams of the parents. In some cases parents want their children to emulate them. Many parents own family businesses or companies and want to continue the tradition.
>
> Some students go to college because they find it difficult to find a job in the business world without further education. In today's business world things have become more complex. More and more society is finding less jobs; therefore, only the highly qualified person can find a job that pays lucratively. Computers, for instance, have taken away some of the jobs that once only humans could perform, but also computers create jobs for those who had been trained properly.

> College serves as a bridge. If the person chooses to put forth the effort to cross the bridge, chances of more and better opportunites await them in the business world.

Responding to her essay, her instructor wrote: "What seems to be missing here is *you*. You write about the topic very objectively. Have you considered including some personal examples?" Judy replied that she tried to be objective because she was taught to write objectively in high school. After she began to write more personally (a more natural gift for feeling types), she wrote a narrative that reflects her strength as a writer, rather than her weakness:

> Everyone has someone they look up to, especially younger children, ages three to six. When I was young, I spent a lot of time with my father. My dad had to babysit during the morning and early afternoon hours so my mom could teach school. We would go for rides to the country store and go for walks in the woods to see frisky, grey squirrels. One day I decided I didn't want to go to Mrs. Floyd's home and wait for mom to pick me up. I wanted to go to work and be like daddy. I followed his footsteps all morning, as if I were his shadow. It finally came time for him to shave for work. There I was standing directly behind him emulating every stroke he made with my imaginary and invisible razor. Needless to say, my father wouldn't allow me to go to work with him, but he promised that one day I could go with him. Now as I'm older I realize I must be careful of actions, because one day I might have someone trying to emulate my actions, too.

At times, instructors can help students to develop by having them write in a mode that draws out their natural strengths and allows them to develop those strengths. Through such practice, Judy was, toward the end of the term, able to write less mechanically even on objective topics, such as analyzing a print advertisement. Following are the first two paragraphs of her analysis of an advertisement for Garanimals, a brand of children's clothing:

> "Designed to go together and built to stay together," is the motto of Garanimals. Garanimals are a system of children's clothing. In this advertisement there are several different ways that the advertisement agency presents the product. Mainly this advertisement is directed toward mothers.
>
> The first thing or focal point that catches your eye is a little all-American boy, probably age six, sitting with a football, wearing a bright red shirt, and smiling ridiculously in the middle of the ad. The advertisement presents an ethical appeal to mothers. For example, the advertisement shows little Timmy all decked out in this Garanimal clothes playing with his dog, Rover. This is an exhibit of durability and happiness that the child can tumble in the grass, but Garanimals will not rip.

Though her writing falters in other ways, Judy has begun to learn how to apply her strengths as a feeling type to writing. Her prose has become more authentic, less mechanical, and more engaging. Her increased use of figurative language ("smiling ridiculously" and "all decked out") signals a development of her feeling function as applied to writing.

Even when instructors do not know their students' MBTI scores, they can still attempt to look past the developing text to the developing writer. They can, for example, look for strengths in early drafts or free writes that are not developed or revised out of later drafts. Ron (ESFJ/Basic) free wrote the following passage, which reflects his preference for a personal approach to writing:

> Free writing, oh how it brings back memories. Sophomore year in high school, first quarter, Mrs. Dougherty, Writing II. One of the best teachers I ever had, one who taught me how to express my feelings on paper, who taught me how to refine my statements into a piece of Art, a person who gave my ego a boost. Where has all the time gone. It's long past Sophomore year, Mrs. Dougherty no longer teaches and here I sit writing at random the first thing my brain releases. Oh what a weird feeling all the many different thoughts that pass through my head. School, the first time in my life I haven't had to wear a uniform to school. The first time in thirteen years I haven't had nuns over my back striving discipline first and academics second. What a wonderful feeling of freedom. The catholic education my parents gave me was a wonderful stepping stone and I really loved my preliminary Education, but for the first time in my education, I am at total peace with myself. I can learn now without having to worry about a uniform violation or whether or not I've done something in another class that is going to earn me Demerits. *Demerits*. A terrible invention that exposes the weakness in the human being. A form of backmail I would say, because if you exceed the limit of the given institutions demerit limit your career with that institution is finished. I say that Demerits did nothing but infuriate me and yet discipline me. Discipline has to come from maturity from within, not from stupid points that signify human ignorance.

From the personal free write, he then developed an objective essay that edited out rather than developed his strengths:

> Demerits in Todays Society.
>
> Throughout history, many forms of discipline have been used to motivate or punish human beings. From the slapping of knuckles with rulers, to burning at the stake. With all forms of discipline taken into consideration, demerits seem to be the least effective.
>
> Receiving points that sanctify a personal failure is in no way a form of motivation, it is an outrage and a sheer form of embarressment. Although

> it is a better way to deal with personal failure rather than bodily harm, in someway it leaves a mental scar.
>
> Personal failure should not be dealt with by points. Some other form of discipline should be taken. Demerits are intended to mold the individual into the model of the given institution, but in many cases, this form of discipline takes away from the ideals and adds to the heartache which in turn causes the individual not to change, but turn into the other direction and when this process takes place, and the given number of points are received, the individual then becomes an outcast which results in drastic self-failure and this part of that persons life will follow them forever. Although demerits may have served their purpose at one time, they are no-longer required in this society. Discipline will always be needed but other measures should stop and look at what the reception of demerits can cause and realize that other methods must be sought. Demerits are as outdated as the club, which no one uses anymore.

Realizing that something valuable was lost in Ron's process of drafting, his instructor wrote to him:

> This is a very good job. The essay, however, might be even better if you wrote closer to your personal experience. I would like to know more about what happened in the class to earn you demerits (as mentioned in your freewrite). How did you feel about that? Would writing about your own experience improve the essay?

Instructors who make such comments on essays, without the benefit of MBTI results, are admittedly acting on hunches. But if they ask their students to respond openly to their comments, they can fairly effectively evaluate the hunches. Ron wrote back:

> Thank you for your objective overview on my essay. The reason I didn't deal with personal experiences in my essay is because where I went to high school, it was tabu to do so. It will take some practice to relate [my] own personal experiences into my essay form and I appreciate your time.

Both in what he says and how he says it, Ron validates the instructor's hunch. He acknowledges that he had written personally in the past and was advised to write more objectively. He also, typical of feeling types, expresses heartfelt appreciation for being understood and accepted as an individual.

Even at the college level, instructors should not assume that students have already developed their natural strengths as writers. Their development as writers may have been stunted by poor instruction or by their own misconceptions about the character of good writing and how one produces it. Extraverts may fail to draw upon their experience, and introverts may fail to plan adequately. Sensing types, rather than writing concretely, beginning with facts and details and moving to ideas from there, may produce essays full of pseudoconcepts. Intuitive types may use their intuitive perception incompetently, writing about flighty, vague, and incomprehensible concepts or may abandon intuition entirely and stick to dull facts. Thinking types may not have learned to organize clearly the content of their message, and feeling types may not feel that it is permissible to write stylishly about what they deeply value. Judging types may exclude material decisively but arbitrarily, and perceiving types may include whatever facts or ideas just happen to be at hand. In order to have a foundation for future growth, in order to help students develop from preferred to unpreferred cognitive processes, an instructor first needs to show students how to write well in their own natural way, to develop strengths that may have lain dormant or been repressed.

CHALLENGE: HELPING WRITERS ACHIEVE BALANCE

Once students gain confidence in and have begun to develop preferred cognitive processes, instructors can challenge them to develop their unpreferred. But it is simply unrealistic to expect a student to become a well-balanced writer on all dimensions of Jung's model during a single course. Even fairly mature writers have great difficulty achieving a balance on some dimensions.

Vygotsky recommended that teachers determine which of a student's mental processes is presently beginning to ripen, to locate the "zone of proximal development," and then center instruction toward helping them to develop that ripening process (Bullock, 1983; Zebroski, 1986). Robert's (ISTJ/Basic) essay, which follows, shows evidence of an immature process emerging into the proximal zone. Most of the essay is objective, even dry, typical of developing ISTJs. But in the third paragraph appears a kind of personal example that comes more frequently and naturally from feeling types, but less often and more awkwardly from thinking types like Robert:

> My main reason to come to college was so that I may have a better outlook on life. Also, I feel that a college education will help me to compete in the employment situation with the other people that are unemployed, because they don't have a college degree.
>
> My second reason was to come to college, because I feel education should be one of your main concerns. If I am going to make it in life I will have to be about the business of learning.

Coming to college was one of the biggests choices that I've made in life, but I did have a little help making that decision, which was my mother. Before I finished high school me and my mother would have a talk about life. She would always say to me if you are going to succeed in life you should further your education. She would say I know it's going to be hard but you have to motivate yourself, be determined to finish college. That's what it takes, self-motivation and determination to be successful in life.

My final reason for coming to college so that I won't wind up like a lot of other people. Today I see so many young people walking the street, no place or people to turn to. As life goes on, I hope they realize that life is too short to let school get the best of them. Finally when they are going to say I wish I had gone to college to be the best.

When talking to students and reading their essays, we need to watch for ripening processes, such as Robert's attempt to develop a more personal approach to the topic. These first awkward attempts to move beyond the security of the familiar into the uncertain terrain of unpreferred processes may be incongruent with the rest of the text, as is Robert's example. If we opt to help the student perfect the text, we might advise him to eliminate the personal example. If, however, we realize that the student is developing an unpreferred process, we can encourage—rather than criticize—the incongruent, awkward passage and provide advice on how to extend this line of development.

We are not suggesting that teachers encourage ISTJs like Robert to write as ENFPs. But we do feel that they can be gently challenged to develop the skills that come more naturally to ENFPs. These skills, even though less refined, can be used to meet the demands of certain rhetorical situations, or can be drawn upon when revising as a means of rounding out a text.

Interventions also work best when they include both support *and* challenge, something like a pat on the back *and* a gentle nudge but clearly not one to the exclusion of the other. The instructor might say to the student, "I like who you are, and I also think you are capable of being better." The theory presented here can help instructors to achieve that balance, for it will allow them to deal with strengths and weaknesses as part of a unified system, as presented in Table 1. For example, Doug (INFP/Basic) wrote the following essay, his first of the quarter, on what bugs him about life:

What bugs me about life.

There are many things in my life that I disapprove of. Not only do they affect my personal being, but also affect everyone in some way. Personally my biggest dislikes are ignorance and hatred towards each other. Everywhere you look in the world you find good examples of this type of

> behavior. The situations range from something as simple as inconsiderate drivers of cars, to the superpowers of the world threatening each other. The single largest fault of people is that they won't accept each other. If everyone would try to work with human nature and understand it, then there would be alot less chao's on this planet.

The strengths of this essay are difficult to ferret out, unless one searches for them systematically. One could either criticize it for a lack of organization (a skill thinking types would tend to develop early), or look for the strength that is opposite this fault: writing enthusiastically about heartfelt beliefs. Taking the latter approach, the instructor wrote:

> Doug,
>
> I get the idea, very clearly, that there are some things about the chaotic world we live in that bug you. Me, too! The thing I like about this essay is that sense of strong values you have, that there is something wrong out there. But I think that the paper is weak in one major way: you feel the need to mention *all* the things that bug you. I appreciate your need to be complete, but I think I would understand your feelings even better if you just selected one gripe and developed it more. Then I could get more connected with your values.

Using Jung's personality construct, the instructor was able to connect with the student by relating to those personal strengths that are evident, if only in nascent form, in the essay, and then suggest a revision related to another preference. Acknowledging and accepting Doug's strong values, his preference for feeling, allows the instructor to make contact with him. Once contact is made, the instructor can suggest a revision, that Doug try to focus on a central idea and develop it. Even when suggesting a revision, the instructor acknowledges the values or strengths behind the process that produced a weak text. Doug's being a perceiving type contributed to an overinclusion of ideas. The instructor said that he appreciated Doug's "need to be complete," before suggesting a textual change. There are strengths to being a perceiving type, which he may need to draw upon in future writing assignments, and an acknowledgment of this can prevent Doug from feeling that he is flawed as a person or a writer. The instructor closes with another appeal to Doug's preference for feeling by saying, "Then I could get more connected with your values." Since feeling types want to be connected with their audience, the comment should provide the motivation for change. In response to the instructor's comments, Doug wrote:

> Your letter made me feel good about myself. I understand the one problem but it is difficult for me to write on one subject and give alot of information.

Table 1. Strategies for Making Contact with Students

Extraversion (E)	**Introversion (I)**
MAKING CONTACT: The best way to make contact with Es is through their preferred channel of communication: talk. They usually respond better to oral than to written feedback. Since they value active experience, they respond well to compliments about the vitality and energy of their writing. WORDS OF PRAISE THAT APPEAL TO Es: experience, vitality, lively, action, doing, initiative.	MAKING CONTACT: Is respond better to any situation when given advance notice and when not expected to "think on their feet." Before talking to Is, it is best to provide them with an agenda, and then follow up later. This will allow them time to think about what they may want to say. Is often respond well to teachers who acknowledge that they have more to say (or write) than they have offered. Is will talk (or write) more when they trust their teacher and when they are not forced to share their ideas. WORDS OF PRAISE THAT APPEAL TO Is: thoughtful, serious, sincere, deep.
Sensory Perception (S)	**Intuitive Perception (N)**
MAKING CONTACT: Ss attend better to communications that begin with the concrete. Facts, concrete examples, and practical solutions appeal to them. They respond well to compliments about being accurate, reliable and precise. WORDS OF PRAISE THAT APPEAL TO Ss: practical, realistic, solid, concrete, sensible, here-and-now, responsible, careful.	MAKING CONTACT: Ns attend better to communications that begin with concepts, theories, or inferences. They like sentences that begin with "What if . . . ?" They value being innovative, original, and theoretical. WORDS OF PRAISE THAT APPEAL TO Ns: innovation, possibilities, hunches, inspiration, fantasy, dream, imagination.
Thinking Judgment (T)	**Feeling Judgment (F)**
MAKING CONTACT: Ts value being logical and objective. They react most favorably to a logical rationale and analytical thought. They prefer criticism that is to the point, rather than criticism that is softened or indirect. Praise should, at least in part, relate to the content of their writing. WORDS OF PRAISE THAT APPEAL TO Ts: objective, analytical, logical, valid, systematic.	MAKING CONTACT: Fs tend to respond well to communication after personal contact has been made. They prefer to chat informally before getting down to business, especially if also E. They respond well to any acknowledgment of them as individuals: learning their name, asking about their interests and values, a smile, a pat on the back, etc. They often respond well to an instructor saying that he or she enjoyed reading their essays. Praise should, at least in part, relate to the process of their writing, e.g., the way that they worded their ideas. WORDS OF PRAISE THAT APPEAL TO Fs: beliefs, values, personal, heartfelt, touching, interesting, us, we, together, invested.

(*continued*)

Table 1. (*Continued*)

Judging (J)	Perceiving (P)
MAKING CONTACT: Js are particularly concerned about wise use of time, and usually respond well to compliments about how efficient, expedient or punctual they are. Js also value being decisive. They tend to view their work, once it is submitted, as finished, and prefer to hear comments about how they can improve the next essay than about how to improve this essay. WORDS OF PRAISE THAT APPEAL TO Js: complete, finished, hard working, punctual, decisive.	MAKING CONTACT: Ps are usually most concerned about being inclusive, so they tend to respond well to compliments about the breadth of their research. They tend to view their work as ongoing. They prefer to hear about how to improve this essay rather than about how to improve the next essay. They also like to see how one project can relate to the next, even though both are unfinished. WORDS OF PRAISE THAT APPEAL TO Ps: thorough, extensive, in-progress, ongoing, adaptable, flexible, open-minded, questioning.

Rather than being demoralized by critical comments, Doug both acknowledges the need to develop new skills and feels confident about his ability to improve.

Perhaps one of the most valuable lessons to be learned from Jung's personality theory is that "weaknesses" are not necessarily aberrant behavior. Developmental models that focus on deficits and faults have, as Thomas Newkirk (1985) recently pointed out, inherent dangers:

> Any developmental theory begins with the assumption that the youngest children in the span being examined are *relatively* disadvantaged, less capable than the older children being studied. The task of the developmentalist is to uncover these limitations and to show how, progressively, they disappear as children "develop." There can be an underlying pathology to this quest, a kind of deficit hunting, a bias toward disadvantage that can and has caused investigators to underestimate the capabilities of young children.

Jung's model, since it is based on individual strengths, does not embody or lead to an underestimation of writers' capabilities. All types of writers have strengths. A simple exercise can illustrate. If MBTI results are available, instructors can sort students' essays by type before reading them. Certain patterns of strengths will emerge. For example, the instructor might realize that ESTJs are particularly skilled at assuming a firm stance on an issue and emphatically arguing their point. Patterns of weaknesses will also emerge. The instructor might discover that the essays of ISTJs tend to be dry and formulaic. But such "weaknesses" are not deficits; they are symptomatic of underdeveloped, childlike, or immature cognitive processes. Jung's model teaches us to reframe our understanding of "weaknesses" rather than attempt to eradicate them.

Jung's system can also help us to place "weaknesses" within the context of the whole writer, to understand that a writer's greatest strength often appears at the opposite end of the same dimension as his or her greatest weakness. Ron, the feeling type discussed in Chapter 3, was very concerned about how he related to his audience, and from this concern he developed a superior style for a basic writer. But his concern for how he could engage his reader diverted attention from the logical development of his content, his major weakness as a writer.

To encourage this writer, and others like him, to develop, we must first appreciate their strengths. We must respect their approach to life and writing. We can then give them that subtle blend of a pat and a nudge. Instead of solely focusing on a weakness ("Your content is terrible"), the instructor might write on the essay: "You have an engaging and expressive style, and I really enjoy reading your essays, but I'd also like for us to talk about how to improve your content." Instead of focusing alone on weaknesses and errors, we can move from the writer's natural strengths (in this case, those of a feeling type) to a development of supportive skills which tend to come more easily to the opposite type (in this case, those that come more naturally to a thinking type).

In the process, we must also provide students with the opportunity to develop both preferred and unpreferred processes. When structuring peer feedback, for example, we can at times pair students of similar type so that they can learn to develop their strengths. After a peer feedback session, one sensing type wrote of her feedback from another student of the same type: "I learned from the papers that I read that I need to include more details and be more concrete." Sensing types are particularly capable of writing concretely, and this sensing type learned to do so from someone who in general approaches writing as she does and who "speaks her language." As another student wrote after being paired with someone of the same type: "I need to revise with someone who knows the way I write. That way I can relate better."

As a writer matures, supportive feedback alone is less valuable. After being paired with a peer of the same type, a student wrote: "Nothing I read would really have a bearing on my paper. The papers have similar ideas to my own." She has apparently learned all she can from other writers of her type who also are at roughly the same level of development. At this point, she needs to begin to develop her unpreferred processes by receiving feedback from writers who are different than she. After being paired with a sensing type, an intuitive type wrote: "I learned that I need to go back and include a few quotes in my paper so that I can back up my ideas." The intuitive type is learning to overcome her weakness (a tendency to ignore the concrete) from a sensing type (who excels at writing concretely).

All students need both support and challenge, but in a different balance. Thinking types are more prone to distrust too much praise; they usually perform better when seriously challenged. Feeling types, on the other hand, benefit from criticism when they know that they have already earned the basic support of the teacher, especially when the teacher acknowledges their personal investment in their writing.

Since writing so often involves an expression of oneself—in process if not always in product—composition teachers frequently come face to face with their students' level of self-esteem. Although teachers should not act like amateur psychologists, they should nonetheless acknowledge that they have a powerful impact on how students feel about themselves as people and writers. As was shown earlier in this chapter, Judy (ISFJ/Basic) and Ron (ESFJ/Basic) learned through the years to follow teachers' admonitions to write only objective, dispassionate prose. Thinking type instructors at their worst are more likely to provide this kind of advice. They may also view attention to individual differences as just so much babying and handholding. However, the approach of Judy's and Ron's most recent instructor, also a thinking type, employed a logically consistent system for understanding differences (Jung's model) to draw on their latent strengths. The results were freeing for them. Feeling type instructors, in contrast, can err on the side of overidentifying with students and their dilemma; they may attempt to nurture all students even to the neglect of their standards of what constitutes good writing.

When commenting on student essays or providing oral feedback, we need to remember the advice of Emig and Sommers. We need to move past the neurotic activity of correcting errors and deal with the essence of a developing text. But we also need to realize that our ultimate goal is not to help a particular student produce a single mature text. Our broader goal is to encourage long-range growth. Students may need to be encouraged to produce some imperfect texts so that they can develop new skills, for maturing as a writer certainly extends beyond the limits of a single text or a single course. The maturation may begin in a basic writing course, continue through advanced writing courses, and be reinforced in content courses and the world of work. It is a life-long process that individuals approach in their own way and at their own speed.

5

Writing Anxiety and Writer's Blocks

Although investigations into writing difficulties—writer's cramp, writing anxiety, or writer's blocks—date to the late 1800s (Boice, 1985), researchers seem to disagree widely on the most fundamental issues. What is writer's cramp, writing anxiety, writing apprehension, writer's block? Do these phenomena overlap or interact? What causes them? How can they be treated?

Even though researchers can not agree on how to answer these questions, progress in the field is nonetheless evident. Or at least, a clear historical trend is emerging: the focus of research on writing difficulties has shifted from the presumed psychopathology of the writer to the study of the writing processes of anxious or blocked writers. Early researchers felt that dysfunctional writers suffered from oral regression or castration anxiety (see Boice, 1985). More recently, researchers have felt that writers have difficulty because their writing process has, in some way or form, gone awry (Fox, 1980; Rose, 1980; Thompson, 1979).

The shift in focus seems appropriate and healthy. Certainly, the writer's neuroses and psychopathology can spill over into his or her writing; in some cases, then, counseling or behavioral treatments can effectively reduce writing anxiety and writer's block (Boice, 1985). However, everyone who has difficulty with writing is not necessarily in possession of or possessed by a troubled psyche. Many writers are stressed or stalled because they cling to ineffective strategies.

Determining which strategies are effective and which are ineffective, however, can be a delicate matter. Not all writers use the same process. Given the variety of approaches across writers, how can we isolate the kinks in an individual's writing process? How can we find strategies that may be more effective for that individual? One option is to begin with an understanding of the individual's personality type. In this chapter, we will use two case studies to show how Jung's personality theory can be used both to diagnose an individual's difficulties with writing and to suggest more productive alternatives.

DEFINING WRITING ANXIETY AND WRITER'S BLOCKS

Writing anxiety and writer's blocks occur together so frequently in individuals that the concepts are difficult to separate, and indeed the terms are often used loosely and interchangeably. They are, nonetheless, phenomena that can be viewed distinctly.

Writing anxiety is a nonspecific, chronic stress reaction to the act of writing or to a genre of writing. It is "nonspecific" because it is not a reaction to a particular writing episode, which Daly and Hailey call "situational anxiety" (1984). Rather, it is a general affective response to all writing or to a broad genre of writing (e.g., poetry, research papers, etc.) It is also "chronic" in that it is a reaction that has developed and persisted over a span of time; it can be distinguished from situational anxiety in that it is not transient or related to the particular events of a particular writing situation.

Writer's block is the inability to make effective decisions during the writing process. While writing anxiety is an affective reaction, or an arousal response, to writing in general, a writer's block is a specific cognitive dysfunction (here, "cognitive" is meant in the more restrictive sense, relating to thinking patterns and decision making skills but not affective states) at a particular point in the writing process. A writer may, for example, experience little anxiety about writing in general, but, when planning a particular essay, be unable to organize the data and become blocked.

The two phenomena are most distinct when we realize that writing anxiety is affective while writer's block is cognitive. Writing anxiety is related to a high level of stress, a negative attitude toward writing, a poor self-concept as a writer, or a low level of confidence in one's writing ability. Writer's block is related to decision making. The writer is unable, for one reason or another to make the kind of effective decisions that allows composition to begin or continue. The two almost certainly interact, but how they interact is difficult to determine.

To show the impact of personality type on writing anxiety and writer's block, we present two case studies of similar types: ESFJ and ENFJ.

CASE STUDY: TRISHA (ESFJ)

Trisha, an ESFJ graduate student in psychology, was experiencing a great deal of anxiety adapting to her program. Her undergraduate degree was not in psychology, and she was a sensing type entering a predominantly intuitive field. She was also a relatively inexperienced writer, but was now faced with frequent and threatening writing assignments.

These new stressors added to a long-standing case of writing anxiety; her score on the Daly–Miller (1975) Test of Writing Apprehension was 92.

During the first of seven weekly sessions (which occurred in her second year as a graduate student), Jensen interviewed her to determine how she was presently going about writing. What was most clear from the initial interview was that Trisha seemed to be a sensing type who wrote as a sensing type. She began her writing process with the concrete (the details and data of her literature review), and it was with the concrete that she felt most comfortable. As she moved sequentially from the data to abstractions (what she called her "opinions"), writing became more difficult. She explained:

> I'm very tied to the research. It's not like I postulate a lot of hypotheses either. I'm much less of an abstract thinker and more tied to, well, this is the topic and let's see what the facts say. I might have an opinion that will guide me in terms of what sources I will look for, but I tend to need to feel very familiar with the facts and the research and then incorporate my opinion, but that's always the hardest part for me to do, is in the conclusion to relate my opinion to the facts. That's very difficult and usually I don't budget enough time, so that I end up being at the most difficult part of the paper for me and end up just sort of sluffing it off and not doing it justice.

One can sense here some of Trisha's difficulty as she attempts to write in her preferred process (focusing on the concrete) but for a predominantly intuitive audience, most of whom value the abstract.

On the other hand, Trisha felt fairly comfortable with her day-to-day professional writing, such as charting, because it was more naturally suited to an extraverted–sensing type. She explained:

Trisha: The other sort of writing I've had to do [at work] is in terms of individual service plans, objective writing on the client's assessment, and that flows for me, and I think that's related to my pragmatic form of reference. I can describe pretty well, but my abstract . . . um . . . and my ideas aren't something that I do well.

Jensen: That sort of writing you do relating to clients and so on, it's sort of like charting?

Trisha: Yea. It's very formatted, in terms of behavioral observation and in terms of rehabilitation plans, and that's easier for me to do.

Jensen: Why is it easier? Is it easier because there is a format or . . . ?

Trisha: I think it's easier because there is a format and also I feel experienced at it and that gives me more conviction to sort of write what I believe, and I know how tied I am to the data, so I have enough, usually, information to make the hypotheses that I do, the plans I do.

Trisha found the academic writing required in her courses more difficult because it was abstract and conceptual. As she explained, "everything was new and changing and so I was writing different papers and it just really got harried; I didn't get that sense of building up." As a sensing type, she preferred to move sequentially from facts and data to concepts (the "building up") and to write practical essays in some standard format. As a graduate student in psychology, she had to develop concepts quickly and constantly write in new and unique ways. The incompatibility between her cognitive style and the demands of her program produced considerable stress.

Some of Trisha's difficulties (also connected to her preference for sensory perception) related to her ongoing development as a writer. She wrote very little in undergraduate school, and those few papers she did write left her with little self-confidence. She said:

> I should probably say that my undergraduate program wasn't demanding academically. The requirements were much more geared to behavioral objectives and that sort of writing style. And I did an independent project, which was like a forty page paper, and I kept running up to everyone and saying, "Tell me how this is writing wise." And I just didn't get very much assistance on that. So I came to this program feeling like, that I don't write very well.

As mentioned in Chapter 2, sensing types, who are inexperienced writers, often feel that writing is rule-governed. They feel that, if teachers would only tell them the steps to good writing, then they could write well. As Trisha said later in the interview, "I never learned to write correctly." By correctly, she means more than "write grammatically correct"; she also means that she never learned the proper procedure or steps to follow that she feels one *must* follow to produce an acceptable finished product.

Just as typical of inexperienced sensing writers, Trisha often became lost in her data:

Jensen: Do you sometimes get lost in that process of researching the topic, of accumulating data?

Trisha: Yes. What's important, what's not. And that seems to change with experience with the same body of literature. Having a good feel for that [body of literature], I better know what my own criteria are. That seems to have helped that, but when I venture into a new area, that is something hard for me to figure out.

Intuitive types naturally ignore data that are not related to their ideas or concepts, but sensing types are more likely to focus on the data early in their writing process and then move to some general concept (see the discussion of SFs and Ranke's approach to history in Chapter 1). As a result, they often have difficulty deciding what is important and what is not. Trisha seems to be struggling with this issue.

Some of Trisha's stress seemed to evolve from another source of dissonance, an incompatibility between her personality type and her writing process. Although all of her MBTI scores were strong (E31, S23, F19, J47), she seemed to be writing in a process more typical of ISTPs. As an extravert, we would expect Trisha to develop ideas by talking with a classmate. We would also expect her to leap into writing with little planning and develop most of her ideas while putting pen to paper. Yet, she used a process more typical of introverts:

Jensen: When you start writing, do you feel like you spend a lot of time thinking about the topic, or do you just say, "It's time to sit down and write," and leap into it?

Trisha: Um. I almost have to spend time thinking about it because the actual act of sitting down to write is usually so stressful that I like to have thought about what it is I want to say, and I like to walk and get the ideas in my head before writing.

She tends to write in isolation and wants to conceptualize the paper before beginning the physical act of writing. (Note that she does pace in extraverted fashion when trying to conceptualize her paper.) She also feels a need to use outlines and rely on them to provide the structure of her essay (more typical of introverted–thinking types):

Jensen: Do you use outlines?

Trisha: I try to, I try to. It really depends. I think I have a better sense of timing and how much time I need to budget with outlines. I think I write better if I do. I think my outlines are very general. I'd like to be more detailed about that.

Jensen: Do you feel if you had a more detailed outline that . . . ?

Trisha: Yes, because I'm so tied to that [the outline]. That would be a way of keeping me tied to the data and just able to write. I think that would enhance my own process.

Trisha, here, seems to believe (almost as one believes in salvation) that a detailed outline would make her writing process easier, but outlining seems difficult. When asked if she uses outlines, she replied, "I try to, I try to." She also does not seem to use outlines as mature EFs do, as an entrée to writing or as a means of generating ideas. She seems to use them as ITs do, to organize thoughts and as a criterion for making organizational decisions, but without much success.

During the second session, Jensen interpreted her MBTI results and discussed how these results related to her writing process. The main purpose of the session, which was more didactic than later sessions, was to provide support for her preferred way of writing and to suggest new approaches to writing that were more compatible with her personality type. The following transcript illustrates that process:

Jensen: Extraverts usually think best when they are talking or doing something active . . . and that tends to be typical of extraverts as writers. They usually think best when they can talk about the topic, when they're blocked quite often they can talk their way out of the block.
Trisha: Right.
Jensen: They also tend to think well when they're in the actual physical act of writing.
Trisha: Yes. Yes.
Jensen: They may not think well when they are sitting as introverts would with their feet up, physically doing nothing. . . .
Trisha: Right.
Jensen: Just doing all of the work inside their heads. . . .
Trisha: Right.
Jensen: But actually doing their writing on paper, extraverts quite often come up with their best ideas in the process of writing.
Trisha: Yes.
Jensen: And I remember one thing you said about your writing process is that you have a structure in mind [before you begin to put words on paper], but it changes when you write. That's real typical of extraverts. Introverts are far more likely to have the whole essay planned out in advance and then it won't change much in the process of writing.
Trisha: Yes.

* * *

Jensen: It's far more likely for introverts to have entire essays planned in their minds before they sit down to write.
Trisha: That's a notion that I have never even experienced, and I don't expect to.
Jensen: Well, you shouldn't expect it. It's not your way of doing things.
Trisha: But I think I value it, just because it doesn't work that way for me. It's sort of awesome.
Jensen: Although it may not be apparent, there can be bad side effects to planning too much, also.

Here, Jensen is trying to help Trisha to understand the values and strengths of an extraverted writing process in hopes that she will begin to feel comfortable with her more natural and preferred approach to writing.

Jensen also used Trisha's MBTI results to help her to distinguish between how she wrote and what she needed to do to write effectively. In the initial interview, Trisha claimed that she needed the "big picture" to write, which is a more naturally intuitive way to compose. In the second session, the following clarification was offered:

Jensen: One thing that you were saying last week, you said several times that you needed the big picture first, then you said at the end [of the interview], "Well, I'm not so sure if I need the big picture first or not."
Trisha: Yea. Yea. That's right.
Jensen: When I asked you to clarify that, it really sounded more to me like it was, not so much big picture, as it was foundation.
Trisha: Oh, that's interesting.
Jensen: I think what sensing types really want, in order to develop their ideas, is that they want them well-founded. What you were talking about in terms of big picture was getting historical perspective. . . . After you've done that, the ideas make a lot more sense to you. . . . What you need is probably more of a concrete context.
Trisha: You're right. That's a nice clarification.

With a better understanding of how she writes best, Trisha should be better able to compose in a less stressful process.

Even a single session like this, in which the writer's results are interpreted and her more preferred, natural writing processs is validated, can powerfully lead to greater confidence and a reduction of writing anxiety. In fact, Trisha began the following session by saying, "I feel like I have been therapized about my writing." But most anxious writers will benefit from a more extended contact with an instructor or counselor who can repeatedly *suggest*—not dictate—options for realigning the writing process with the writer's personality type.

Jensen continued to meet with Trisha for five more sessions. During these weekly meetings, her writing process was discussed further and writer's blocks were analyzed, but much of the discussion centered on how she, as a sensing type, could adapt to her intuitive professors. For example, her reaction papers were often criticized for being too detailed. As a sensing type, she would begin papers by concentrating on facts and details and inductively build toward general conclusions or concepts. Her concepts, which emerged in the final paragraph or two, were only discussed briefly. Even though she revised extensively, she was usually, as SJs often are, quite tied to the basic structure of her first draft. Her papers changed, but they remained too detailed and fairly concrete. Jensen tried to suggest ways to separate her process from her product, so that she could write in a process that was comfortable and natural but yet end up with product that suited her professors. Rather than write lengthy and time-consuming drafts about facts and details in an attempt to develop concepts, Jensen suggested that she talk or free write about her data, in a more naturally extraverted–sensing process, until she developed her abstractions. Then she could write a rough draft that thoroughly discussed abstractions rather than one that only touched upon them in the final paragraph.

Trisha was also experiencing some writer's blocks. She sometimes developed abstract ideas early in her writing process but had difficulty "holding onto them" long enough to develop them (ES). As she said, sometimes "I get a very, very weak hold on the idea." Even when she could reflect on abstract ideas, she was blocked until she could validate them with the empirical results of research studies (S). She either spent time generating a number of ideas, spinning her wheels (E), or reading far more research studies than necessary (typical of Ss' writing on abstract research topics). Trisha herself felt the need to balance her sensory perception with intuition, as the following dialogue illustrates:

Trisha: I think that, even though I say that I rely so much on the data, there's a real part of me that has that opinion, that it seems like it gets lost in there because I can't substantiate it somehow, so I think that those two processes are trying to come together somehow, and I'd like to see them a little more balanced. I don't mind being way towards data most of the time, but I do want it to be more balanced.

Jensen: I think that will happen. One of the things I really like about the Myers–Briggs, and I think that it is a theory that is borne out in experience, is that it is not a limiting theory. It is not saying you're a sensing type and cannot do the other. It says that both are in you. It's just a matter of how can you get access to the other side of you. And it sounds like one of the ways that you get access to your intuition is by building up through a lot of data, through that sequential process, and there are probably other ways to get there, too.

Trisha: Yea.

Jensen: One of the ways that the theory says you can get access to an unpreferred process is in the service of one of your preferred processes. An example of that would be, if you're an extravert, it would be easier for you to get access to your intuition when you're talking about something, rather than sitting down functioning like an introvert.

Trisha: Yea. True. That makes sense.

Jensen: As a feeling type, probably it's much easier for you to use your intuition once you've established that your values, what's important to you, are connected to the project. . . .

Trisha: That makes sense.

Jensen: Then, I think it will be an easier process, less of a struggle.

After applying this advice to her next writing assignment, a research paper for a family therapy course, Trisha reported that she experienced fewer blocks:

Trisha: I really learned through this whole thing to actually trust my ability to conceptualize about power [the topic of her paper]. . . . These were ideas that I could really keep in my head. It was amazing. And I was really never able to work on a paper in my head as much as I have with this. The amazing thing is that I read through my notes and then I write. I don't sit and say, "where is this sentence" and "where is this sentence?" It was tighter in my head. It was amazing.

Jensen: How did it get tighter in your head?

Trisha: Mary [an ENTP classmate] came over and we talked. . . . I asked her about my assumptions, and inferences, and opinions. I had all of the facts, but before I got to the writing phase, it's like, do I have this clear, and she said, yep, yep, that makes sense, and a little fine tuning, and I asked her if that was her experience of what it was like to be with me at that time [Mary had previously observed Trisha write], and she said, yea, that mostly it didn't seem real blocked [this time].

By talking about her ideas with a friend whom she trusted (a natural process for an EF), she was both able to reflect on the ideas longer (as an introvert does naturally) and trust them (as an intuitive type does naturally). She also seems to have more of a big picture about the paper (which is more natural to intuitve types), so she didn't have to agonize so much over where each sentence should be placed. Her greater balance between her preferred and unpreferred processes seems to have helped her to circumvent the blocks that usually halt her writing process.

CASE STUDY: JOHN (ENFJ)

John, a successful business executive in his early 40s, is an example of a writer who seems to have developed an effective and healthy approach to writing. He has learned to adapt to the kind of writing he must do on the job, and he has learned how to work efficiently on a novel at home. As a result, he seems to experience very little writing anxiety and few writer's blocks.

At work, John analyzes market trends and writes periodical reports, which include extensive graphs, so that his company can make adjustments to the fluctuating demand for its products. As he talked about his business writing, it seemed that he is an intuitive type writing for a predominantly sensing audience. He values the data on market trends that he has been collecting for almost 20 years and naturally wants to explore the implications of this data base in his reports. But his audience (which seems to be predominantly SJ in an environment that values efficiency) prefers the bare facts in a concise format:

John: I'm one of those who continuously gets talked to about the length of my writing.

Jensen: Too long?

John: Yea. People at work don't have the time or patience to go through the detail that I'm capable of giving them. . . . If I give them everything that I used to give them, they wouldn't read it. So, consequently what I have to give them is what they do need, which is the basic summaries. And they'll read those. Later on in meetings, there will be problems because they didn't read all of the information that I could have given them. So it's something that I keep wrestling with. . . . Part of me wants to impart to them all of the knowledge of the world. But I'm not allowed to in business circles. My audience won't read it.

Although John clearly wants to "impart the knowledge of the world," to give his audience the full predictive force of the data bank that he so values, he realizes that he must adapt to his audience's need to be concise. John also spoke of how he, early in his career, assumed that his audience would understand the implications of his data (much is often assumed in the communication of intuitive types) and was continually astonished to find that they did not: "People at work don't have the time or patience to go through the detail that I'm capable of giving them" (by "detail," John does not seem to refer to data for its own sake, but to all of the possible implications he can draw from that data). He learned that he needed to state his conclusions overtly in a clear format. He seemed in general very attuned to the needs of his audience and how he needed to adapt to that audience.

One might think that NFs like John (who tend to be idealistic, expressive, creative, symbolic in their writing) would have difficulty adapting to the routine, prosaic, stick-to-the-facts writing of the business world, and this is often the case. But John seems to have found ways to make his work-related writing more personal. For example, he personalizes his graphs by "signing" them in a secret way:

> I see a lot of things in print, but they're business things. I've gotten some credibility in the world of industry. And I've seen some of the things I do in print. My graphs are being used in publications, *stolen.* I always put a little marker in them, like a weaver puts an error in his work. I have a signature in my graphs.

John has found his own unique way of personalizing the objective and anonymous writing that he does on the job, and he seems to derive a great deal of personal satisfaction from seeing others value his work, even if they value it by stealing it.

In his writing of a novel, John seems to have developed a creative process that more suits his personality type. The novel's genesis was closely connected to the development of the central character (who is like James Bond but more sensitive and vulnerable), and it has been the central character, rather than some objective structure (on which an NT might rely), that drives the creative process. He said: "The plot can flow, because I worked so hard on creating the character that his capabilities are wide." As an NF, John feels most comfortable focusing on the characters, but he also at times almost symbolically fuses with his subject matter (see the discussion of NFs in Chapter 1):

> I feel so much for the characters in my writing. I really feel them. I feel what they're going through. The settings themselves are incidental.

He so identifies with the characters that he even has difficulty killing them off.

John also, as is compatible with his preference for extraversion, plans little and discovers most of his content when in the process of putting words on paper. He keeps a brief, four- or five-word synopsis of each chapter; then, before he begins a session of writing, he quickly reviews the synopses to get back into the flow of the plot. He may have a general idea of how the next chapter will materialize, but most of his ideas seem to develop while writing. When asked if he plans before beginning a chapter, John responded:

> I pretty well have an idea, well, the last thing I wrote, the last sentence was the end of the preparation stage [of a mission that the central character would lead], and it finally got to that moment of doing it and his last words were, "Let's do it." I know what the next chapter has got to be. It's the action of doing it. So when I sit down, how all this is going to work, I don't know, but it'll work. And it'll flow. And it'll come. I know that. But it doesn't happen as it was supposed to.

He is open to discovering ideas and to changing his general plan once he begins writing, and, as a feeling type, he is very concerned about how his audience will react to the text that he is producing:

> I've sat down and said, where do we go from here, and write it out. The characters go from here to there to there, and you haven't set yourself a solid structure. So where do I go from here? And sometimes that has been a block. Because I say do I go on with the same stuff, and if I do, the reader is going to be bored. I want to keep the reader interested, I want to keep it moving along, I want to keep the characters developing.

It seems that John has learned to make organizational and structural decisions as feeling types prefer to, by following "the flow" (with his novel, "the flow" seems to be more than the flow of his thoughts; it is also how his characters naturally develop) and by imagining how readers will respond to his text.

John seems to have found a comfortable and workable writing process, which is well suited to his personality type, and he has also learned how to deal with the kind of blocks that writers of his type tend to experience. He has always been very creative, but, when younger, he failed to follow through on his creative efforts. He wrote a children's book and more than 100 songs, but never published them. His creative process was usually halted by premature criticism or the threat of criticism:

Jensen: It seems like you've been creative in all of these different areas, and in different situations you've been close to publication of some kind. And then that hasn't come through. Do you have any idea why?

John: In a way I do. In the first place, the novel I'm working on right now was something that I told the idea of to a friend of mine, who turned out to be an editor for Doubleday. I was in the Reserves with him. I didn't know who he was. And he offered me . . . he said, give me four chapters and an outline and I'll give you two grand right now, and it scared the living fire out of me. . . . I don't know whether I have a fear of rejection or whatever, but it's like I get to a critical point and get some rejection and I back off of it and go on to something else.

Feeling types tend to internalize criticism more than thinking types. In order to deal with this threat to his creative process, John has learned to curb his extraverted tendency to talk about his novel, even with close relatives. Thus, he avoids the premature criticism that might disrupt his writing.

Early in his process of writing the novel, he also found that "life distractions" (his job, family, and other interests) interfered with his writing. To deal with the "life distractions" that are particularly appealing to extraverts, he relied on his strength as a judging type and developed a schedule for writing. His plan was to devote 1 night per week and 2 Sundays per month to writing. He discussed the schedule with his family (so that they would respect his time to write) and he then marked the times for writing sessions off on his calendar (which is publicly displayed on the refrigerator). When he completes a session, he circles it. If an important event interferes with his schedule, he "trades" time by rescheduling his writing for another night or day. He only allows himself two "reschedules" per month, which prevents him from being too loose with his writing time. The schedule seems to be especially effective. Using it, John had, at the time he was interviewed, written 22 chapters, or about 300 pages of text.

On a few occasions, John's process of writing his novel began to falter.

One time he became locked into revising earlier chapters. He began to feel that the revisions might be very disruptive because he might become bored with writing and abandon the manuscript. He felt that he needed the thrill of discovering new ideas to maintain an interest in the project, so he made the decision to avoid revisions until the entire novel was finished. Earlier in the process of working on the novel, he was also occasionally distracted by research. Once he realized that the research was taking time away from writing, he began to limit it.

The only other minor block that he has experienced was solved just as expediently. About $1\frac{1}{2}$ hours into each writing session, he invariably hit a "dead spot." If he stayed with the writing, he found himself frustrated and unable to write. He discovered that the easiest way to deal with this "dead spot" was to take a break, go downstairs, get a cup of coffee, talk to his wife for a few minutes, and then return to writing. As an extravert, he probably began to feel restless for some physical activity. Rather than stay with the planned schedule, as immature judging types tend to do, he has learned to walk away from the writing, take a very active break (talking to his wife) and then return his manuscript fresh and ready to write.

CONCLUSION

We do not want to over interpret the differences between Tricia's and John's approaches to writing. Even though they are similar in personality type, they still differ on one dimension of Jung's model. Also, John is clearly a more mature writer. Thus, a detailed comparison of the two case studies might be misleading.

The salient differences that we would like to emphasize are that John seems to write in a process that is more naturally suited to his personality type (at least when writing his novel), and as a more mature writer he also seems to have found ways to adapt to a discourse community that is not entirely compatible with his personality type (as he has done at work). Tricia, who experiences more writing anxiety, seems to be still learning how she writes best as she struggles to adapt to the demands of her graduate program, issues that John has already successfully resolved. But how are these conclusions related to pedagogy in the field of composition?

Classroom instructors may seldom have the time or opportunity for the kind of intervention Jensen made with Tricia, and we certainly do not suggest that instructors intensely counsel each student in their class. Many students will have developed a healthy, effective writing process on their own, adopting the advice that works for them and rejecting the advice that does not. Other students, for a variety of reasons, may develop and rigidly adhere to ineffective strategies. These students can be helped even within the structure of a composition course. Kleine (1986) has his students use MBTI results as a heuristic to explore their writing process and then has them write an essay describing that process. He feels that the exercise helps students to explore new options to composing, provides permission for students to write as they naturally prefer to, and increases their metacognitive knowledge of how they approach writing. Even without administering the MBTI, instructors can use Jung's model of personality and the information presented in Chapter 2 to suggest new options for anxious or blocked writers.

If instructors can encourage students to write in a process that is comfortable to them, that is well suited to their personality type, or at least be open to students exploring a wide variety of approaches to writing, then fewer students will probably develop writing anxiety. If instructors encourage students to learn to write in a more balanced way, to employ primarily their preferred cognitive processes but also to consult and develop their less preferred processes, then students will probably be more effective decision-makers and experience fewer blocks.

Finally, instructors should realize that adapting to a new discourse community, whether it be a composition class, an academic program, or a job, can be very stressful, even for bright, capable writers. Michel Foucault, in an interview with Paul Rabinow, spoke of the difficulties he had earlier in his career. The French intelligentsia, the discourse community to which he was attempting to adapt, was simply unwilling to regard the kind of issues that Foucault was exploring as valid and worthwhile. Foucault's work "was met with a great silence among the French intellectual left." Without certain political openings, Foucault said that he would probably "never have had the courage" to continue his work (Rabinow, 1984, pp. 51–53). Foucault's difficulty in adapting to a discourse community (which he prefers to call a "discourse regime") seems more based in ideological differences than in differences among personality types, but it is intriguing that a thinker of Foucault's stature could be shut out of the intellectual community. If he experienced such difficulties, and was almost ready to abandon his line of research, then certainly the average writer might experience a great deal of stress adapting—or attempting to adapt—to a discourse community that is incompatible with his or her personality type. Certainly, one of our roles as composition instructors should be to prepare students to be more adaptable. We can best do this by helping them to understand how they write best, by encouraging them to appreciate their strengths as a writer, but also by helping them, in unthreatening situations, to explore new options to writing and becoming more well-balanced writers.

Jung's model also seems to have some value in defusing the tension of adapting to a new discourse community. It seemed to help Tricia to know that some of her difficulties with learning to write for psychology professors were simply related to differences in personality type, rather than to some personal inadequacy. The issue then could be reframed from "what is wrong with me" to "how can I adapt to this audience."

6
The Evaluation of Writing

Evaluation—with numerous sticky, often political issues, surrounding it—has nobly served as the professional neurosis of composition teachers and researchers for over a decade. And if ever a neurosis were justifiable, this is it, for valid evaluation is—or has at least been perceived as being—essential to the credibility of composition pedagogy. If teachers disagree radically on what constitutes good writing, how can they expect student writers to progress as they move from one teacher to the next? One teacher may encourage a student to write more personally. The next term, just as the student is beginning to feel secure with the new approach, the next teacher may forbid the use of "I." Whatever progress was made is quickly erased, the residue being a jaded, bewildered student.

We are equally sensitive about the rating of essays for placement and research (Hillocks, 1986, pp. 100–102). If we cannot reliably and validly rate essays, then our placement of students into and out of remedial classes seems to lack authority. Likewise, without sound ratings, most research results are questionable. Even though raters *of similar background* (perhaps, also of similar personality type) have, on occasion, achieved very high inter-rater reliability (Cooper, 1977), this does not ensure validity. Raters of similar background may be in mutual agreement about particularly boneheaded evaluations.

Ironically, composition theorists perceive the need to research the writing process, but not the process of evaluating writing. We need to understand better the string of affective responses, conclusions, and judgments that occur as an evaluator reads a text. We also need to understand better how this process affects the product of evaluation, the feedback given to the student and the scores that raters assign to the text. To make some tentative hypotheses about how Jung's model can be used to study the process of evaluation, we draw on three sources: the responses of 26 high school English teachers to Glenda's (ESFJ/Basic) and Paulette's (ISTP/Basic) essays quoted in Chapter 3 (references to this body of data will be designated by HS); the comments made during rating sessions for the exit exams of the developmental writing program at Georgia State University (GSU); and studies by Sheryl Gowen (1984) and Katya McCall Walter (1984).

We will argue that a rater's or teacher's personality type will tend to have an effect on how he or she evaluates essays, but we would also like to suggest that Jung's model can be used to alert teachers and raters to some sources of their biases and the egocentric ways they may respond to texts.

EXTRAVERSION–INTROVERSION

Of the 26 high school teachers who responded to Glenda's and Paulette's essays, 8 were extraverts. Five of the 8 commented on what they perceived to be Glenda's lack of initiative. None of the 18 introverts commented on either writer's initiative (HS). Extraverts, who leap into experience with little planning, value initiative; introverts, who plan before acting, value reflection. The raters' type seems to have affected how they reacted to Glenda as a person, perhaps as a writer as well.

These type-related values, though often subtly manifested or submerged beneath seemingly objective criticism, may radically affect evaluations. One extravert (ENFP/HS) wrote of Glenda's essay: "I wonder what Glenda's problem is. If Paulette was such a special friend last quarter and the girls are at the same school, why haven't they met? Is Glenda afraid to take the initiative to find Paulette?" One might in general expect that Glenda, the extravert, would show more social initiative than Paulette, the introvert, and this would probably be true for a large sample. If so, extraverted raters and teachers may have a general tendency to value more highly the writing of extraverted writers who exhibit initiative.

Introverted raters also seemed to show type-related bias in their evaluations. An introvert (INFJ/HS) disliked Glenda's essay because she felt that Glenda did not "reveal much of herself." She felt, on the other hand, that Paulette had "much insight about herself and her motivations." The introvert values insight, or reflection, more than initiative.

Whether extraverted or introverted, it seems that raters' basic orientation to life can affect how they evaluate a text.

SENSING–INTUITION

The Sensing–Intuition dimension will probably prove to have an enormous impact on evaluation. The impact will likely be felt differently at a high school level, where roughly 30% of composition teachers appear to be sensing types, than on the college level, where around 10% are sensing types.

The most interesting difference between sensing and intuitive evaluators is that the sensing types tend to evaluate the concrete text, the words on paper, while intutive types tend to evaluate the concrete text in light of the inferences they may make from it. When asked to respond to Paulette's essay, a sensing type (ESFJ/HS) wrote:

> The reader gets the idea that a positive attitude toward work, whatever it may be, is necessary to succeed. The reader is told that Paulette was able to develop this attitude because of her friend in the Remedial Reading course. We also see her reason for staying in the course to begin with—a few people talked to her and she found someone who also had a problem like she had.
>
> Paulette also had a more or less summary paragraph at the end, containing the main idea of the theme.
>
> Even though the theme wasn't written that well grammatically, the ideas were conveyed quite well (HS).

Throughout, the evaluator stays close to what was directly stated in the text and how it was encoded. Her comments on the content are a fairly close paraphrase of Paulette's essay. In addition to content, she comments on mechanics, the text's structure, and clarity. The values that seem to be behind these comments are that good essays should be grammatically correct, should follow a set structure or at least guidelines (viz., state the "main idea" early), and directly state, rather than imply, the message.

Intuitive types, in contrast, are less attentive to the concrete text, which seems to hold value only for the inferences it inspires. An INTP (HS) wrote of Paulette's essay:

> I feel that Paulette is an insecure person who draws to the people around her. Since she sees others as responsible for her success, she will also be able to blame them for her failures. Also her goals are unrealistic. It takes more than determination and taking good notes to be a good student. It is evident from her paper that she lacks many of the basic skills necessary to excell in college level work.

Only in the last sentence does the evaluator mention the concrete text, and even there it is to make an inference about Paulette's skills in general. Intuitive types, since they attend less to the concrete text, are less likely to evaluate it in terms of mechanics, prescribed text structure and clarity. For example, if transitions or words are missing from the concrete text, the intuitive teacher will often supply them. Intuitives are also more likely to make evaluations, whether consciously or not, on the basis of their impressions: what they infer the writer to be like, what they infer the writer's intent to be, and how they believe the text could be improved.

We have observed that intuitive types often infer the writer's intention and then evaluate the essay on whether or not it achieves that intention (GSU). Evaluating by inferred intentions or aims has some utility; it allows for a more flexible set of evaluative criteria, rather than a rigid reliance on criteria fixed to static or artificial modes. But evaluating by inferred intention or aim is only as valid as the inference. If the writer never intended to do what the intuitive evaluator infers as his or her aim, or if the evaluator has failed to infer the writer's intention, then the evaluation that evolves from that faulty inference can hardly be considered valid.

Each approach needs to be studied and valued. Sensory instructors are probably very good at helping students to refine the concrete text, while intuitive instructors may be better at helping students to understand the possibilities of their text, how it might be revised.

And all instructors are capable of providing well-rounded feedback. A sensing teacher (ESTJ/HS) wrote the following response to Glenda's essay:

> Glenda and Paulette needed each other during their Remedial Reading course. Because of a change in class schedules, they don't see each other during second quarter. It seems that Glenda should call or contact Paulette to continue the positive re-inforcement in their friendship.

The sensing type begins concretely, with a paraphrase, but then moves from the concrete to make an inference about what Glenda should do. At their best, instructors who are sensing types will also make inferences, which will probably be well grounded by the text.

Each type can also use its preference inappropriately. An intuitive teacher (ENFP/HS) responded to Paulette's essay in this way:

> When I first read Paulette's essay, I was struck by the feeling of an individual who is coming to terms with herself. She is recognizing not only her faults, but the ingredients essential to her personality to work through these problems. Only time will tell how strong her determination and success are, but at least she is actively trying to improve herself and her future. This ability to change despite the odds, recognizing opportunities for growth through negative experiences is essential for mature development. Too often individuals aspire to dreams which when left unrealized result in a falling back on old routines or like-my-parents' patterns. They subvert feelings which could generate change, relying on conventional

> patterns to which to structure their lives. Only by following at least a few of our gut feelings, taking an occassional chance, can we discover new facets to life and reveal aspects of our personality which have been overlooked or not touched upon. Paulette's essay is of a girl who is discovering that life is a process; individuals are not products who are battered by life. Rather our lives are here for us to create as we experience and grow within our environment.

This response, actually more of a philosophical treatise, exemplifies how far afield the inferences of intuitive evaluators may be from the concrete text. If evaluators' inferences are too dissociated from what is actually written, then they may poorly communicate with the writer or fail to agree with other raters. Indeed, intuitive raters seem to disagree often because each rater is essentially evaluating his or her own idosyncratic text (the text that he or she inferred) rather than the concrete text that the writer produced (GSU).

THINKING–FEELING

The Thinking–Feeling dimension, since it explains opposite ways of making judgments and decisions, will probably, more than any other dimension, explain how raters evaluate what they have perceived. Instructors' preferences on this dimension can also greatly influence their style of giving feedback.

Thinking types seem to value good content and organization over good style. In their own writing they frequently prefer to develop ideas by logic rather than personal examples. Similarly, when evaluating others' writing, they prefer to read an essay with logical arguments rather than personal examples, which they may feel are "merely subjective," mushy, sentimental, or egocentric (GSU). They often feel that objective writing reflects a higher stage of development than expressive writing. At their best, thinking types will deliver what Peter Elbow (1981, pp. 140–151) calls criteria-based feedback, which is objectively based on a set of standards given to the students before they write. At their worst, their feedback may be harsh or inappropriately sarcastic (GSU).

Feeling types value the more personal qualities of writing. They often value style (sentence variety, phrasing, diction, etc.) over content. They also value writing that is personal, authentic, honestly expressive, genuine, and interesting (HS). Especially when also extraverted, they often view writing that has a "voice," in which the writer's unique personality is expressed in both style and content, as being at a higher level of development than writing that seems objectively sterile, technically clear but dull (GSU).

At their best, feeling types will provide what Elbow (1981, pp. 140–151) calls response-based feedback, which is based on the instructor's subjective responses to the essay. Unfortunately, "subjective" feedback is often viewed pejoratively, as being synonymous with "unfair" or "biased." Sound subjective responses, however, can be quite important to a writer's development. Unless writers know when they move their audience (including their teacher), make them laugh, cry, or morally outraged, they may fail to develop effective strategies.

Feeling instructors are also quite good at providing empathic responses that can help them make contact with their students. For example, a feeling type (INFJ/HS) wrote on Glenda's essay:

> It sounds like Paulette is a very special friend. I hope that you are able to find her soon.

At their worst, feeling instructors are so empathic that they may be afraid to criticize. Another feeling type (INFP/HS) wrote on Paulette's essay:

> It would scare me to touch this paper. A positive attitude is great, but it is not *all* you need to succeed. If Paulette perceives helpful criticism as negativism, I'd have to talk to her before grading the paper.

This instructor might deliver some sensitive and encouraging feedback in person, or she might needlessly hold back, either by not making critical comments or by softening criticisms until they are unclear or wishy-washy. In actuality, Paulette, a thinking type, was quite good at accepting criticism. As is typical of thinking types, she frequently solicited it.

JUDGING–PERCEIVING

The most interesting facet of how this dimension relates to evaluation is that judging types (especially if also T) rate essays more quickly than perceiving types (GSU). The more decisive judging types feel comfortable in reading a few paragraphs of an essay and then "holistically" rating it. Perceiving types, who value thoroughness over decisiveness, usually feel that rating an essay without a comprehensive reading borders on malpractice (GSU).

As they quickly rate essays, judging types seem to prefer writing that comes to a definite conclusion and that is concise. Judging types will often criticize the longer, more inclusive essays of perceiving types, such as Paulette's, for rambling (HS, GSU). In so doing, they may overlook the possibly rich potential in what appear to be unrelated ideas and data. They may feel that shorter, even poorly developed, essays reflect a comparatively higher stage of development than essays that seem to include seemingly unrelated ideas and data.

Perceiving types are more likely to value essays that fully explore, rather than resolve, an issue. They may feel that longer essays, even when overinclusive, reflect a higher stage of development than short, concise essays (GSU).

One might expect that judging instructors could easily help perceiving students to develop a sense of parsimony, and that perceiving instructors could easily help judging students to further develop their topics, but the reverse seems to be true (GSU). Judging types naturally limit their topics and content; what they do consciously, what they have had to learn as they matured as writers, is to develop a topic more completely. They thus seem to feel more comfortable working with students who, like themselves, write short, underdeveloped, rough drafts than with those who write rambling, overinclusive drafts. Similarily, perceiving instructors, as they matured, had to learn to trim their essays. Since deleting data is a skill that they now consciously employ, they seem to feel more comfortable when teaching students to cut the length of their essays than when teaching to expand.

Though we have only noticed this phenomenon with the Judging–Perceiving dimension, instructors in general may feel more comfortable teaching students similar to themselves in type because these students follow a developmental pattern close to their own. In other words, those skills that they consciously learned are what they feel most comfortable teaching. If this assumption is accurate, it may have some bearing on the evaluative process. Instructors may feel less frustrated when teaching students whose personality type is similar to their own because they will better understand these students' developmental pattern. Instructors may become more frustrated when teaching students whose personality type is dissimilar to their own because these students will yet need to learn skills that seem, to the instructors, so fundamental. Those students who are easier to teach may receive the highest grades.

CONCLUSION

Two studies have already used the MBTI to suggest that our evaluation of student writing is far more egocentric than we might like to believe.

Walter (1984), after studying the distribution of type in upper-level English, journalism, and business communication courses, discovered that those students who were similar in type to both their instructors and to the modal type of their discipline tended to receive the highest grades. Gowen (1984) investigated the influence of raters' personality type and level of experience on their scoring of student essays. She found that the raters' type was a significant variable but level of experience was not. These studies, along with the observations made in this chapter, suggest that raters and instructors may have a natural tendency to more highly value and reward the writing of students whose personality type is similar to their own.

If teachers do indeed prefer the essays written by students with a personality type similar to their own, we may need to question some of our research techniques. When we strive to achieve reliability during holistic scoring sessions, do we discard valid responses? If most of the raters are NTs, will the ratings done by STs, SFs, and NFs tend to be discarded more frequently? Will subtle standards naturally develop that favor NT writings?

We also need to question the evaluation of student essays in the classroom. Are the weaknesses of some types of students ignored and the strengths of other students ignored? If we rigidly adhere to our values in grading essays, how will it affect our students' development?

Certainly, more research is needed in this area, but we also need to expand the use of Jung's model in teacher education programs. Our evaluation of writing need not be so egocentric. In a number of settings, Jung's model has been found to be an effective tool for exploring the source of our evaluations and learning to appreciate a wider range of texts.

7
Understanding Groups of Writers*

In *The Mismeasure of Man* Stephen Jay Gould (1981) initiates his masterful debunking of intelligence testing with an explanation of what he terms the reification fallacy:

> The argument [against the current practice of intelligence testing] begins with one of the fallacies—*reification*, or our tendency to convert abstract concepts into entities (from the Latin *res*, or thing). We recognize the importance of mentality in our lives and wish to characterize it, in part so that we can make the divisions and distinctions among people that our cultural and political systems dictate. We therefore give the word "intelligence" to this wondrously complex and multifaceted set of human capabilities. This shorthand symbol is then reified and intelligence achieves its dubious status as a unitary thing. (p. 24)

As Gould outlines it here, the process of reification begins—not with biology—but with political and social pigeonholes. In part to explain—at times, justify—why certain ethnic groups were found predominantly in the lower socioeconomic classes, psychologists developed the concept of a "general factor" of intelligence, which could not by any means explain the complex nature of cognitive skills. The abstraction, Gould feels, was the first step toward reification. Once the specious, conceptually mushy, and reductionistic abstraction was formulated, it was reified. Psychologists, exhibiting all the vigor of lunatics pounding square pegs into round holes, struggled to locate "general intelligence" at a particular point of the brain or tie it to what they felt were "racial genes." A spuriously conceived abstraction became a concrete, palpable thing.

Though the comparison should not be pushed too far, the field of composition may be developing its own reification fallacy. As with intelligence testing, the reificaton of the basic writer begins with our cultural and political systems. Though the "underprepared student"—also called subfreshman, remedial student, developmental student and nontraditional student—has perhaps always been with us, current notions about

* This chapter orginally appeared as an article by G. H. Jensen in the *Journal of Basic Writing*.

the college basic writer date to the early 1970s. As a large number of underprepared students entered colleges and universities, primarily an effect of open admissions and desegregation policies, faculty were faced with teaching what seemed to be an atypical group of students. As Mina Shaughnessy reflected in *Errors and Expectations*, "the essays these students wrote during their first weeks of class stunned the teachers who read them" (1977, p. 3).

Since these underprepared students (whether at Shaughnessy's CUNY or at other institutions) seemed academically, socially, and culturally apart from their peers, teachers and researchers naturally wanted to understand how and why they differed. They observed and studied the students in their classes and reported their findings. Shaughnessy, one of the first to characterize basic writers, wrote that they equate correct writing with good writing and that they feel an urgency "to meet their teachers' criteria" (1977, pp. 8–9). Such "folk psychologizing," which is ultimately reductionistic and may lead to reification, was not typical of her work; she preferred to focus on the wide range of "styles to being wrong" (1977, p. 40). Even in a basic writing class, which might at first seem relatively homogeneous, Shaughnessy found a range of errors and a diversity in the processes that produced them.

Rather than amplify Shaughnessy's most consistent message, that basic writers are a diverse lot, those researchers who followed seem more intrigued by her characterizations. They have preferred to peg isolated personality traits on the basic writer. Lunsford (1979) studied a number of basic writers and concluded that "they have not attained that level of cognitive development which would allow them to form abstractions or concepts." Perl (1979) investigated the writing processes of unskilled writers and felt that they frequently "began writing without any secure sense of where they were heading, acknowledging only that they would 'figure it out' as they went along." They also, she found, tended to be so concerned about "error-hunting" that they broke the "rhythms generated by thinking and writing." Pianko (1979), after comparing 10 remedial and 7 traditional students, concluded that the remedial students planned a shorter period of time before writing and paused less frequently. Sommers (1981), after comparing the writing processes of an unskilled freshman writer and a skilled adult writer, stated that unskilled writers are most concerned about applying rules or filling in a set organizational structure while skilled writers are most concerned about the relationship between developing a structure and discovering meaning. More recently, Troyka (1982) tested nontraditional students, discovering that they, at least those in her sample, are field-dependent. They are holistic thinkers, highly gregarious and concerned about the social context or getting along with other people. Her article was unusual in that she actually tested her subjects for cognitive style, and, rather than point to their deficiencies as other writers had, she emphasized their strengths.

As can be seen from this brief overview of the literature, a gross characterization of the students in basic writing classes seems to be emerging. This composite characterization is of a gregarious writer who talks but does not think, who does not value planning, who has difficulty developing concepts, is overly concerned about correctness, likes to please the teacher, and prefers the basic five-paragraph theme. Such characterizations are dangerous in part because they lead to reification, which, as we will discuss later, can have adverse effects on how well we teach basic writers. Yet, the characterization of the basic writer should also be criticized in and of itself. It is simply too much of a portrait in broad strokes to account for the diversity among basic writers, and it too heavily emphasizes their faults.

How does this characterization relate to Jung's model of personality, and would looking at the basic writer through this model alert us to some of his or her strengths? As described in the literature, the basic writer seems to be an extraverted–sensing–feeling type. Extraverts, when still immature, as basic writers often are, may be less reflective than introverts (Pianko to remedial writers), but they are quite good at generating ideas by talking about their topics. Extraverts also tend to figure out what they want to say as they are writing (Perl to unskilled writers), a trait that, when applied to mature writers, Murray (1978) canonizes as "writing as process of discovery." Sensing types, especially those who are cognitively immature, tend to have more difficulty developing concepts than intuitive types (Lunsford to the basic writer). They are often very concerned about following directions or fulfilling the teacher's expectations (Shaughnessy to the basic writer), and, when inexperienced as writers, they tend to equate correct writing with good writing (Shaughnessy). They also prefer prescribed organizational patterns, which help them to know what the teacher expects, over original patterns (Sommers to unskilled writers). If these descriptions were slightly reworded, they might describe a good technical writer, and indeed sensing types are found in large numbers in technical fields such as engineering. Sensing types, and good technical writers, usually stick to the facts, rather than make flighty hunches, attempt to follow directions accurately, and try to produce grammatically correct prose in a widely accepted format. Even though it is unfortunate that most researchers characterize basic writers by their weaknesses alone, it is interesting that all of these isolated traits form a relatively accurate description of the faults of an ESF. But does this composite personality of the basic writer accurately describe the students in a basic writing program or a basic writing class?

Table 1 is a type table of 188 students in 11 composition classes of the developmental studies program at Georgia State University. Only a glance at the type table will reveal that the 16 possible personality types described by the MBTI are not equally represented in this sample. Introverts only slightly outnumber extraverts (which is in itself interesting, because in the general population extraverts outnumber introverts by three to two), but sensing types, thinking types, and judging types outnumber their opposites by about two to one. Given the preponderance of certain types, it is easy to understand how a teacher or researcher might characterize the group, rather than appreciate their diversity. Some of the instructors in this program have described the basic writer at Georgia State as being concrete and very structured learners, which is typical of ISTJs and grossly accurate of this population. It is also a description that would roughly, in a gut-level, first impression way, fit what the literature reports as current notions about the basic writer. The only striking difference that a casual observer might notice would be that the typical Georgia State student—an ISTJ—would tend to be less social than the basic writer found in the literature—an ESF. If, however, we demand more accuracy, the characterization of the basic writer found in the literature only describes those students in the ESFP and ESFJ cells of the table, or 11% of this sample.

Table 2 provides the distribution of another population, students in a basic writing class at the University of Illinois at Chicago. The rather small sample is somewhat different from the sample in Table 1. This class has slightly more extraverts than introverts and a predominance toward feeling types. The typical student in the Georgia State sample, to the casual observer, would probably seem more like an ISTJ, and the typical student in the University of Illinois at Chicago sample would probably seem more like an ESFJ. It is difficult to say, from this limited amount of data, whether or not the differences between the two tables reflect differences between the two programs. The class illustrated in Table 2 may simply be atypical of that program. With the limited data available, we can only say that differences exist, that it is unlikely that all basic writing programs will draw the same kinds of students or that classrooms in each program will be exact microcosms of the program.

At the most fundamental level, the characterizations of the basic writer found in the literature are inaccurate because they are overgeneralizations from what would seem to be naturally biased samples. The samples are naturally biased toward some personality type, as are almost all samples. Perl's and Pianko's samples seem to have been predominantly extraverts, Lunsford's and Sommers's predominantly sensing types. Since these authors are working with students at different institutions, each of which probably has its own criteria for placing students into basic

Table 1. Students in Developmental Composition Georgia State University (11 Classes Fall 1982 to Winter 1985) (N = 188)

DISTRIBUTION OF COMBINED PREFERENCES

SENSING TYPES with THINKING	SENSING TYPES with FEELING	INTUITIVE TYPES with FEELING	INTUITIVE TYPES with THINKING	
ISTJ *n* = 40 % = 21 ••••••• ••••••• ••••••• ••••••• ••••••• •••••	ISFJ *n* = 12 % = 6 ••••••• •••••	INFJ *n* = 2 % = 1 ••	INTJ *n* = 4 % = 2 ••••	JUDGING / INTROVERTS
ISTP *n* = 12 % = 6 ••••••• •••••	ISFP *n* = 9 % = 5 ••••••• ••	INFP *n* = 4 % = 2 ••••	INTP *n* = 14 % = 7 ••••••• •••••••	PERCEPTIVE / INTROVERTS
ESTP *n* = 15 % = 8 ••••••• ••••••• •	ESFP *n* = 5 % = 3 •••••	ENFP *n* = 10 % = 5 ••••••• •••	ENTP *n* = 7 % = 4 •••••••	PERCEPTIVE / EXTRAVERTS
ESTJ *n* = 24 % = 13 ••••••• ••••••• ••••••• •••	ESFJ *n* = 15 % = 8 ••••••• ••••••• •	ENFJ *n* = 6 % = 3 ••••••	ENTJ *n* = 9 % = 5 ••••••• ••	JUDGING / EXTRAVERTS

DISTRIBUTION OF ISOLATED PREFERENCES

E	= 48%	(*n* = 91)
I	= 52%	(*n* = 97)
S	= 70%	(*n* = 132)
N	= 30%	(*n* = 56)
T	= 66%	(*n* = 125)
F	= 34%	(*n* = 63)
J	= 62%	(*n* = 117)
P	= 38%	(*n* = 71)

Code

E = Extraverts
I = Introverts

S = Sensing Types
N = Intuitive Types

T = Thinking Types
F = Feeling Types

J = Judging Types
P = Perceiving Types

• = one student

Developed by Isabel Briggs Myers

Table 2. Students in Remedial Composition University of Illinois at Chicago (1 Class Fall 1984) (N = 14)

DISTRIBUTION OF COMBINED PREFERENCES

SENSING TYPES		INTUITIVE TYPES			
with THINKING	**with FEELING**	**with FEELING**	**with THINKING**		
ISTJ *n* = 0 % = 0	ISFJ *n* = 4 % = 29 ••••	INFJ *n* = 0 % = 0	INTJ *n* = 0 % = 0	JUDGING	INTROVERTS
ISTP *n* = 0 % = 0	ISFP *n* = 0 % = 0	INFP *n* = 1 % = 7 •	INTP *n* = 1 % = 7 •	PERCEPTIVE	INTROVERTS
ESTP *n* = 0 % = 0	ESFP *n* = 1 % = 7 •	ENFP *n* = 1 % = 7 •	ENTP *n* = 2 % = 14 ••	PERCEPTIVE	EXTRAVERTS
ESTJ *n* = 2 % = 14 ••	ESFJ *n* = 2 % = 14 ••	ENFJ *n* = 0 % = 0	ENTJ *n* = 0 % = 0	JUDGING	EXTRAVERTS

DISTRIBUTION OF ISOLATED PREFERENCES

E	= 57%	(*n* = 8)
I	= 43%	(*n* = 6)
S	= 64%	(*n* = 9)
N	= 36%	(*n* = 5)
T	= 35%	(*n* = 5)
F	= 65%	(*n* = 9)
J	= 57%	(*n* = 8)
P	= 43%	(*n* = 6)

Code

E	= Extraverts
I	= Introverts
S	= Sensing Types
N	= Intuitive Types
T	= Thinking Types
F	= Feeling Types
J	= Judging Types
P	= Perceiving Types
•	= one student

Developed by Isabel Briggs Myers

writing programs, we should not assume that any abstraction of the basic writer generated from a biased sample will be an accurate description of the writers in all programs. Pianko's and Perl's comments about the basic writer cannot be generally applied to students at Georgia State, who are more typically introverts. Rather than being unreflective, as Pianko found with her sample, the Georgia State writer is more likely to be so reflective that he or she is distant from experience and produces a lifeless prose. Rather than leaping into writing with little planning, as was typical of Perl's sample, the Georgia State writer may plan too long. But we cannot even talk about the typical Georgia State writer.

At another level, the characterizations are inaccurate because they cannot adequately account for the diversity found in even a single program, class or sample. Even though 70% of the students in Table 1 are sensing types, 30% of them are intuitives. Even though ISTJs—the program's modal personality type—comprise 21% of the population, every one of the 16 possible types is represented. Even when dealing with a single population, or a single class, it is dangerous, and more reductionistic than descriptive, to characterize the basic writer.

But characterizations are very difficult to avoid, as we have seen. Researchers naturally want to describe their populations and resort to a kind of home-grown personality theory to do so. As long as we are going to describe groups of writers, we might as well use sound personality theory. We can then describe the population more accurately, be more aware of the limitations of any description, and perhaps even avoid the reification fallacy.

Reification can naturally—almost inevitably—occur when we begin to believe that our characterizations are accurate descriptions, when we begin to believe that our notions about the shared traits of some group of writers are more significant than their individual differences, or that these notions embody *the* salient characteristic that separates that group from all other groups. Pianko, for example, seems to believe that basic writers are less reflective than traditional students. As stated before, we believe that her characterization of basic writers is reductionistic, just as Gould feels that the concept of a "general intelligence factor" fails to account for the wide range of human capabilities. Reductionistic abstractions are, Gould feels, dangerous in and of themselves, but, when they are reified, when they become a concrete thing, as when intelligence was tied to "racial genes," the faulty abstractions assume even more power over how we think and act (1981, p. 24). In the following passage, Pianko (1979) takes that extra dangerous step; she reifies the basic writer:

> Although it is unlikely that a single teaching strategy or several strategies in concert will be able to immediately alter behavioral patterns already

> embedded in a student's writing habits, there are certainly a few basic shifts in teaching emphasis which could simply and organically alter a student's writing sense and consciousness. (p. 278)

Pianko seems to be saying that the basic writer (or, in her study, the remedial writer) is innately, organically different than his or her peers. She suggests that teachers "organically alter a student's . . . consciousness." We believe that it is important for instructors to help students develop as writers, but it seems to us that organically altering their consciousness is bit overzealous.

The reification can be more subtle, as in Sommers's study (1981). She compared one unskilled writer to one skilled writer. The assumption behind her research design is that the differences between any basic writer and any professional writer are more significant than differences between their personality type or cognitive style. In the context of Jung's model of personality, the two writers seem to have different personality types. Rita, the unskilled writer, seems to be an ESF, and Walter, the skilled writer, seems to be an ENT (from the information supplied, it is difficult to hypothesize about the two writers' preference on the Judging–Perceiving dimension). If this conjecture is accurate, Sommers may be describing the differences between a sensing–feeling writer and an intuitive–thinking writer, rather than the differences between an unskilled and skilled writer. Would her conclusions be the same if she compared an unskilled ESFP with a skilled ESFP, or an unskilled ENTJ with a skilled ENTJ?

Sommers asserts that her two case studies are "representative" of each cohort, and she goes on to state that the differences between the two writers are illustrative of "the fundamental differences between the revision strategies of unskilled and skilled writers." Does not the fact that she can find what she feels to be a typical case imply that she has already reified the basic writer? Is not Rita, her unskilled writer, the concrete embodiment of her notions about how unskilled writers revise? Should we assume that all basic writers will write as Rita does? Should we teach all of our basic writers as if they were Rita?

Our intention here is not to single out Sommers, whose research is insightful, but to raise some questions about general research practices in the field of composition. Other researchers have, like Sommers, used comparative designs to study the differences between "high-apprehensives" and "low-apprehensives" (Selfe, 1984) and "high-blockers" and "low-blockers" (Rose, 1984, pp. 44–69). Researchers have also investigated the writing processes of advanced writers (Hairston, 1984) and good writers (Stallard, 1974). These studies would have been more valid, and we believe more interesting, if the authors better understood the heterogeneity of their sample populations. If a researcher were comparing the writing process of, for example, one Eskimo to that of one WASP, the probability that these two writers will have different personality types, and thus different cognitive styles, is quite high. If personality type affects how one writes, as we believe it does, then the researcher would be discovering the differences between two personality types as well as any differences that might exist between the typical Eskimo and the typical WASP. Even when researchers are using relatively large samples, the chance that these samples are biased in regards to personality type or cognitive style must be considered. We could compare the writing processes of 30 Eskimos to 30 WASPs, but, even if randomly selected, the samples would likely be biased. As data in the MBTI manual (Myers & McCaulley, 1985) illustrate, it is rare for any group, whether it be nurses or surgeons, teachers or journalists, to have an equal representation of all personality types. For example, nurses are predominantly sensing–feeling types, and surgeons are predominantly sensing–thinking types.

Researchers may argue that a bias in their sample that reflects a bias in the population offers no threat to the validity of their studies. And they might be right if we taught only entire samples or populations. We do not; we teach individuals. We might, for example, want to determine what kind of topics are best for basic writers. We could then have a group of basic writers, 70% of whom might be sensing types, write on a selection of topics and find that the group as a whole wrote better and with less anxiety when given concrete, factual, and detailed topics. We could then decide to administer nothing but concrete, factual, and detailed topics, and about 70% of the population would be pleased with our decision. The intuitive types, who consitute 30% of the population, might be less pleased. They would probably prefer to write on more open-ended, abstract, and creative topics. If researchers controlled for personality type, we would be able to understand better how we might help each individual student develop.

Using personality or cognitive style theory to appreciate both the biased distribution and the diversity of basic writing classes, advanced writing classes, or other groups of writers may help us to avoid faulty inferences, but it also holds a danger. It may lead to yet another kind of pigeonholing or reification. We may begin to believe that Jungian personality theory can explain all human behavior, which it cannot, or that those students who are called sensing types are somehow a different biological creature than those who are called intuitive types. Jung's theory of type posits that people prefer certain psychological processes, not that they possess certain innate and unalterable static traits. A person's preference, whether for sensory or intuitive perception, only provides a push to behave in a certain way; the preference does not determine behavior. Sensing types may prefer concrete perception through their senses, but they also, like intuitives, are capable of using their imagination to make hunches and explore possibilities. If misused, personality and cognitive style theories can be as reductionistic as "folk psychologizing."

This plea for an appreciation of the diversity and strengths of students in basic writing classes or other classes, is more an echo than a manifesto. Troyka (1982) emphasized the strengths, rather than the faults, of basic writers. Shaughnessy (1977) asked that teachers treat their students as individuals when she wrote about the different styles to being wrong. Shaughnessy (1976) also warned that just because "teachers use the word 'remedial,' we cannot be at all certain that they mean the same thing by it." Within one program, students will differ from class to class, and the composition of students in different programs will vary with admission and placement policies. We should not believe that there is any one way to define, signify, label, identify, or teach those students who are called basic, remedial, or developmental writers. Though, as Gould (1981, p. 252) says, "the temptation to reify is powerful . . . it is a temptation that we must resist, for it reflects an ancient prejudice of thought, not a truth of nature."

Conclusion and Topics for Research

In this volume, we have suggested that personality type is one of the factors that influences how individuals write in specific situations. To begin to describe how this factor impacts on writing we have concentrated on one theoretical model (Jung's theory of psychological types) and one measure of this theoretical model (the MBTI). We have discussed how personality type can possibly—or tends to—influence writing processes, texts, development, instruction, and evaluation. Our purpose has not been to review all of the research in the field of composition as Hillocks (1986) did recently, but to argue that a new line of research, one that concentrates on individual differences, would be fruitful and useful. Since our discussion has been focused and necessarily limited, we feel the need to end with a few qualifications.

First, no one factor could possibly explain the complexity of any facet of the teaching of writing. If we only look at writing processes, many factors must be considered in addition to personality type:

The Topic or Writing Task: Some topics seem to allow the writer a great deal of flexibility in his or her approach to the writing task: thus, with these topics, the effects of personality type may be readily apparent. Other topics or tasks so direct and restrict the writer that the effects of personality type may be virtually erased.

Instruction: The advice that many instructors give presents a fairly limited view of how individuals go about writing. Thus, many students may write as they were taught to write, rather than in a process that is naturally suited to their personality type.

Context: The context, the social situation in which one writes, can also exert an influence on the writer, perhaps forcing him or her to abandon a preferred approach to writing, or nudging him or her to develop a less preferred approach to writing.

Development: As writers develop, they seem to exhibit a greater flexibility in how they approach writing. They seem to be better able to adapt to a variety of topics and contexts.

Anxiety: Anxiety also seems to influence process. An anxious writer may abandon a preferred approach to writing or more rigidly adhere to ineffective writing strategies.

Given this array of factors that could possibly influence how one writes, it is understandable that not all introverts always plan extensively before writing or that not all extraverts invariably leap into writing with little planning. We are not surprised that personality type sometimes fails to predict behavior; we also find it reassuring that Jung's theory is not deterministic.

Second, as the task of writing is too complex to be explained by any one factor, so too are people too complex to be explained by any one theory. Jung's model is powerful, but it cannot—and does not purport to—explain all individual differences. Writers of the same type, therefore, will not employ a process that is identical in every detail, nor will they produce identical texts. If we investigated the writing processes of one type, say ISTJs, we would no doubt find many similarities *and* much variation.

Much more research is needed to understand how personality type influences various aspects of writing, when it influences writing, and when it does not influence writing.

Even though the hypotheses raised in this volume have been refined over 6 years of clinical and classroom experience, only a few have been empirically tested and these only in pilot studies. Some broad areas of needed research can be suggested.

We need hard data on how each dimension of Jung's model affects particular aspects of the writing process. In Chapter 2, we suggested that Jung's model can explain many of the individual differences in writing processes documented by Emig, Britton, and others. The hypotheses raised in Chapter 2 should be empirically tested and further refined. When testing these hypotheses, researchers should be careful to examine how an interaction of dimensions may influence the variable under study. For example, a researcher may wish to test the hypothesis that introverts spend more time planning than extraverts. If the researcher's sample of extraverts is also predominantly a sample of perceiving types, and his or her sample of introverts is also predominantly judging in preference, then the results may be affected by the skew of the sample. The push to meet deadlines, which is so characteristic of judging types, may shorten the length of the introverts' natural tendency to plan; the natural reluctance to reach closure associated with a perceiving preference may lengthen the planning of this particular group of extraverts. Whenever possible, researchers should control for such interactions by comparing samples that are identical (or balanced) except on the dimension under study. For example, the researcher could compare samples of ESFJs and ISFJs. Or, the researcher could test for interactions.

The effect of personality type on individual writing processes that is least understood is that of the interactions of dimensions. The MBTI identifies 16 personality types and can potentially identify 16 writing processes. To understand and appreciate these writing processes more fully, case studies of writers representing all 16 personality types are needed.

In Chapter 2, we also attempted to outline how Jung's model might synthesize many of the conflicting theories on the teaching of composition, as Jung used his theory of personality types to explain differences between the psychoanalytic approaches of Freud and Adler (Homans, 1979, pp. 93–95). Diametrically opposed theoretical approaches may both be valid if we view them as teaching styles that can appeal to opposite types of students. One style might be appropriate for an extravert, another for an introvert. But we need to know more about how Jung's model relates to the teaching of composition, how a teacher's instructional style and credo interacts with a student's learning style and writing process. We have observed that writers function best when early drafts draw upon their preferred cognitive processes, with later drafts drawing upon unpreferred processes to round out the composition. If this finding is supported by future studies as it has been through years of observation, then it can provide the writing teacher with a system for delivering the appropriate intervention for an individual writer at a particular point in his or her writing process. We suspect that teachers, especially novices, may, in general, advise students to write as they do, instead of adapting their advice to the needs of the individual writer. The effects of "mismatched" advice on a student's development, on his or her attitude toward writing, and on the genesis of writing anxiety or writer's blocks all deserve attention. Yet, a simple mismatch of teaching and learning styles may not be the most crucial factor; a lack of appreciation for the talents and strengths of a certain type, a teacher's failure to nurture a student's latent gifts, may even more profoundly retard growth.

In order to understand the effects of teaching on the development of writing skills, we must first understand what it means to develop as a writer. We need to study writers of different ages with varying levels of writing experience to see if Jung's model can explain some features of writing growth. We have suggested that writers become more skillful as they develop both their preferred and unpreferred processes. Young writers may find it difficult to write in a way that requires them to use those cognitive processes which come less naturally to them. Our observations suggest that they should first be encouraged to discover their preferred processes and then move to their unpreferred. This hypothesis needs to be tested empirically. In so doing, the interaction of personality type with the developmental models of Piaget, Vygotsky, Perry, Moffett, and others should be explored.

The conceptual framework of Jung's model will, we believe, ultimately tell us a great deal about how we evaluate writing. If we better understand why we evaluators fail to agree, we may be able to improve the reliability and validity of holistic scoring and the effectiveness of instructor responses to student essays.

Finally, we need to re-evaluate current research methodology. In research on pausing (Matsuhashi, 1981), for example, measuring the length and frequency of pauses may have more meaning if the effect of personality type is considered.

We hope that research into the influence of personality type or cognitive style on writing processes and texts will lead to a greater appreciation for individual differences in writing. Despite the excellent work of Emig, Britton, Graves, and others, textbooks and, one would expect, many teachers still present a fairly prescriptive and limited view of how one should go about writing and what sort of text is acceptable. The writers of textbooks and teachers too often fall prey to the biases of their own personality type and do not always consider how others, individuals of a different personality type, may think, learn, or write best.

APPENDIX 1

Additional Information About Jung's Model and Learning Styles

PREFERENCE COMBINATIONS THAT PROVIDE USEFUL INSIGHT INTO LEARNING STYLES

As discussed in Chapter 1, the combination and interaction of preferences is complicated. Those who are new to Jung's personality model should not expect to understand quickly how preferences combine into each of the 16 types. They should first strive to understand the four sets of preferences in isolation, then how certain pairs of preferences interact, and finally how preferences on all four dimensions interact.

In the following two sections, we will discuss two simplified approaches to the interaction of preferences. Gordon Lawrence stresses the interaction of the first two dimensions (E–I with S–N), while David Keirsey's temperament theory emphasizes certain combinations of the last three dimensions (S–N with either T–F or J–P).

Lawrence's Quadrants: ES, IS, IN, EN

Gordon Lawrence (1982) has offered the conclusion that the first two dimensions of Jung's model were the most important to learning styles. His conclusion, besides being supported by research (Lawrence, 1984), is theoretically sound. The first dimension, Extraversion–Introversion, indicates whether the student thinks best while actively involved in the external world or while reflecting in the internal world. The second dimension, Sensing–Intuition, describes two ways of perceiving. Education necessarily has much to do with one's style of perceiving.

Extraverted Sensing (ES). ESs are the most frequently found type among students at the elementary and secondary level, due primarily to the preponderance of extraverts and sensing types in our society. These students tend to approach learning for its practicality. They are pragmatists, wanting to direct their abundant energy into interacting with a tangible reality. They are often described as "being at home with the world." They, above all other types, learn best by doing first, with considering, reading, and writing to follow. They absolutely need to experience life before they can understand it.

Introverted Sensing (IS). Also attuned to tangible reality are the IS types, but with a difference. As introverts, they are active principally in their minds, rather than in outwardly observable behavior. They are thus often referred to as the careful compilers of information. "Slow but sure" is their motto, and they can invariably produce data based on their concrete observations whenever asked, but they usually need to be asked. And it is best to expect their answer a bit *after* the delivery of the question, for their inner powers of sorting and retrieving data need time to operate before producing their findings.

Introverted Intuitive (IN). Similarly inwardly directed are the IN types, but what goes on inside is mediated by a very different perceptual process than for the IS. These types are the ones whose inner intuition roams freely into previously unexplored terrain. Opposites to the ES types and least frequently found among elementary and secondary students, they need to understand life before they can fully experience it. Often called the academic types, they are drawn to the realm of abstractions and symbols that represent reality rather than experiential reality itself. "Reality" in its raw form is almost immediately processed through an inner filter that reads between the lines to hypothesize about what is *not* there, but could be there if only . . . . For the IN, knowledge is important for its own sake. They often feel more at home with education once they reach college or graduate school.

Extraverted Intuitive (EN). Lastly, the EN types are the innovators. They seek knowledge for the inspiration it brings toward significant change. Full of both initiative and enthusiasm, they tend to be impatient with the slow and methodical. They make quick "intuitive" leaps into the realm of the possible, but, unlike the INs, they are equally quick to put their intuitive leaps to work interacting with the external world.

Keirsey's Temperaments: SJ, SP, NF, NT

After years of studying ancient Greek descriptions of human temperament, David Keirsey (1978) discovered Myers's work on types. He wrote that the four basic Greek temperaments, which have been redefined over the centuries with varying labels, had been described in Myers's work with the interaction between Sensing and either Judging (SJ) or Perceiving (SP) and between Intuition and either Feeling (NF) or Thinking (NT). These four clusters of types have been used to describe both teaching and learning styles (Golay, 1982).

Epimethean (SJ). Keirsey's Epimethean (SJ) temperament is one of steadiness. Reliable, responsible, and well organized, SJ types tend to be among our most hard-working students. Indeed, they often believe that true learning has not taken place unless toil and sweat are involved. At times, they are considered traditionalists, and are the stabilizing supporters of institutions and organizations, the very glue of society. They learn best when orderly plans are explicitly presented. They are highly represented among elementary school teachers. As teachers, they tend to conduct orderly classrooms.

Dionysian (SP). In contrast, the Dionysian (SP) temperament combines an attention for the concrete (S) with an open orientation to the external world (P). This particular combination tends to contribute to a kind of free-wheeling sensual love affair with the tangible world around them. In academic pursuits, however, their emphasis on the verifiable and real with such a loose approach to the external world often creates difficulties. As one advances in education, abstract complexities (N) are increasingly emphasized. Lacking the organizational tendencies of the SJ, the SPs tend not to be able to compensate for their natural attention to the concrete. Unless their strengths are acknowledged, they are at risk academically more than any other two dimension combination. These strengths are found in free-wheeling roles as negotiators, where, without advance warning, they can quickly diagnose a problem and offer a practical solution. They are also often called trouble-shooters. Unfortunately, their gift for dealing with the unexpected is often neglected in schools, and they are found in high numbers among school dropouts. It is important to note, however, that many SPs are quite successful in school. More research is needed to understand how the successful SP adapts and why the unsuccessful SP does not.

Apollonian (NF). Keirsey's next temperament, the Apollonian (NF), is one that values learning for the service it can bring to humanity. They are often catalysts and facilitators. Their intuitive attention to subtle cues which are read between the lines (N) is put in the service of people (F). They are intense idealists, operating best from the heart, and they value highly the challenge of motivating others to become as personally invested in an issue as are they. As teachers, they tend to go out of their way to give special attention to individual students in need. While equal in numbers to SJs in teacher-training programs, they may despair when caught in the routine and structure of traditional American schools and leave teaching after a few years. Frequently, they return to graduate school to become counselors or college professors.

Promethean (NT). Keirsey's Promethean temperament (NT) combines an interest in the big picture and abstractions (N) with an objective logic

(T). As a result, they conceive of analytical systems to explain things. Understanding the world through critical analysis is of high priority to NT learners, and they may often intimidate SJ, SP and NF types with their rather aloof knowledge. Their insight is less personally focused than that of the NF, directed instead toward the inanimate. Not surprisingly, they are found in large numbers among conceptual scientists and mathematicians. They learn best through challenge, competition, and intellectual investigation. As teachers, they bring challenges to their students as well.

Though these simplified approaches to how MBTI dimensions interact can be useful, especially to the novice, they need to be used with even greater caution than the entire four dimensions of the model. When looking at interactions between only two dimensions, we subtract a great deal of the power from Jung's model and are more likely to label than describe people. These combinations are most useful when employed to form insights that can then be refined by considering the additional effects of the other dimensions of the complete model.

It is also important not to underestimate the ability of any type, even SPs who are highly represented in high school dropouts. Even though SPs may have more difficulty adapting to the predominantly intuitive world of higher education, many do adapt and even go on to become college professors. The following passage was written by an ESTP college professor who is familiar with Jung's model. He describes his writing process as it contrasts to the processes of types who are more traditionally successful in academia:

> As an EP writer, I do best with a word processor, which allows me to write in a conversational manner and then go back and revise. As an ESP, I really have to revise since I use too many monsyllable words. . . . The word processor is also a great help because handwriting slows my mind down. If I try to keep up with my rate of thought, my writing becomes even more like chicken scratch. By the way, this is a rewrite. The first copy was nearly unreadable.
>
> I know of two INTJ's that can write final copy without outlines and rough drafts. It is interesting to watch them work. They organize all of their thoughts in their head and then begin to write when they have their organization complete. I'm sure there must be some disadvantages of writing completely from memory, but they are both fairly successful at what they do. I couldn't pull it off!

The ESTP professor is successful in part because he learned to write in a process that suits his own personality type, not because he has tried to learn to write like INTJs.

A COMPILATION OF MBTI RESEARCH ON LEARNING STYLES

Gordon Lawrence (1984) reviewed 36 studies of learning style that made use of the MBTI and synthesized the statistically significant findings in the following tables. They are included here to demonstrate possibilities for research on type and learning styles. Readers should consult Lawrence's article for a discussion of the implications of the findings. In the tables, the letter of the type preference with the strongest significant correlation for each variable is italicized.

Table 1. Correlation of MBTI Continuous Scores with Needs, As Measured by Edwards Personal Preference Schedule

Achievement (intellectual)	IN*T*.
Order	IST*J*
Exhibition	E..P
Autonomy	.*N*TP
Affiliation	E.*F*.
Dominance	E.T.
Nurturance	..*F*.
Change	.NT*P*
Endurance	..T*J*

Among these, the need most strongly associated with each preference is:

Pref.	Value	r
E	Dominance	.28
S	Order	.34
T	Endurance	.30
J	Order	.49
I	Achievement	.15
N	Autonomy	.31
F	Nurturance	.51
P	Autonomy	.31

Sample: 236 male freshmen

Table 2. Correlation of MBTI Continuous Scores with Scales of the Personality Research Inventory

	Cornell Engrs.	H.S. Boys
Tolerance of Complexity	.NFP	
Impulsiveness	EN.P	EN.P
Talkativeness	ENT.	E.TJ
Gregariousness	ES..	ES..
Attitude to Work	E.TJ	EN.J
Artistic	.NFP	
Liking to Use Mind	.NT.	ENT.

Sample: 507 Cornell freshmen engineers and 722 Massachusetts high school males

Table 3. Correlation of MBTI Scores with Faculty Ratings

Thorough	...J
Responsible	...J
Dependable	...J
Performs up to capacity	...J
Meets deadline	...J
Works steadily	...J
Fond of work	...J
Industrious	...J
Completes undertakings	...J
Good on details	...J
Deep	.N..
Shows originality	.N..
Imaginative	.N..
Good at analyzing	.N..
Good grasp of abstract	.N..
Independent	.N..
Competitive	E..J
Active	E...
Strong	E...
Gregarious	ES.J
Potential leader	E.F.
Carefree	E...
Pleasant	ESF
Expresses self well	E.F.
Willing to take direction	.S.J
Cooperative	.S.J

Sample: 249 male college students

Table 4. Relationships Found Between Various Attitude and Aptitude Measures and the MBTI Preferences

Extraversion	Introversion
exhibition	intellectual achievement
dominance	solitary
talkativeness	verbal reasoning
active	ideational fluency
gregarious	reality distance
reality closeness	reading (particularly at college level)
Sensing	**Intuition**
order	autonomy, independence
gregariousness	artistic; aesthetic interests; creativity
field-dependent	liking to use mind; intellectuality
economic interests	field-independent
reality closeness	reality distance
practical outlook	managing abstract symbols
see learning for practical use	imagination
carefulness in problem solving	theorectical orientation
	reading
	quickness in problem solving
Thinking	**Feeling**
theoretical interests	social interests
endurance	affiliation
	nurturance
Judging	**Perceiving**
order	autonomy
endurance	change
attitude to work (achievement orientation)	impulsiveness
	tolerance of complexity

Table 5. Learning Preferences Associated With Dimensions of MBTI Type

Extraversion	Introversion
talking, discussion	reading/verbal reasoning
psychomotor activity	time for internal processing
working with a group	working individually
Sensing	**Intuition**
tasks that call for carefulness, thoroughness and soundness of understanding	tasks that call for quickness of insight and in seeing relationships
going step by step	finding own way in new material
tasks that call for observing specifics	tasks that call for grasping general concepts
tasks that call for memory of facts	tasks that call for imagination
practical interests	intellectual interests (independent of intelligence)
	reading
Thinking	**Feeling**
logical organization of teacher	personal rapport with teacher
objective material to study	learning through personal relationships
Judging	**Perceiving**
work in steady, orderly way	work in flexible way, follow impulses
formalized instruction	informal problem solving
prescribed tasks	discovery tasks
drive toward closure, completion	managing emerging problems

Table 6. Learning Preferences Associated With MBTI Types by Quadrants

IS_ Types	IN_ Types
demonstrations	serious reading
labs	tutorials
computer-assisted instruction	independent study
films, audiovisual aids	systematically organized courses
facts, facts, and more facts	
dislike independent study	
ES_ Types	**EN_ Types**
television	reading
reports to class on topics selected by students	self-instruction
scheduling one's time	courses that put one on one's own initiative
having a schedule and sticking to it	working on group projects
orderly work on goals set in advance	meeting a lot of people
	opportunities to be creative and original

Table 7. Learning Preferences Associated With MBTI Types By Function Combinations

.ST. Types	.SF. Types
demonstrations labs television having a plan and sticking to it	student-led demonstrations or presentations instruction with personal involvement television films and audiovisuals having a study schedule
.NF. Types	**.NT. Types**
learn through personal relationships dislike impersonal, didactic instruction highly value faculty feedback value student enthusiasm low-friction student-led discussions opportunities to be creative and original	organized teacher lectures self-instruction reading systematically organized courses

Table 8. Learning Preferences Associated With MBTI Types By Perception And Attitude Combinations

.S.P Types: Structured exploratory observation, hands-on

.S.J. Types: Structured didactic, sensory rich instruction

.N.P Types: Low structure, inductive instruction

N.J. Types: Moderate to high structure, "serious" instruction

APPENDIX 2

The Distribution of Type in Education

Findings from research employing the MBTI have provided insight into the makeup of both the general American population and specific segments of education. Some of these findings are summarized below.

Extraversion–Introversion. The most recent reports of type distributions employing samples as large as 32,000 (McCaulley, Macdaid, & Kainz, 1985) show that extraverts outnumber introverts in the general American population by approximately a three-to-two ratio, with somewhat higher percentages among females and somewhat lower among males. There is, however, a more even balance of Es and Is among public schoolteachers, though distributions vary a bit with specializations (Hoffman & Betkouski, 1981). A relatively small sample of 39 college composition teachers who attended preconference workshops at the Conference on College Composition and Communication show almost two-thirds to be introverts. Samples of students indicate that there are more extraverts in high school populations than college populations.

Sensing–Intuition. According to McCaulley et al. (1985), sensing types significantly outnumber intuitives in the general American population by almost three to one. As with the Extraversion–Introversion dimension, sensing types and intuitive types are found in roughly even numbers among high-schoolteachers (Hoffman & Betkouski, 1981). However, the percentage of sensing types drops considerably for both teachers and students as one goes up the academic ladder. In samples of college students, intuitives outnumber sensing types, except when the samples are of "returning students" or adult learners. Even at their best, sensing types tend to put into practice what they have learned in high school before going on to college. Studies tend to show that a higher percentage of dropouts are sensing types, especially those who also prefer perceiving (Myers, 1964), but Myers (1980) has suggested that their difficulties are not so much related to innate academic ability as to how they are taught. In general, intuitives seem to perform better than sensing types in traditional academic settings, as indicated by the predominance of intuitive types found in samples of honors students, national merit finalists and Rhodes scholars (McCaulley, 1974). Judging from the CCCC sample, about 90% of college composition teachers appear to prefer intuition; the few who prefer sensing tend also to prefer introversion, thinking, and judging.

Thinking–Feeling. This is the one dimension of the MBTI that has consistently shown male–female differences, with 60% of the males reporting a preference for thinking and 65% of females reporting a preference for feeling (McCaulley et al., 1985). Among public schoolteachers, there are more feeling types, in part because a larger percentage of these teachers are females but also because feeling types are naturally drawn to fields that emphasize human service (Lawrence, 1982). One's preference on this dimension seems to have little effect on academic performance, but one's clarity of preference does. McCaulley (unpublished) found that high school students with a clear and unambivalent preference, whether for thinking or feeling, had higher GPAs. Almost 70% of the college composition teachers in the CCCC sample preferred thinking, even though 58% of the sample was female.

Judging–Perceiving. Between 55% and 60% of most estimates of the general American population tend to prefer judging over perceiving (McCaulley et al., 1985). Public schoolteachers and especially school administrators tend to prefer judging, a planful orientation suited to much of education (Lawrence, 1982). For students, the slight preference toward judging remains relatively constant through all levels of formal education, but GPAs in subjects where productivity is important are found to be higher among judging types (McCaulley & Natter, 1974).

Table 1. Composition Teachers: Preconference Workshop Participants at Conference on College Composition and Communication, 1983 and 1984 (Total = 39)

SENSING TYPES with THINKING	SENSING TYPES with FEELING	INTUITIVE TYPES with FEELING	INTUITIVE TYPES with THINKING	
ISTJ $n = 4$ % = 10% XXXXXXXXXX	ISFJ $n = 0$ % = 0%	INFJ $n = 3$ % = 8% XXXXXXXX	INTJ $n = 10$ % = 26% XXXXXXXXXX XXXXXXXXXX XXXXXX	JUDGING / INTROVERTS
ISTP $n = 0$ % = 0%	ISFP $n = 0$ % = 0%	INFP $n = 5$ % = 13% XXXXXXXXXX XXX	INTP $n = 3$ % = 8% XXXXXXXX	PERCEPTIVE / INTROVERTS
ESTP $n = 0$ % = 0%	ESFP $n = 0$ % = 0%	ENFP $n = 3$ % = 8% XXXXXXXX	ENTP $n = 3$ % = 8% XXXXXXXX	PERCEPTIVE / EXTRAVERTS
ESTJ $n = 0$ % = 0%	ESFJ $n = 0$ % = 0%	ENFJ $n = 1$ % = 2% XX	ENTJ $n = 7$ % = 18% XXXXXXXXXX XXXXXXXX	JUDGING / EXTRAVERTS

X = 1%.

E	= 14	(36%)
I	= 25	(64%)
S	= 4	(10%)
N	= 35	(90%)
T	= 27	(69%)
F	= 12	(31%)
J	= 25	(64%)
P	= 14	(36%)

Table 2. High School English Teachers (Total = 179)

SENSING TYPES with THINKING	SENSING TYPES with FEELING	INTUITIVE TYPES with FEELING	INTUITIVE TYPES with THINKING	
ISTJ *n* = 14 % = 8% XXXXXXXX	ISFJ *n* = 17 % = 10% XXXXXXXXXX	INFJ *n* = 17 % = 10% XXXXXXXXXX	INTJ *n* = 9 % = 6% XXXXXX	INTROVERTS JUDGING
ISTP *n* = 3 % = 2% XX	ISFP *n* = 2 % = 1% X	INFP *n* = 18 % = 11% XXXXXXXXXX X	INTP *n* = 14 % = 8% XXXXXXXX	INTROVERTS PERCEPTIVE
ESTP *n* = 0 % = 0%	ESFP *n* = 2 % = 1% X	ENFP *n* = 22 % = 12% XXXXXXXXXX XX	ENTP *n* = 5 % = 3% XXX	EXTRAVERTS PERCEPTIVE
ESTJ *n* = 9 % = 6% XXXXXX	ESFJ *n* = 12 % = 7% XXXXXXX	ENFJ *n* = 21 % = 12% XXXXXXXXXX XX	ENTJ *n* = 14 % = 8% XXXXXXXX	EXTRAVERTS JUDGING

E =	85	(47%)
I =	94	(53%)
S =	59	(33%)
N =	120	(67%)
T =	68	(40%)
F =	111	(60%)
J =	113	(63%)
P =	66	(37%)

X = 1%.
Source: Myers and McCaulley (1985)

Table 3. Writers and Journalists (Total = 530)

	SENSING TYPES with THINKING	SENSING TYPES with FEELING	INTUITIVE TYPES with FEELING	INTUITIVE TYPES with THINKING
INTROVERTS — JUDGING	ISTJ $n = 23$ % = 4% XXXX	ISFJ $n = 21$ % = 4% XXXX	INFJ $n = 23$ % = 4% XXXX	INTJ $n = 44$ % = 8% XXXXXXXX
INTROVERTS — PERCEPTIVE	ISTP $n = 7$ % = 1% X	ISFP $n = 12$ % = 2% XX	INFP $n = 72$ % = 14% XXXXXXXXXX XXXX	INTP $n = 47$ % = 9% XXXXXXXXX
EXTRAVERTS — PERCEPTIVE	ESTP $n = 13$ % = 3% XXX	ESFP $n = 19$ % = 4% XXXX	ENFP $n = 92$ % = 17% XXXXXXXXXX XXXXXXX	ENTP $n = 39$ % = 7% XXXXXXX
EXTRAVERTS — JUDGING	ESTJ $n = 26$ % = 5% XXXXX	ESFJ $n = 18$ % = 3% XXX	ENFJ $n = 47$ % = 9% XXXXXXXXX	ENTJ $n = 27$ % = 5% XXXXX

E	= 281	(53%)
I	= 249	(47%)
S	= 139	(26%)
N	= 391	(74%)
T	= 226	(43%)
F	= 304	(57%)
J	= 229	(43%)
P	= 301	(57%)

X = 1%.
Source: Myers and McCaulley (1985)

APPENDIX 3

Handouts on Personality and Writing

EXTRAVERSION AND WRITING

Process: Extraverts generate ideas best by talking about the topic, interviewing people, or actively experiencing the topic. They tend to leap into writing with little planning, using trial and error. Free writing is a good method of developing ideas (especially if N), for extraverts will think better when writing quickly, impulsively, and uncritically. They tend to develop more ideas while writing than introverts. When writing in class, their essays may reflect confusion in the early paragraphs and clarity in the latter paragraphs. They usually pause when blocked (especially if J), and the blocks are best overcome by activity (such as writing about having nothing to write about). They may even "write" better by speaking their first drafts into a tape recorder. If they perform traditional prewriting strategies (such as outlining), they can often do so more easily *after* writing a first draft as a means of clarifying rather than generating ideas. Discussing drafts with others helps them both to realize the need for revision and to understand what needs to be revised. Some (especially if J) may not revise unless they receive spoken feedback. Their first drafts tend to need editing out of unrelated material. Those ideas that remain can be written about in greater depth.

Strengths: Extraverts tend to generate more ideas (if N) or facts (if S) than introverts and will generate them faster. They tend to excel at writing about experience.

Weaknesses: They may write fragmentally (touching on too many ideas) or superficially. They may lack awareness of the audience if that audience is not a part of their active outer experience.

Blocks: Extraverts may become blocked if they are often unable to develop an inner dialogue with themselves. The block can be overcome by carrying on an outer dialogue (discussing the topic with someone) or by simulating an outer dialogue (pretending to give a speech, or simulating a debate). They may also become blocked as a result of having generated shallow ideas or too many ideas (especially if also N and P). Sometimes they may generate ideas so quickly that they fail to realize they have good ideas (especially if S); they may need to tell their ideas to someone who can help them isolate and identify important ideas. Extraverts will also benefit from using their introversion (by planning an outline or getting away from a first draft to contemplate revisions); they may be more willing to use their introversion when isolated from possible distractions or in a comfortable position (in a bed or hot bath). Some extraverts find it easier to think through a topic when involved in a routine task, such as washing dishes.

INTROVERSION AND WRITING

Process: The introvert's basic writing process follows the prewriting–writing–rewriting pattern. Introverts plan before writing and want most of their ideas clarified before writing. They make outlines (especially if T), brainstorm (if N), or perform prewriting exercises. They tend not to generate ideas during class discussions but rather after the class discussion. When receiving oral feedback, they may become confused as they realize the flaws in their writing plans. The confusion will more likely be resolved after they have been allowed to think about the problem in isolation. Since they need time and solitude for concentration, they are at a disadvantage when required to write in class (unless they have anticipated the topic and thought about it in advance). When they begin to write, they stop frequently to anticipate the direction of the essay. They may become dissatisfied with a first sentence or a transition not because it is poorly written but because they are not yet sure where it is going. Despite frequent stops to anticipate the direction of the paper, their writing flows at a more even pace—once they finally begin—than extraverts because they are usually better at creating an inner dialogue. The paper also has usually been planned in advance. They spend more time than extraverts between drafts considering revisions. They may, as a result, revise more extensively. Throughout the writing process, they tend to write alone, asking for advice only from close friends or during private sessions with teachers. When revising, they may need to relate their ideas to experience.

Strengths: Introverts tend to excel at writing about ideas (especially if N). They tend to have the needed distance from their audience to gain a perspective for whom they are writing.

Weaknesses: They may (especially if T), present their ideas dryly unless they learn to connect them to experience. Since they tend to have less outer experience than extraverts, they may lack the information needed to analyze or connect with an audience.

Blocks: Introverts often become bored with writing because they plan so thoroughly that writing becomes a process of transcribing what has been written mentally. They may become blocked when they cannot see where the paper is going (especially if N) or when they want to have the entire paper planned in their minds before beginning to write (especially if P). The blocks can be overcome by writing temporarily in an extraverted way, by trial and error, or by writing to discover what they want to write about. Such activities work best if the introvert can see how they can free up their *inner* block. They may tend not to ask for advice when having trouble writing, which may unnecessarily prolong the block.

SENSING AND WRITING

Process: Sensing types tend to prefer explicit detailed and specific directions. When given general directions, they need to interpret them by making them more concrete. They generate ideas best from direct experience (if E) or concrete observation (if I). Their preferred prewriting exercises move from the collection of sensory data to the development of abstract concepts in a step-by-step process. Their first drafts tend to be a recording of facts that may not be related to a central theme or idea. They feel more comfortable when following a specific pattern that is what the teacher wants or is "tried and true," such as the five-paragraph theme. Their focus on isolated specifics often causes them to have a concrete coherence without a global cohesion of the topic. One word may cohere to the next until they drift off the topic. At the sentence level, they may lose sight of their point, writing sentences in which clauses are not logically connected. Even during a first draft, they closely attend to mechanics (grammar, spelling, handwriting, etc.). Similarly, they often tend to view revising as merely "correcting" or proofreading. They should be encouraged, when revising, to explain the implications of the data presented in the first draft by adding or rewriting topic sentences, thesis statements, summaries, and so forth.

Strengths: Sensing types excel at presenting factual information. As a result, they may excel at writing descriptions and technical reports.

Weaknesses: They may fail to present the idea behind the observation. They may fail to see the unique demands of each assignment and adjust to those demands.

Blocks: Sensing types may follow previously used patterns or "rules" too rigidly. When the pattern or "rule" does not meet the demands of the present assignment, they become blocked. They may also become blocked when they fail to interpret general directions. Unless given a general principle to separate important from unimportant details, they may become overwhelmed by large amounts of data. If too concerned about mechanics, sensing types can have the development of their thoughts interrupted.

INTUITION AND WRITING

Process: Intuitive types tend to write best when given general directions from which they can create their own goals. Developing a unique approach to the topic is an important part of their prewriting phase. They generate ideas quickly, almost unconsciously. At their best they tend also to write quickly, letting one idea trigger another and paying little attention to mechanics. They will tend to innovate organizational patterns. In the first drafts, they present generalities without examples. Their revisions may be more effective if they resolve the unnecessary complexities of their ideas, check their facts, and, as a *last* step, clean up the mechanics of spelling, punctuation, and the like.

Strengths: Intuitives tend to excel at presenting theories and concepts and at devising new and unusual approaches to writing.

Weaknesses: They tend to forget to include concrete examples and may not provide the reader with background information. They may also fail to follow directions closely.

Blocks: Intuitives sometimes become blocked through trying to make even a simple writing task (such as a memo) unique. As they generate ideas, they may become blocked by the escalating complexity of the topic (especially if P). In such cases, they need to get back to earth, to apply their ideas to concrete situations, which both tests and simplifies their abstractions.

THINKING AND WRITING

Process: Thinking types tend to select topics that can be written about with distance rather than self-involvement. They organize their ideas (if N) or data (if S) into systems. In their introductions, they often establish a point of view and then argue against it. They tend to make organizational decisions by following a structure (such as an outline). If the structure dictates the inclusion of material, it is included. If not, it is excluded. Unsurprisingly, their essays often read like an outline. While writing they tend to focus on the content rather than how the material is presented to the audience. They value feedback that is given with a clear rationale (such as, "It is important for you to provide more details so that your reader will better understand your ideas"). In revising, they may need to enliven their writing with some personal examples and qualify blunt statements.

Strengths: Thinking types tend to excel at writing logically, objectively, and analytically. Their essays are often well organized.

Weaknesses: They may regard their beliefs as being universally held (especially if E) and thus be abrasive or dogmatic. They may objectify ideas and examples to a point where they lack personal interest. As a result, readers may regard their writing as being cold.

Blocks: Thinking types may become blocked when not given a clear rationale and regard an assignment as an "academic exercise." They may also become blocked when they perceive that they are treated unfairly (such as with arbitrary grading practices). They may find it difficult to write on topics that draw upon feelings or personal experience. If they are unable to adopt or develop an organizational structure, they may find it difficult to make organizational decisions.

FEELING AND WRITING

Process: Feeling types prefer topics that they can care about; they often complain about topics that are "boring." Thus, deciding how a writing project is of value to them is an important part of their prewriting phase. While writing, they tend to draw upon personal experience (an inner experience if I and outer if E). Their introductions will often begin with a personal example. They rely less on structure than thinking types. They often begin with a sentence and then follow "the flow" (their own subjective thought process). They also make organizational decisions by anticipating the reader's reaction to their prose. If they feel that the reader needs additional information, they will include it, even when it violates a structure or outline. In general, they tend to focus more on how the message is delivered to the audience than on content. They write best when given personal encouragement and feedback that focuses on the possible reactions of the audience (such as, "How do you feel that your audience will react to this statement?") If overly criticized, they may wish to ignore revising or writing in general; when revising, they may need to clarify the content and improve their organization.

Strengths: Feeling types tend to excel at topics that draw upon feelings, and thus are good at making contact with the audience. They qualify their statements, but their writing will usually reflect a deep personal conviction. Their writing often contains personal examples and reflects a concern to make their writing interesting.

Weaknesses: Their writing may lack a clear organizational structure (especially E, S, or P) and be overly sentimental (especially if E).

Blocks: Feeling types may become blocked when trying to follow an outline or when too rigidly following an organizational pattern (especially if S). They find it difficult to write critically if they believe that the criticisms may hurt someone's feelings. They may also become blocked if their personal values are not involved. Often their concern to make their writing interesting will cause them to struggle to find the exact word or phrase, the precise opening sentence, that will capture the reader's attention.

JUDGING AND WRITING

Process: Judging types tend to limit their topics very quickly and set goals that are manageable. They devote time to setting process goals (how to get it done), which ideally include plans to stop at key intervals to analyze and revise objectives. Since they want to complete the first draft expediently, they may divide the paper in sections (especially if I and T) so that it can be written more easily and make organizational and stylistic decisions quickly. Their first drafts tend to be short with ideas stated emphatically and without qualification (especially if T). The organization may be clear, but the content may lack development. When revising, they need to re-evaluate decisions that may have been made hastily or arbitrarily, more thoroughly analyze their ideas, expand their writing to clarify or qualify, and improve transitions.

Strengths: Judging types tend to write quickly, meet deadlines and produce more writing.

Weaknesses: They may be overly emphatic, set goals that are unambitious (especially if S), and too rigidly adhere to their original plans.

Blocks: Judging types may begin writing before they have collected enough information or generated adequate ideas; if so, they may become blocked during a first draft because they do not have enough to write about. Since they tend to stick to their plans, they may force themselves to sit and stare at a blank sheet of paper for hours. They are better off delaying the writing to think more about the topic or more thoroughly research it. Since they tend not to revise goals and plans, they may become blocked when those goals or plans prove faulty. They may become blocked when a teacher forces them to write more broadly than they want to.

PERCEIVING AND WRITING

Process: Perceiving types tend to select broad topics and dive into research without limiting them. Topics will usually be limited only as the deadline approaches. They want to research or analyze the topic thoroughly before beginning to write and may feel that there is always one more book or article to read. They may have difficulty dividing the essay into sections, and thus may need a large block of time to devote to writing. When writing, they pause frequently to consider numerous alternatives (especially if N) and to ponder over organizational or stylistic decisions. Their first drafts tend to be long and thorough but also too inclusive. When revising, they may need to cut down the length of the paper or to refocus its direction.

Strengths: Perceiving types tend to investigate their topics thoroughly and present carefully considered ideas.

Weaknesses: They may write on topics that are too broad or may lose sight of their original goals while writing. As a result, their writing may lack a clear thesis. They may also only begin to write when an external deadline is approaching, which may leave them no time for revision.

Blocks: Perceiving types may become blocked if they fail to limit their topic adequately or limit it too late in the writing process. Their need to be thorough may cause blocks when they try to be too inclusive. Large amounts of material can be overwhelming (especially if S) or hard to organize (especially if F).

APPENDIX FOUR

Descriptions of the Sixteen Types*

ESTJ: EXTRAVERTED THINKING WITH SENSING

ESTJ people use their thinking to run as much of the world as may be theirs to run. They like to organize projects and then act to get things done. Reliance on thinking makes them logical, analytical, objectively critical, and not likely to be convinced by anything but reasoning. They tend to focus on the job, not the people behind the job.

They like to organize facts, situations, and operations related to a project, and make a systematic effort to reach their objectives on schedule. They have little patience with confusion or inefficiency, and can be tough when the situation calls for toughness.

They think conduct should be ruled by logic, and govern their own behavior accordingly. They live by a definite set of rules that embody their basic judgments about the world. Any change in their ways requires a deliberate change in their rules.

They are more interested in seeing present realities than future possibilities. This makes them matter-of-fact, practical, realistic, and concerned with the here-and-now. They use past experience to help them solve problems and want to be sure that ideas, plans, and decisions are based on solid fact.

They like jobs where the results of their work are immediate, visible, and tangible. They have a natural bent for business, industry, production, and construction. They enjoy administration, where they can set goals, make decisions, and give the necessary orders. Getting things done is their strong suit.

Like the other decisive types, ESTJs run the risk of deciding too quickly before they have fully examined the situation. They need to stop and listen to the other person's viewpoint, especially with people who are not in a position to talk back. This is seldom easy for them, but *if* they do not take time to understand, they may judge too quickly, without enough facts or enough regard for what other people think or feel.

ESTJs *may* need to work at taking feeling values into account. They

---

****Source:*** Isabel Briggs Myers, *Introduction to Type* (1987).

may rely so much on their logical approach that they overlook feeling values—what they care about and what other people care about. If feeling values are ignored too much, they may build up pressure and find expression in inappropriate ways. Although ESTJs are naturally good at seeing what is illogical and inconsistent, they may need to develop the art of appreciation. One positive way to exercise their feeling is to appreciate other people's merits and ideas. ESTJs who make it a rule to mention what they like, not merely what needs correcting, find the results worthwhile both in their work and in their private lives.

ENTJ: EXTRAVERTED THINKING WITH INTUITION

ENTJ people use their thinking to run as much of the world as may be theirs to run. They enjoy executive action and long-range planning. Reliance on thinking makes them logical, analytical, objectively critical, and not likely to be convinced by anything but reasoning. They tend to focus on the ideas, not the person behind the ideas.

They like to think ahead, organize plans, situations, and operations related to a project, and make a systematic effort to reach their objectives on schedule. They have little patience with confusion or inefficiency, and can be tough when the situation calls for toughness.

They think conduct should be ruled by logic, and govern their own behavior accordingly. They live by a definite set of rules that embody their basic judgments about the world. Any change in their ways requires a deliberate change in their rules.

They are mainly interested in seeing the possibilities beyond what is present, obvious, or known. Intuition heightens their intellectual interest, curiosity for new ideas, tolerance for theory, and taste for complex problems.

ENTJs are seldom content in jobs that make no demand upon their intuition. They are stimulated by problems and are often found in executive jobs where they can find and implement new solutions. Because of their interest in the big picture, they may overlook the importance of certain details. Since ENTJs tend to team up with like-minded intuitives who may also underestimate the realities of a situation, they usually need a person around with good common sense to bring up overlooked facts and take care of important details.

Like the other decisive types, ENTJs run the risk of deciding too quickly before they have fully examined the situation. They need to stop and listen to the other person's viewpoint, especially with people who are not in a position to talk back. This is seldom easy for them, but *if* they do not take time to understand, they may judge too quickly, without enough facts or enough regard for what other people think or feel.

ENTJs *may* need to work at taking feeling values into account. Relying so much on their logical approach, they may overlook feeling values—what they care about and what other people care about. If feeling values are ignored too much, they may build up pressure and find expression in inappropriate ways. Although ENTJs are naturally good at seeing what is illogical and inconsistent, they may need to develop the art of appreciation. One positive way to exercise their feeling is through appreciation of other people's merits and ideas. ENTJs who learn to make it a rule to mention what they like, not merely what needs correcting, find the results worthwhile both in their work and in their private lives.

ISTP: INTROVERTED THINKING WITH SENSING

People with ISTP preferences use their thinking to look for the principles underlying the sensory information that comes into awareness. As a result, they are logical, analytical, and objectively critical. They are not likely to be convinced by anything but reasoning based on solid facts.

While they like to organize facts and data, they prefer not to organize situations or people unless they must for the sake of their work. They can be intensely but quietly curious. Socially they may be rather shy except with their best friends. They sometimes become so absorbed with one of their interests that they can ignore or lose track of external circumstances.

ISTPs are somewhat quiet and reserved, although they can be quite talkative on a subject where they can apply their great storehouse of information. In everyday activities they are adaptable, except when one of their ruling principles is violated, at which point they stop adapting. They are good with their hands, and like sports and the outdoors, or anything that provides a wealth of information for their senses.

If ISTPs have developed their powers of observing the world around them, they will have a firm grasp on the realities of any situation, and show a great capacity for the important and unique facts of a situation. They are interested in how and why things work and are likely to be good at applied science, mechanics, or engineering. ISTPs who do not have technical or mechanical interests often use their talents to bring order out of unorganized facts. This ability can find expression in law, economics, marketing, sales, securities, or statistics.

ISTPs *may* rely so much on the logical approach of thinking that they overlook what other people care about and what they themselves care about. They may decide that something is not important, just because it isn't logical to care about it. If ISTPs always let their thinking suppress their feeling values, their feeling may build up pressure and find expression in inappropriate ways. Although good at analyzing what is wrong, ISTPs sometimes find it hard to express appreciation. But if they try, they will find it helpful on the job as well as in personal relationships.

ISTP people are in some danger of putting off decisions or of failing to follow through. One of their outstanding traits is economy of effort. This trait is an asset if they judge accurately how much effort is needed; then they do what the situation requires without fuss or lost motion. *If* they cannot judge accurately, or if they just don't bother, then nothing of importance gets done.

INTP: INTROVERTED THINKING WITH INTUITION

People with INTP preferences use their thinking to find the principles underlying whatever ideas come into their awareness. They rely on thinking to develop these principles and to anticipate consequences. As a result, they are logical, analytical, and objectively critical. They are likely to focus more on the ideas than the person behind the ideas.

They organize ideas and knowledge rather than situations or people, unless they must for the sake of their work. In the field of ideas they are intensely curious. Socially, they tend to have a small circle of close friends, and like being with others who enjoy discussing ideas. They can become so absorbed with an idea that they can ignore or lose track of external circumstances.

INTPs are somewhat quiet and reserved, although they can be quite talkative on a subject to which they have given a lot of thought. They are quite adaptable so long as their ruling principles are not violated, at which point they stop adapting. Their main interest lies in seeing possibilities beyond what is present, obvious, or known. They are quick to understand and their intuition heightens their insight, ingenuity and intellectual curiosity.

Depending on their interests, INTPs are good at pure science, research, mathematics, or engineering; they may become scholars, teachers, or abstract thinkers in fields such as economics, philosophy, or psychology. They are more interested in the challenge of reaching solutions to problems than of seeing the solutions put to practical use.

Unless INTPs develop their perception, they are in danger of gaining too little knowledge and experience of the world. Then their thinking is done in a vacuum and nothing will come of their ideas. Lack of contact with the external world may also lead to problems in making themselves understood. They want to state the exact truth, but often make it so complicated that not everyone can follow them. If they can learn to simplify their arguments, their ideas will be more widely understood and accepted.

INTPs *may* rely so much on logical thinking that they overlook what other people care about and what they themselves care about. They may decide that something is not important, just because it isn't logical to care about it. *If* INTPs always let their logic suppress their feeling values, their feeling may build up pressure until it is expressed in inappropriate ways.

Although they excel at analyzing what is wrong with an idea, it is harder for INTPs to express appreciation. But if they try, they will find it helpful on the job as well as in personal relationships.

ESFJ: EXTRAVERTED FEELING WITH SENSING

People with ESFJ preferences radiate sympathy and fellowship. They concern themselves chiefly with the people around them and place a high value on harmonious human contacts. They are friendly, tactful, and sympathetic. They are persevering, conscientious, orderly even in small matters, and inclined to expect others to be the same. They are particularly warmed by approval and sensitive to indifference. Much of their pleasure and satisfaction comes from the warmth of feeling of people around them. ESFJs tend to concentrate on the admirable qualities of other people and are loyal to respected persons, institutions, or causes, sometimes to the point of idealizing whatever they admire.

They have the gift of finding value in other people's opinions. Even when these opinions are in conflict, they have faith that harmony can somehow be achieved and they often manage to bring it about. To achieve harmony, they are ready to agree with others' opinions within reasonable limits. They need to be careful, however, that they don't concentrate so much on the viewpoints of others that they lose sight of their own.

They are mainly interested in the realities perceived by their five senses, so they become practical, realistic, and down-to-earth. They take great interest in the unique differences in each experience. ESFJs appreciate and enjoy their possessions. They enjoy variety but can adapt well to routine.

ESFJs are at their best in jobs that deal with people and in situations where cooperation can be brought about through good will. They are found in jobs such as teaching, preaching, and selling. Their compassion and awareness of physical conditions often attracts them to health professions where they can provide warmth, comfort, and patient caring. They are less likely to be happy in work demanding mastery of abstract ideas or impersonal analysis. They think best when talking with people, and enjoy communicating. They have to make a special effort to be brief and businesslike and not let sociability slow them down on the job.

They like to base their plans and decisions upon known facts and on their personal values. While liking to have matters decided or settled, they do not necessarily want to make all the decisions themselves. They run some risk of jumping to conclusions before they understand a situation. *If* they have not taken time to gain first-hand knowledge about a person or situation, their actions may not have the helpful results they intended. For example, ESFJs beginning a new project or job may do things they assume should be done, instead of taking the time to find out what is really wanted or needed. They have many definite "shoulds" and "should nots," and may express these freely.

ESFJs find it especially hard to admit the truth about problems with people or things they care about. *If* they fail to face disagreeable facts, or refuse to look at criticism that hurts, they will try to ignore their problems instead of searching for solutions.

ENFJ: EXTRAVERTED FEELING WITH INTUITION

People with ENFJ preferences radiate sympathy and fellowship. They concern themselves chiefly with the people around them and place a high value on harmonious human contacts. They are friendly, tactful, and sympathetic. They are persevering, conscientious, and orderly even in small matters, and inclined to expect others to be the same. ENFJs are particularly warmed by approval and are sensitive to indifference. Much of their pleasure and satisfaction comes from the warmth of feeling of people around them. ENFJs tend to concentrate on the admirable qualities of other people and are loyal to respected persons, institutions, or causes, sometimes to the point of idealizing whatever they admire.

They have the gift of being able to see value in other people's opinions. Even when opinions are in conflict, they have faith that harmony can somehow be achieved, and they often manage to bring it about. To bring harmony, they are ready to agree with others' opinions within reasonable limits. They need to be careful, however, not to concentrate so much on the viewpoints of others that they lose sight of their own.

They are mainly interested in seeing the possibilities beyond what is present, obvious, or known. Intuition heightens their insight, vision, and curiosity for new ideas. They tend to be interested in books and are moderately tolerant of theory. They are likely to have a gift of expression, but may use it in speaking to audiences rather than in writing. They think best when talking with people.

They are at their best in jobs that deal with people, and in situations that require building cooperation. ENFJs are found in jobs such as teaching, preaching, counseling, and selling. They may be less happy in work demanding factual accuracy, such as accounting, unless they can find a personal meaning in their work. They have to make a special effort to be brief and businesslike and not let sociability slow them down on the job.

They base their decisions on their personal values. While they like to have matters decided or settled, they do not necessarily want to make all the decisions themselves. ENFJs run some risk of jumping to conclusions before they understand a situation. *If* they have not taken time to gain first-hand knowledge about a person or situation, their actions may not have the helpful results they intended. For example, ENFJs beginning a new project or job may do things they assume should be done, instead of taking the time to find out what is really wanted or needed. They have many definite "shoulds" and "should nots," and may express them freely.

ENFJs find it especially hard to admit the truth about problems with people or things they care about. *If* they fail to face disagreeable facts, or refuse to look at criticism that hurts, they will ignore their problems instead of searching for solutions.

ISFP: INTROVERTED FEELING WITH SENSING

People with ISFP preferences have a great deal of warmth, but may not show it until they know a person well. They keep their warm side inside, like a fur-lined coat. When they care, they care deeply, but are more likely to show their feeling by deeds rather than words. They are very faithful to duties and obligations related to things or people they care about.

They take a very personal approach to life, judging everything by their inner ideals and personal values. They stick to their values with passionate conviction, but can be influenced by someone they care deeply about. Although their inner loyalties and ideals govern their lives, ISFPs find these hard to talk about. Their deepest feelings are seldom expressed; their inner tenderness is masked by a quiet reserve.

In everyday activities they are tolerant, open-minded, flexible, and adaptable. If one of their inner loyalties is threatened though, they will not give an inch. They usually enjoy the present moment, and do not like to spoil it by rushing to get things done. They have little wish to impress or dominate. The people they prize the most are those who take the time to understand their values and the goals they are working toward.

They are interested mainly in the realities brought to them by their senses, both inner and outer. They are apt to enjoy fields where taste, discrimination, and a sense of beauty and proportion are important. Many ISFPs have a special love of nature and a sympathy with animals. They often excel in craftsmanship, and the work of their hands is usually more eloquent than their words.

They are twice as good when working at a job they believe in, since their feeling adds energy to their efforts. They see the needs of the moment and try to meet them. They want their work to contribute to something that matters to them—human understanding, happiness, or health. They want to have a purpose beyond their paycheck, no matter how big the check. They are perfectionists whenever they care deeply about something, and are particularly suited for work that requires both devotion and a large measure of adaptability.

The problem for *some* ISFPs is that they may feel such a contrast between their inner ideals and their actual accomplishments that they burden themselves with a sense of inadequacy. This can be true even when they are being as effective as others. They take for granted anything they do well and are the most modest of all the types, tending to underrate and understate themselves.

It is important for them to find practical ways to express their ideals; otherwise they will keep dreaming of the impossible and accomplish very little. *If* they find no actions to express their ideals, they can become too sensitive and vulnerable, with dwindling confidence in life and in themselves. Actually, they have much to give and need only to find the spot where they are needed.

INFP: INTROVERTED FEELING WITH INTUITION

People with INFP preferences have a great deal of warmth, but may not show it until they know a person well. They keep their warm side inside, like a fur-lined coat. They are very faithful to duties and obligations related to ideas or people they care about. They take a very personal approach to life, judging everything by their inner ideals and personal values.

They stick to their ideals with passionate conviction. Although their inner loyalties and ideals govern their lives, they find these hard to talk about. Their deepest feelings are seldom expressed; their inner tenderness is masked by a quiet reserve.

In everyday matters they are tolerant, open-minded, understanding, flexible, and adaptable. But if their inner loyalties are threatened, they will not give an inch. Except for their work's sake, INFPs have little wish to impress or dominate. The people they prize the most are those who take the time to understand their values and the goals they are working toward.

Their main interest lies in seeing the possibilities beyond what is present, obvious, or known. They are twice as good when working at a job they believe in, since their feeling puts added energy behind their efforts. They want their work to contribute to something that matters to them—human understanding, happiness, or health. They want to have a purpose beyond their paycheck, no matter how big the check. They are perfectionists whenever they care deeply about something.

INFPs are curious about new ideas and tend to have insight and long-range vision. Many are interested in books and language and are likely to have a gift of expression; with talent they may be excellent writers. They can be ingenious and persuasive on the subject of their enthusiasms, which are quiet but deep-rooted. They are often attracted to counseling, teaching, literature, art, science, or psychology.

The problem for *some* INFPs is that they may feel such a contrast between their ideals and their actual accomplishments that they burden themselves with a sense of inadequacy. This can happen even when, objectively, they are being as effective as others. It is important for them to use their intuition to find ways to express their ideals; otherwise they will keep dreaming of the impossible and accomplish very little. If they find no channel for expressing their ideals, INFPs may become overly sensitive and vulnerable, with dwindling confidence in life and in themselves.

ESFP: EXTRAVERTED SENSING WITH FEELING

ESFP people are friendly, adaptable realists. They rely on what they can see, hear, and know first-hand. They good-naturedly accept and use the facts around them, whatever these are. They look for a satisfying solution instead of trying to impose any "should" or "must" of their own. They are sure that a solution will turn up once they have grasped all of the facts.

They solve problems by being adaptable, and often can get others to adapt, too. People generally like them well enough to consider any compromise they suggest. They are unprejudiced, open-minded, and tolerant of most everyone—including themselves. They take things as they are and thus may be very good at easing a tense situation and pulling conflicting factions together.

With their focus on the current situation and realistic acceptance of what exists, they can be gifted problem solvers. Because they are not necessarily bound by a need to follow standard procedures or preferred methods, they are often able to see ways of achieving a goal by "using" the existing rules, systems, or circumstances in new ways, rather than allowing them to be roadblocks.

They are actively curious about people, activities, food, objects, scenery, or anything new presented to their senses. Their expert abilities in using their senses may show in: (a) a continuous ability to see the need of the moment and turn easily to meet it, (b) the skillful handling of people and conflicts, (c) the ability to absorb, apply, and remember great numbers of facts, or (d) an artistic taste and judgment.

They make their decisions by using the personal values of feeling rather than the logical analysis of thinking. Their feeling makes them tactful, sympathetic, interested in people, and especially good at handling human contacts. They may be too easy in matters of discipline. They learn far more from first-hand experience than from books, and do better in actual situations than on written tests. Abstract ideas and theories are not likely to be trusted by ESFPs until they have been tested in experience. They may have to work harder than other types to achieve in school, but can do so when they see the relevance.

ESFPs do best in careers needing realism, action, and adaptability. Examples are health services, sales, design, transportation, entertainment, secretarial or office work, food services, supervising work groups, machine operation, and many kinds of troubleshooting.

ESFPs are strong in the art of living. They get a lot of fun out of life, which makes them good company. They enjoy their material possessions and take the time to acquire and care for them. They find much enjoyment in good food, clothes, music, and art. They enjoy physical exercise and sports, and usually are good at these.

How effective they are depends on how much judgment they acquire. They may need to develop their feeling so that they can use their values to provide standards for their behavior, and direction and purpose in their lives. *If* their judgment is not developed enough to give them any character or stick-to-it-iveness, they are in danger of adapting mainly to their own love of a good time.

ESTP: EXTRAVERTED SENSING WITH THINKING

People with ESTP preferences are friendly, adaptable realists. They rely on what they see, hear and know first-hand. They good-naturedly accept and use the facts around them, whatever these are. They look for a satisfying solution instead of trying to impose any "should" or "must" of their own. They are sure a satisfying solution will turn up once they have grasped all the facts.

They solve problems by being adaptable, and often can get others to adapt, too. People generally like them well enough to consider any compromise they suggest. They are unprejudiced, open-minded, and tolerant of most everyone—including themselves. They take things as they are and thus may be very good at easing a tense situation and pulling conflicting factions together.

They are actively curious about objectives, scenery, activities, food, people, or anything new presented to their senses. Their expert abilities in using their senses may show in: (a) a continuous ability to see the need of the moment and turn easily to meet it, (b) the ability to absorb, apply, and remember great numbers of facts, (c) an artistic taste and judgment, or (d) the handling of tools and materials.

With their focus on the current situation and realistic acceptance of what exists, they can be gifted problem solvers. Because they are not necessarily bound by a need to follow standard procedures or preferred methods, they are often able to see ways of achieving a goal by "using" the existing rules, systems, or circumstances in new ways, rather than allowing them to be roadblocks.

They make their decisions by using the logical analysis of thinking rather than the more personal values of feeling. Their thinking enables them to crack down when the situation calls for toughness, and also helps them grasp underlying principles. They learn more from first-hand experience than from study or reading, and are more effective in actual situations than on written tests. Abstract ideas and theories are not likely to be trusted by ESTPs until they have been tested in experience. They may have to work harder than other types to achieve in school, but can do so when they see the relevance.

ESTPs do best in careers needing realism, action, and adaptability. Examples are engineering, police work, credit investigation, marketing, health technologies, construction, production, recreation, food services, and many kinds of troubleshooting.

ESTPs are strong in the art of living. They get a lot of fun out of life, which makes them good company. They enjoy their material possessions and take the time to acquire them. They find much enjoyment in good food, clothes, music, and art. They enjoy physical exercise and sports, and usually are good at these.

How effective they are depends on how much judgment they acquire. They may need to develop their feeling so that they can use their values to provide standards for their behavior, and direction and purpose in their lives. *If* their judgment is not developed enough to give them any character or stick-to-it-iveness, they are in danger of adapting mainly to their own love of a good time.

ISTJ: INTROVERTED SENSING WITH THINKING

People with ISTJ preferences are extremely dependable and have a complete, realistic, and practical respect for the facts. They absorb, remember, and use any number of facts and are careful about their accuracy. When they see that something needs to be done, they accept the responsibility, often beyond the call of duty. They like everything clearly stated.

Their private reactions, which seldom show in their faces, are often vivid and intense. Even when dealing with a crisis they look calm and composed. Not until you know them very well do you discover that behind their outer calm they are viewing the situation from an intensely individual angle. When ISTJs are "on duty" and dealing with the world, however, their behavior is sound and sensible.

ISTJs are thorough, painstaking, systematic, hard-working, and careful with particulars and procedures. Their perseverance tends to stabilize everything with which they are connected. They do not enter into things impulsively, but once committed, they are very hard to distract or discourage.

ISTJs often choose careers where their talents for organization and accuracy are rewarded. Examples are accounting, civil engineering, law, production, construction, health careers, and office work. They often move into supervisory and management roles.

If they are in charge of something, their practical judgment and valuing of procedures makes them consistent and conservative, assembling the necessary facts to support their evaluations and decisions. They look for solutions to present problems in the successes of the past. With time they become masters of even the smallest elements of their work, but don't give themselves any special credit for this knowledge.

They *may* encounter problems if they expect everyone to be as logical and analytical as they are. They then run the danger of inappropriately passing judgment on others or overriding less forceful people. A useful rule is for them to use their thinking to make decisions about inanimate objects or their own behavior, and to use their perception to understand others. If they use their senses to see what really matters to others, so that it becomes a fact to be respected, they may go to generous lengths to help.

Another problem may arise *if* the ISTJ's thinking remains undeveloped. They may retreat, becoming absorbed with their inner reactions to sense-impressions, with nothing of value being produced. They may also tend to be somewhat suspicious of imagination and intuition, and not take it seriously enough.

ISFJ: INTROVERTED SENSING WITH FEELING

People with ISFJ preferences are extremely dependable and devotedly accept responsibilities beyond the call of duty. They have a complete, realistic, and practical respect for the facts. When they see from the facts that something needs to be done, they pause to think about it. If they decide that action will be helpful, they accept the responsibility. They can remember and use any number of facts, but want them all accurate. They like everything clearly stated.

Their private reactions are often vivid and intense, and sometimes quite unpredictable to others. These private reactions seldom show in their faces, and even when dealing with a crisis, they can look calm and composed. Not until you know them very well do you discover that behind their outer calm they are looking at things from an intensely individual angle, often a delightfully humorous one. When ISFJs are "on duty" and dealing with the world, however, their behavior is sound and sensible.

ISFJs are thorough, painstaking, hard-working, and patient with particulars and procedures. They can and will do the "little" things that need to be done to carry a project through to completion. Their perseverance tends to stabilize everything with which they are connected. They do not enter into things impulsively, but once in, they are very hard to distract or discourage. They do not quit unless experience convinces them they are wrong.

ISFJs often choose careers where they can combine their careful observation and their caring for people, as in the health professions. Other fields attractive to ISFJs are teaching, office work, and occupations that provide services or personal care. ISFJs show their feeling preference in their contacts with the world. They are kind, sympathetic, tactful, and genuinely concerned, traits that make them very supportive to persons in need.

Because of their concern for accuracy and organization, ISFJs often move into supervisory roles. If they are in charge of something, their practical judgment and appreciation of what works make them conservative and consistent. They take care to collect the facts necessary to support their evaluations and decisions. As they gain experience, they compare the present problem to past situations.

For an ISFJ, problems may arise if their judgment is not developed. *If* their feeling preference remains undeveloped, they will not be effective in dealing with the world. They may instead retreat, becoming silently absorbed in their inner reactions to sense-impressions. Then nothing of value is likely to come out. Another potential problem is that they tend to be somewhat suspicious of imagination and intuition and not take it seriously enough.

ENTP: EXTRAVERTED INTUITION WITH THINKING

People with ENTP preferences are ingenious innovators who always see new possibilities and new ways of doing things. They have a lot of imagination and initiative for starting projects and a lot of impulsive energy for carrying them out. They are sure of the worth of their inspirations and tireless with the problems involved. They are stimulated by difficulties and most ingenious in solving them. They enjoy feeling competent in a variety of areas and value this in others as well.

They are extremely perceptive about the attitudes of other people, and can use this knowledge to win support for their projects. They aim to understand rather than to judge people.

Their energy comes from a succession of new interests and their world is full of possible projects. They may be interested in so many different things that they have difficulty focusing. Their thinking can help them select projects by supplying some analysis and constructive criticism of their inspirations, and thus add depth to the insights supplied by their intuition. Their use of thinking also makes ENTPs rather objective in their approach to their current project and to the people in their lives.

ENTPs are not likely to stay in any occupation that does not provide many new challenges. With talent, they can be inventors, scientists, journalists, troubleshooters, marketers, promoters, computer analysts, or almost anything that it interests them to be.

A difficulty for people with ENTP preferences is that they hate uninspired routine and find it remarkably hard to apply themselves to the sometimes necessary detail unconnected with any major interest. Worse yet, they may get bored with their own projects as soon as the major problems have been solved or the initial challenge has been met. They need to learn to follow through, but are happiest and most effective in jobs that permit one project after another, with somebody else taking over as soon as the situation is well in hand.

Because ENTPs are always being drawn to the exciting challenges of new possibilities, it is essential that they develop their judgment. *If* their judgment is underdeveloped, they may commit themselves to ill-chosen projects, fail to finish anything, and squander their inspirations on incompleted tasks.

ENFP: EXTRAVERTED INTUITION WITH FEELING

People with ENFP preferences are enthusiastic innovators, always seeing new possibilities and new ways of doing things. They have a lot of imagination and initiative for starting projects, and a lot of impulsive energy for carrying them out. They are stimulated by difficulties and are most ingenious in solving them. ENFPs can get so interested in their newest project that they have time for little else. Their energy comes from a succession of new enthusiasms and their world is full of possible projects. Their enthusiasm gets other people interested too.

They see so many possible projects that they sometimes have difficulty picking those with the greatest potential. Their feeling can be useful at this point to help select projects by weighing the values of each. Their feeling judgment can also add depth to the insights supplied by their intuition.

The ENFP's feeling preference shows in a concern for people. They are skillful in handling people and often have remarkable insight into the possibilities and development of others. They are extremely perceptive about the attitudes of others, aiming to understand rather than judge people. They are much drawn to counseling, and can be inspired and inspiring teachers, particularly where they have freedom to innovate. With talent, they can succeed in almost any field that captures their interest—art, journalism, science, advertising, sales, the ministry, or writing, for example.

A difficulty for ENFPs is that they hate uninspired routine and find it remarkably hard to apply themselves to the sometimes necessary detail unconnected with any major interest. Worse yet, they may get bored with their own projects as soon as the main problems have been solved or the initial challenge has been met. They may need to learn to follow through and finish what they have begun, but are happiest and most effective in jobs that permit one project after another, with somebody else taking over as soon as the situation is well in hand.

Because ENFPs are always being drawn to the exciting challenges of new possibilities, it is essential that they develop their feeling judgment. *If* their judgment is undeveloped, they may commit themselves to ill-chosen projects, fail to finish anything, and squander their inspirations by not completing their tasks.

INTJ: INTROVERTED INTUITION WITH THINKING

People with INTJ preferences are relentless innovators in thought as well as action. They trust their intuitive insights into the true relationships and meanings of things, regardless of established authority or popularly accepted beliefs. Their faith in their inner vision can move mountains. Problems only stimulate them—the impossible takes a little longer, but not much. They are the most independent of all the types, sometimes to the point of being stubborn. They place a high value on competence—their own and others'.

Being sure of the worth of their inspirations, INTJs want to see them worked out in practice, applied and accepted by the rest of the world; they are willing to spend any time and effort to that end. They have determination, perseverance, and will drive others almost as hard as they drive themselves. Although their preference is for intuition, they can, when necessary, focus on the details of a project to realize their vision.

INTJs often value and use confidently their intuitive insights in fields such as science, engineering, invention, politics, or philosophy. The boldness of their intuition may be of immense value in any field, and should not be smothered in a routine job.

Some problems *may* arise from the INTJ's single-minded concentration on goals. They may see the end so clearly that they fail to look for other things which might conflict with the goal. Therefore they need to actively seek the viewpoints of others.

INTJs may neglect their feeling values to the point of ignoring other people's values and feelings. If they do, they may be surprised by the bitterness of their opposition. An INTJ's own feeling values have to be reckoned with also, for if too much suppressed, they may build up pressure and find expression in inappropriate ways. Their feeling needs to be used constructively, such as through appreciation of other people. Given their talent for analysis, appreciation may be hard for INTJs, but they will find it helpful on the job as well as in personal relationships.

To be effective, INTJs must develop their thinking to supply needed judgment. *If* their judgment is undeveloped, they will be unable to criticize their own inner vision, and will not listen to the opinions of others. They will therefore be unable to shape their inspirations into effective action.

INFJ: INTROVERTED INTUITION WITH FEELING

People with INFJ preferences are great innovators in the field of ideas. They trust their intuitive insights into the true relationships and meanings of things, regardless of established authority or popularly accepted beliefs. Problems only stimulate them—the impossible takes a little longer, but not much.

They are independent and individualistic, being governed by inspirations that come through intuition. These inspirations seem so valid and important that they sometimes have trouble understanding why everyone does not accept them. Their inner independence is often not conspicuous because INFJs value harmony and fellowship; they work to persuade others to approve of and cooperate with their purposes. They can be great leaders when they devote themselves to carrying out a sound inspiration, attracting followers by their enthusiasm and faith. They lead by winning (rather than demanding) acceptance of their ideas.

They are most content in work that satisfies both their intuition and their feeling. The possibilities that interest them most concern people. Teaching particularly appeals to them, whether in higher education, or through the arts or the ministry. Their intuition provides insight into the deeper meanings of the subject and they take great satisfaction in aiding the development of individual students.

When their interests lie in technical fields, INFJs may be outstanding in science, or research and development. Intuition suggests new approaches to problems and feeling generates enthusiasm that sparks their energies. Intuition powered by feeling may be of immense value in any field if not smothered in a routine job.

Some problems *may* result from the INFJ's single-minded devotion to inspirations. They may see the goal so clearly that they fail to look for other things that might conflict with the goal. It is also important that their feeling is developed, since this will supply necessary judgment. If their judgment is undeveloped, they will be unable to evaluate their own inner vision and will not listen to feedback from others. Instead of shaping their inspirations into effective action, they may merely try to regulate everything (small matters as well as great ones) according to their own ideas, so that little is accomplished.

References

Baden, R. (1975). Pre-writing: The relationship between thinking and feeling. *College Composition and Communication, 26*, 368–370.

Bakhtin, M. M. (1981). In M. Holquist (Ed.), *The dialogic imagination: Four essays* (C. Emerson & M. Holquist, Trans.) Austin: University of Texas Press.

Bakhtin, M. M. (1986). In C. Emerson & M. Holquist (Eds.), *Speech genres and other late essays* (V. W. McGee, Trans.) Austin: University of Texas Press.

Berkenkotter, C. (1984). Student writers and their sense of authority over texts. *College Composition and Communication, 35*, 312–319.

Boice, R. (1985). Psychotherapies for writing blocks. In M. Rose (Ed.) *When a writer can't write* (pp. 182–218). New York: Guilford Press.

Bradford, A. N. (1983). Cognitive immaturity and remedial writers. In J. N. Hays, P. A. Roth, J. R. Ramsey, & R. D. Foulke (Eds.), *The writer's mind: Writing as a mode of thinking* (pp. 15–24). Urbana: National Council of Teachers of English.

Briggs, K. C. (1926, Dec. 22). Meet yourself: How to use the personality paint box. *New Republic, 49*, 129–133.

Briggs, K. C. (1928, Dec. 5). Up from barbarism. *New Republic, 57*, 61–63.

Britton, J., Burgess, T., Martin, N., McLeod, A., & Rosen, H. (1975). *The development of writing ability (11–18)*. London: Macmillan Education.

Brown, G., & Yule, G. (1983). *Discourse analysis*. Cambridge: Cambridge University Press.

Bullock, C. (1983, March). *Lev Vygotsky, language development, and composition teaching*. Presentation at Conference on College Composition and Communication, Detroit.

Chafe, W. (1986). Writing in the perspective of speaking. In C. R. Cooper & S. Greenbaum (Eds.), *Studying writing: Linguistic approaches* (pp. 12–39) Beverly Hills, CA: Sage.

Ching, M. K. L. (1986, Spring). The effect of psychological type upon the composing process of university faculty. *Bulletin of Psychological Type, 8*, 34–37.

Cooper, C. R. (1977). Holistic evaluation of writing. In C. R. Cooper & L. Odell (Eds.), *Evaluating writing: Describing, measuring, judging* (pp. 3–31). Urbana, IL: National Council of Teachers of English.

Daly, J. A. & Hailey, J. L. (1984). Putting the situation into writing research: State and disposition as parameters of writing apprehension. In R. Beach and L. S. Bridwell (Eds.), *New directions in composition research* (pp. 259–273). New York: Guilford.

Daly, J. A., & Miller, M. D. (1975). The empirical development of an instrument to measure writing apprehension. *Research in the Teaching of English, 9*, 242–249.

D'Angelo, F. J. (1975). *A conceptual theory of rhetoric*. Cambridge, MA: Winthrop.

Davis, M. T., & Schroeder, C. C. "New students" in liberal arts colleges: Threat or challenge? In J. Watson and R. Stevens (Eds.), *Pioneers and pallbearers: Perspectives on liberal education* (pp. 147–168). Macon, GA: Mercer University Press.

DeNovellis, R., & Lawrence, G. (1983). Correlations of teacher personality variables (Myers–Briggs) and classroom observational data. *Research in Psychological Type, 6*, 37-46.

DeVito, A. J. (1985). The Myers–Briggs Type Indicator. In O. K. Buros (Ed.), *The ninth mental measurement yearbook* (pp. 1030–1032). Highland Park, NJ: Gryphon.

DiTiberio, J. K. (1983, Autumn). The person behind the student: The Myers–Briggs approach to learning styles. *Learning Styles Network Newsletter*, 4–6.

Ebbitt, W. R., & Ebbitt, D. R. (1978). *Writer's guide and index to English*. Glenview, IL: Scott, Foresman.

Elbow, P. (1973). *Writing without teachers*. New York: Oxford University Press.

Elbow, P. (1981). *Writing with power*. New York: Oxford University Press.

Elbow, P. (1985). The shifting relationships between speech and writing. *College Composition and Communication, 36*, 283–303.

Elifson, J. M., & Stone, K. R. (1985). Integrating social, moral, and cognitive developmental theory: Implications of James Fowler's epistemological paradigm for basic writers. *Journal of Basic Writing, 4*, 24–37.

Emig, J. (1971). *The composing processes of twelfth graders*. Urbana, IL: National Council of Teachers of English.

Faigley, L. (1980). Names in search of a concept: Maturity, fluency, complexity, and growth in written syntax. *College Composition and Communication, 31*, 291–300.

Flower, L., & Hayes, J. R. (1981). A cognitive process theory of writing. *College Composition and Communication, 32*, 365–387.

Flower, L. & Hayes, J. R. (1980). The cognition of discovery: Defining a rhetorical problem. *College Composition and Communication, 31*, 21–32.

Fox, R. F. (1980). Treatment of writing apprehension and its effects on composition. *Research in the Teaching of English, 14*, 39–49.

Gilligan, C. (1982). *In a different voice: Psychological theory and women's development.* Cambridge, MA: Harvard University Press.

Gleason, B., & Mano, S. (1986). Issues in development: An interview with Louise Wetherbee Phelps. *The Writing Instructor, 5*, 45–50.

Golay, K. (1982). *Learning patterns and temperament styles*. Newport Beach, CA: Manas-Systems.

Gorrell, R. M. (1983). How to make Mulligan Stew: Process and product again. *College Composition and Communication, 34*, 272–277.

Gould, S. J. (1981). *The mismeasure of man.* New York: Norton.

Gowen, S. (1984). *Writing, rating, and personality type.*Presentation at Ninth Annual University System of Georgia Developmental Studies Conference, Athens.

Graves, D. H. (1975). An examination of the writing process of seven year old children. *Research in the Teaching of English, 9*, 227–241.

Grinder, J., & Bandler, R. (1976). *The structure of magic II*. Palo Alto, CA: Science and Behavior Books.

Hairston, M. (1984). Working with advanced writers. *College Composition and Communication, 35*, 196–208.

Hays, J. N. (1983). The development of discursive maturity in college writers. In J. N. Hays, P. A. Roth, J. R. Ramsey, & R. D. Foulke (Eds.), *The writer's mind: Writing as a mode of thinking* (pp. 127–144). Urbana, IL: National Council of Teachers of English.

Hillocks, G., Jr. (1986). *Research on written communication: New directions for teaching*. Urbana, IL: National Council of Teachers of English.

Hoffman, J. L., & Betkouski, M. (1981). A summary of Myers–Briggs Type Indicator research applications in education. *Research in Psychological Type, 3*, 3–41.

Homans, P. (1979). *Jung in context: Modernity and the making of a psychology*. Chicago: University Press of Chicago.

Hunt, K. W. (1977). Early blooming and late blooming syntactic structures. In C. R. Cooper and L. Odell (Eds.), *Evaluating writing: Describing, measuring, judging* (pp. 91–104). Urbana, IL: National Council of Teachers of English.

Jensen, G. H. (1986). The reification of the basic writer. *Journal of Basic Writing, 5*, 52–64.

Jensen, G. H. (1987). Learning styles. In J. A. Provost & S. Anchors (Eds.), *Applications of the Myers–Briggs Type Indicator in higher education* (pp. 181–208). Palo Alto, CA: Consulting Psychologists Press.

Jensen, G. H., & DiTiberio, J. K. (1983, Spring). The MBTI and writing blocks. *MBTI News, 5*, 14–15.

Jensen, G. H., & DiTiberio, J. K. (1984). Personality and individual writing processes. *College Composition and Communication, 35*, 285–300.

Jung, C. G. (1921). *Psychological types* [trans. 1923]. Princeton, NJ: Princeton University Press.

Kant, I. (1950). *Prolegomena to any future metaphysics*. Indianapolis: Bobbs-Merrill.

Kaplan, M. A. (1966). Before they write. *College Composition and Communication, 17*, 157–160.

Keefe, J. W. (1982). Assessing student learning styles: An overview. In *Student learning styles and brain behavior* (pp. 43–53). Reston, VA: National Association of Secondary School Principals.

Keirsey, D., with Bates, M. (1978). *Please understand me: An essay on temperament styles*. Del Mar, Ca: Prometheus Nemesis Books.

Kinneavy, J. L. (1971). *A theory of discourse*. Englewood Cliffs, NJ: Prentice-Hall.

Kleine, M. (1986). *Developing a writer's self-knowledge with the Myers–Briggs Type Indicator*. Presentation at Conference on College Composition and Communication, New Orleans.

Knefelkamp, L. (1984). *Developmental stages: Different patterns, different voices*. Presentation at the Conference on Education and Training for Human Development, Memphis.

Kuhn, T. S. (1962). *The structure of scientific revolutions.* Chicago: University of Chicago Press.

Lauer, J. (1975). Heuristics and composition. In W. R. Winterowd (Ed.), *Contemporary rhetoric: A conceptual background with readings* (pp. 79–90). New York: Harcourt, Brace and Jovanovich.

Lauer, J. (1982). Writing as inquiry: Some questions for teachers. *College Composition and Communication, 33,* 89-93.

Lawrence, G. (1979/1982). *People types and tiger stripes: A practical guide to learning styles.* Gainesville, FL: Center for Applications of Psychological Type.

Lawrence, G. (1982). Personality structure and learning style: Uses of the Myers-Briggs Type Indicator. In *Student learning styles and brain behavior* (pp. 92–105). Reston, VA: National Association of Secondary School Principals.

Lawrence, G. (1984). A synthesis of learning style research involving the MBTI. *Journal of Psychological Type, 8,* 2–15.

Loomis, M. (1982). A new perspective for Jung's typology. *Journal of Analytical Psychology, 27,* 59–69.

Lowen, W. (1982). *Dichotomies of the mind: A systems science model of the mind and personality.* New York: John Wiley & Sons.

Lunsford, A. A. (1979). Cognitive development and the basic writer. *College English, 41,* 38–46.

Lunsford, A. A. (1980). The content of basic writers' essays. *College Composition and Communication, 31,* 278–290.

McCaulley, M. H. Type and education. Unpublished manuscript.

McCaulley, M. H. (1974). *The Myers–Briggs Type Indicator and the teaching–learning process.* Gainesville, FL: Center for Applications of Psychological Type.

McCaulley, M. H. (1980). Isabel Briggs Myers: Her life. *MBTI News, 2,* 2–5.

McCaulley, M. H., Macdaid, G. P., & Kainz, R. I. (1985). Estimated frequencies of the MBTI types. *Journal of Psychological Type, 9,* 3–9.

McCaulley, Mary H., & Natter, F. L. (1974). *Psychological (Myers–Briggs) type differences in education.* Gainesville, FL: Center for Applications of Psychological Type.

MacDonald, S. P. (1984). Can I write about my life? *The Writing Instructor, 3,* 140–148.

Macrorie, K. (1959). *The perceptive writer, reader, and speaker.* New York: Harcourt, Brace and Jovanovich.

Macrorie, K. (1970). *Telling writing.* Rochelle Park, NJ: Hayden.

Manchester, W. (1983). *The last lion: Winston Spencer Churchill.* New York: Dell.

Matsuhashi, A. (1981). Pausing and planning: The tempo of written discourse production. *Research in the Teaching of English, 15,* 113–134.

Merleau–Ponty, M. (1964). *Signs* (R. C. McCleary, Trans). Evanston, IL: Northwestern University Press.

Mill, J. S. (1973). *Utilitarianism.* Garden City, NJ: Anchor.

Miller, S. (1980). Rhetorical maturity: Definition and purpose. In A. Freedman & I. Pringle (Eds.), *Reinventing the rhetorical tradition* (pp. 119–127). Conway, AR: L & S Books.

Mitroff, I. I., & Kilmann, R. H. (1978). *Methodological approaches to social sciences.* San Francisco: Jossey-Bass.

Moffett, J. (1965). I, you, and it. *College Composition and Communication, 16*, 243–248.

Moffett, J. (1968). *Teaching the universe of discourse*. Boston: Houghton Mifflin.

Moffett, J., & Wagner, B. J. (1976). *Student-centered language arts and reading, K–13*. Boston: Houghton Mifflin.

Murray, D. M. (1968). *A writer teaches writing*. New York: Houghton Mifflin.

Murray, D. M. (1978a). Write before writing. *College Composition and Communication, 29*, 375–381.

Murray, D. M. (1978b). Internal revision: A process of discovery. In C. R. Cooper & L. Odell (Eds.), *Research on composing: Points of departure* (pp. 85–103). Urbana, IL: National Council of Teachers of English.

Murray, D. M. (1980). Writing as process: How writing finds its own meaning. In T. R. Donovan & B. W. McClelland (Eds.), *Eight approaches to teaching composition*. Urbana, IL: National Council of Teachers of English.

Myers, I. B. (1962/1987). *Introduction to type*. Palo Alto, CA: Consulting Psychologists Press.

Myers, I. B. (1964). *Relation of psychological type to dropouts in nursing*. Gainesville, FL: Center for Applications of Psychological Type.

Myers, I. B. (1977). Making the most of individual gifts. *MBTI News, 2*, 2, 3–6.

Myers, I. B. (1980). *Gifts differing*. Palo Alto, CA: Consulting Psychologists Press.

Myers, I. B., & McCaulley, M. H. (1985). *Manual: A guide to the development and use of the Myers–Briggs Type Indicator*. Palo Alto, CA: Consulting Psychologists Press.

Navia, L. E., & Kelly, E. (1980). *Ethics and the search for values*. Buffalo, NY: Prometheus.

Newkirk, T. (1985). The hedgehog or the fox: The dilemma of writing development. *Language Arts, 62*, 593–603.

Nichols, D. C. (1966). The five-paragraph essay: An attempt to articulate. *English Journal, 55*, 903–908.

North, S. M. (1987). *The making of knowledge in composition: Portrait of an emerging field*. Upper Montclair, NJ: Boynton/Cook.

O'Donnell, R. C. (1976). A critique of some indices of syntactic maturity. *Research in the Teaching of English, 10*, 31–38.

O'Donnell, R. C., Griffin, W. J., & Norris, R. C. (1967). *Syntax of kindergarten and elementary school children: A transformational analysis*. Urbana, IL: National Council of Teachers of English.

Perl, S. (1979). The composing process of unskilled college writers. *Research in the Teaching of English, 13*, 317–336.

Perry, W. (1968). *Forms of intellectual and ethical development in the college years, a scheme*. New York: Holt, Rinehart, & Winston.

Pianko, S. (1979). Reflection: A critical component of the composing process. *College Composition and Communication, 30*, 275–278.

Provost, J. A., & Anchors, S. (1987). *Applications of the Myers–Briggs Type Indicator in higher education*. Palo Alto, CA: Consulting Psychologists Press.

Rabinow, P. (Ed.). (1984). *The Foucault reader*. New York: Pantheon.

Rohman, G. D. (1965). Pre-writing: The stage of discovery in the writing process. *College Composition and Communication, 16*, 106–112.

Rose, M. (1980). Rigid rules, inflexible plans, and the stifling of language: A cognitivist analysis of writer's block. *College Composition and Communication, 31*, 389–401.

Rose, M. (1984). *Writer's block: The cognitive dimension*. Carbondale, IL: Southern Illinois University Press.

Schumacher, G. M., Klare, G. R., Cronin, F. C., & Moses, J. D. (1984). Cognitive activities of beginning and advanced college writers: A pausal analysis. *Research in the Teaching of English, 18*, 169–187.

Selfe, C. L. (1984). The predrafting process of four high- and four low-apprehensive writers. *Research in the Teaching of English, 18*, 45–64.

Selzer, J. (1983). The composing processes of an engineer. *College Composition and Communication, 34*, 178–187.

Selzer, J. (1984). Exploring options in composing. *College Composition and Communication, 35*, 276–284.

Shaughnessy, M. P. (1976). Basic writing. In G. Tate (Ed.), *Teaching composition: Ten bibliographical essays* (pp. 137–167). Fort Worth: Texas Christian University Press.

Shaughnessy, M. P. (1977). *Errors and expectations*. New York: Oxford University Press.

Shuy, R. W. (1981). Toward a developmental theory of writing. In C. H. Frederiksen & J. F. Dominic (Eds.), *Writing: The nature, development and teaching of written communication* (Vol. 2, pp. 119–132). Hillsdale, NJ: Erlbaum.

Sommers, N. (1981). Intentions and revisions. *Journal of Basic Writing, 3*, 41–49.

Sommers, N. (1982). Responding to writing. *College Composition and Communication, 33*, 148–156.

Stallard, C. K. (1974). An analysis of the writing behavior of good student writers. *Research in the Teaching of English, 8*, 206–218.

Sternglass, M. (1982). Applications of the Wilkinson model of writing maturity to college writing. *College Composition and Communication, 33*, 167–175.

Stewart, D. C. (1983). *Some history lessons for composition teachers*. Chairs address at Conference on College Composition and Communication, Detroit.

Stuckey, E. (1983). Basic insights: An interview with Andrea A. Lunsford. *The Writing Instructor, 2*, 57–65.

Thompson, M. O. (1979). *Writing anxiety and freshman composition*. Presentation at Annual Meeting of the Northeastern Conference on English in the Two Year College.

Troyka, L. Q. (1982). Perspectives on legacies and literacy in the 1980's. *College Composition and Communication, 33*, 252–262.

Vygotsky, L. S. (1962). *Thought and language*. Cambridge, MA: M.I.T. Press.

Walter, K. M. (1984). *Writing in three disciplines correlated with Jungian cognitive styles*. PhD Thesis, University of Texas at Austin.

Wheelwright, J. B., Wheelwright, J. H., & Buehler, H. A. (1964). *Jungian type survey: The Grey–Wheelwright Test*. San Francisco: Society of Jungian Analysts of Northern California.

White, H. (1973). *Metahistory: The historical imagination in nineteenth-century Europe*. Baltimore, MD: Johns Hopkins University Press.

White, H. (1978). *Tropics of discourse: Essays in cultural criticism.* Baltimore, MD: Johns Hopkins University Press.

Young, R. (1976). Invention: A topographical survey. In G. Tate (Ed.), *Teaching composition: Ten bibliographical essays* (pp. 1–43). Fort Worth: Texas Christian University Press.

Zebroski, J. T. (1986). The uses of theory: A Vygotskian approach to composition. *The Writing Instructor, 5*, 57–65.

Author Index

Subject Index